$\mathcal{B}$UILDING BRIDGES

BUILDING BRIDGES

Pope John Paul II and the Horizon of Life

Lena Allen-Shore

With a Foreword by
Archbishop Stanislaw Dziwisz

NOVALIS

© 2004 Novalis, Saint Paul University, Ottawa, Canada

Cover design: Caroline Gagnon
Cover image: © GIANSANTI GIANNI/CORBIS SYGMA
Interior photographs: All photographs from the collection of Lena Allen-Shore
Layout: Richard Proulx, Francine Petitclerc

Business Office:
Novalis
49 Front Street East, 2nd Floor
Toronto, Ontario, Canada
M5E 1B3

Phone: 1-800-387-7164
Fax: 1-877-702-7775 or (416) 363-9409
E-mail: cservice@novalis.ca
www.novalis.ca

Library and Archives Canada Cataloguing in Publication

Allen-Shore, Lena
    Building bridges: Pope John Paul II and the horizon of life / Lena
Allen-Shore.

ISBN: 2-89507-551-4

    1. John Paul II, Pope, 1920- 2. Popes--Biography. 3. Allen-Shore,
Lena. 4. Jews--Poland--Biography. 5. Peace. I. Title.

BX1378.5.A64 2004   282'.092   C2004-904380-3

Printed in Canada.

The Scripture quotations contained herein are from (or are slightly adapted from) the New Revised Standard Version of the Bible, copyrighted 1989 by the Division of Christian Education of the National Council of the Churches of Christ in the United States of America, and are used by permission. All rights reserved.

A version of this book was published in 2003 by Cathedral Press, Box 777, Baltimore, Maryland, 21203 under the title: *Building Bridges: Pope John Paul II and the Horizon of Life*. Novalis thanks Cathedral Press for its assistance in the preparation of this revised and reformatted edition of that work.

We acknowledge the financial support of the Government of Canada through the Book Publishing Industry Development Program (BPIDP) for our publishing activities.

5   4   3   2   1   08   07   06   05   04

For the LORD God is a sun and shield;
he bestows favor and honor.
No good thing does the LORD withhold
from those who walk uprightly.
O LORD of hosts,
happy is everyone
who trusts in you.

Psalm 84: 11-12

Let the heavens be glad, and let the earth rejoice;
let the sea roar, and all that fills it;
let the field exult, and everything in it.
Then shall all the trees of the forest sing for joy
before the LORD; for he is coming,
for he is coming to judge the earth.
He will judge the world with righteousness,
and the peoples with his truth.

Psalm 96: 11-13

With My Prayer of Thanks

Thank you, God, the Creator of life,
for allowing me to write this book, *Building Bridges*.

Contents

Foreword

L ena Allen-Shore is a poet fascinated with nature, as God created it. As a philosopher, as a writer of poetry and songs, and as a professor she tries to instill in her audience the basic rights that all people are entitled to possess, by their very being.

Most importantly, as a mother she has a passion for issues related to peace and justice. In many ways, over many years, she has courageously and eloquently expressed her thoughts and ideas on these interrelated subjects.

Lena first wrote to Pope John Paul II in 1978, shortly after his election as Pontiff. Her letter compared their experiences during the Second World War and expressed hope for a better and more just tomorrow. That letter marked the beginning of a friendship between two people who share similar cultural roots, but whose biographies are particularly different.

Both the Holy Father and Lena express themselves in various languages, as well as in their shared Polish language, and they also share various literary skills, especially poetry. They both, in their own way, continue to be advocates for those less fortunate.

As Lena travels the world, she strives to solve problems with love, compassion and prayer. She reminds people of the events of the past in order that they might become more vigilant to the present. She has often been able to see for herself the emotional reaction of an audience to her writings and lectures whereby others clearly understood her plea.

In French, Lena published her first book of poems, *L'Orage dans mon coeur* (Storm in my Heart), followed by more poems, *Le pain de la paix* (Bread of Peace); a novel, *Ne me demandez pas qui je suis* (Don't Ask Me Who I Am); essays, *Langue universelle, Fraternité et Culture* (Universal Language: Brotherhood and Culture) and another collection of poems, *Le Dieu qui chante* (The Singing God).

In English, she wrote *Ten Steps in the Land of Life*, on how to find meaning in life. She has written a book about Rembrandt, as well as a book of short stories (in collaboration with her father) about the Holocaust, *Rendezvous with Love*, in which she describes her way of seeing love. That book contains a poem that reads almost as a prayer, "And God Prayed at Dawn."

Over the years, Lena has been present at many Vatican-sponsored events that bring together people of all faiths.

I remember Lena during the visit of the Holy Father to Yad Vashem in Jerusalem. I remember her in Assisi, in the midst of so many faiths, traditions and denominations who were praying for peace in the world. I remember her attending the Concert of Reconciliation, which brought Jews, Muslims and Christians together in Rome in 2004.

In this book, *Building Bridges*, she tells the story of two very different lives, lived almost parallel during the same difficult period of history. The portrait that emerges of the Wojtyla family, as well as her own, is one of great tenderness, in spite of the dangers and difficulties during the Holocaust.

With rare insights, she writes about the Holy Father and compares their experiences of those tragic years. Both sojourned through great personal loss. They kept their abiding faith in God with strong convictions that peace is attainable, not only in theory but in everyday living.

Lena, who is Jewish, sees in the Holy Father a person of great spiritual strength as he encourages people all over the world to realize their own responsibility to nurture world peace.

Lena Allen-Shore adeptly demonstrates in the pages of this book that joy and hope are possible as people of all faiths build bridges together.

Archbishop Stanislaw Dziwisz
Secretary to Pope John Paul II
July 2004

My Words of Thanks

Reflection

The history of humankind is the history of human lives.

The history of humankind describes those who are responsible for this history.

The history of humanity does not search for the sources of good and evil.

Each one of us has parents.

The first people who guide children on the road of life are their parents, their father and mother.

In honour of Karol and Emilia Wojtyla

I think of the parents of Pope John Paul II, the late Emilia and Karol Wojtyla, and I believe that they were the source of the strength of goodness in their son. They taught him how to love those around him and bestowed on him the strength of love for God and for every human being, each created in the image of God.

Writing this book, I thought often of Wadowice, the home of His Holiness John Paul II. I thought about his childhood, youth and his parents. It seemed to me that as I was writing, I was addressing to them many questions, and they helped me understand the personality of their son.

In honour of my parents, Jakub and Lusia Herzig

I think about my parents, about my childhood and youth. My parents taught my brother, Adam, and me about people of good will and about those who still had not learned how to be human beings, created in the image of God.

This book would have been impossible to complete without the generous support of His Excellency Archbishop Stanislaw Dziwisz at the Vatican. I think of him as the very sensitive, sincere, and warm-hearted man who gave me courage while I was writing my book.

I consider it a privilege to have known His Eminence Cardinal William Keeler of Baltimore. He strengthened me and endowed me with hope that my book would reach many people and find understanding for the ideas it contains.

In December 2000, Mr. Michael Dubruiel, Editor of *Our Sunday Visitor*, wrote me a letter after reading my manuscript and wanted to know what had prompted me to write a book about the Holy Father. He was interested in my life and encouraged me to write about my relationship with Pope John Paul II. After a few weeks I agreed to take up this challenge. I prayed to God to help me in my effort; this book that you now hold in your hands is the result. In it I will try to show how two people born in the same country and at almost the same time in history shaped their characters. One of them is the Holy Father, the shepherd of millions of people; the other is me, a woman who wanders with her life through different countries and dreams about a better and more just world.

My thoughts also go to my very dear cousin, the late Dr. Albin Schiff of Philadelphia, who often listened to my ideas and encouraged me to write about Pope John Paul II.

And now I think about the late Cardinal of Philadelphia John Krol, who during one of our conversations before his death said, "If you want so much to meet His Holiness John Paul II, I think you should go to Rome and visit the Holy Father."

I think of my very dear friend, the late Rev. Father Joseph Papin, Professor in the Theology Department at Villanova University, who believed in my writing and brought me from Montreal to Philadelphia to finish my studies.

I also thank Monsignor Michael Carroll in Philadelphia, who helped me in my research many, many times, especially concerning St. Francis of Assisi and St. John of the Cross.

My thoughts go to my very dear professor of history in high school in Jaslo, Poland, the late Jan Lisowski, who in my youth encouraged me to write.

I thank the friend of my childhood and youth, Dziuta Schoenborn-Zurek in Krakow, who sent me books about St. Teresa of Avila and St. John of the Cross in Polish.

I thank Andrzej and Zosia Kontkiewicz in Warsaw for long years of friendship and for always caring for my wellbeing.

My thoughts go to my dear friend Bronia Winicki-Klibanski in Jerusalem, a hero of resistance in Poland during the war. During our long years of friendship, she often gave me courage to believe in my dreams.

I thank my friends Catherine and Bob Thomas in Ottawa for their outstanding preparation of the manuscript.

I thank my friend Dr. Margaret Jaskulek for meticulous proofreading. I thank my friend Marta Radzinska for helping me choose photographs for this book.

I thank my friend Jo Anne Deglin for her help on countless occasions of everyday life.

I thank my friend Ela Krynska for assisting me in my daily chores.

I am very grateful to the editor of Cathedral Press, Daniel Medinger, and his collaborator, Patti Medinger, who became my friends while working on the preparation of the first edition of this book, and I am thankful to Gabriella Ferraro of the Cathedral Press for her creative work – the illustrations included in the original version of this book.

I am thankful to Ronald I. Cohen in Ottawa for introducing my work to Kevin Burns at Novalis in Canada.

My gratitude goes to Kevin Burns, commissioning editor at Novalis, who provided me with many thoughtful remarks concerning this second edition of *Building Bridges*. I admire his depth and sincerity.

I thank my brother, Adam Herzig, whose presence in my life I consider a blessing from God.

I thank my son Michel, who always endows me with courage.

Finally, my special thanks go to my son Jacques, who gave me the initial idea for writing *Building Bridges* and who helped me to draw this story to a fitting close.

Karol Wojtyla as a baby

Karol Wojtyla
and his mother, Emilia

Karol Wojtyla and his father, Karol Wojtyla Senior

Karol Wojtyla (second row, second from right) with his classmates (1930)

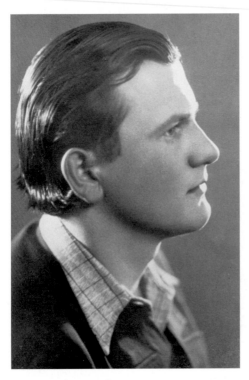

Karol Wojtyla as a young man

Lena's parents, Jakub and Lusia Herzig, with Lena and her brother, Adam

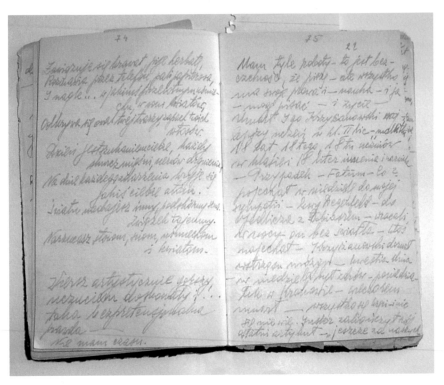

Lena's 1938 diary – see pages 137-138

Lena at the beginning
of the war (1939)

Lena's cousin Albin Schiff (1939)

Lena, Adam, Irka Niemiec and her friend (Surochow, 1943)

The painting of Vlastimil Hoffman – the only one that was saved from
the Herzigs' collection, currently in Adam's possession in Philadelphia

Lena and her parents

Adam Herzig (1945)

Lena during the war

Lena (1945)

Lena's father, Jakub, and her son Michel in Paris (1951)

Lena's mother, Lusia

Lena's husband Sigmond Shore. They married in 1946, and had two sons, Michel and Jacques. Sigmond died in 1967 in Montreal.

Lena and her son Michel in Paris (1949)

Lena and her son Jacques in Montreal (1959)

Lena and Michel during the launching in 1964 of her book
of poems *Le Pain de la Paix* (Bread of Peace), published in 1964.

Lena's husband John Edward Greenberg. They married in 1974.
John Edward died in 1990.

Lena with Michel and Jacques in Philadelphia (1990)

Lena returns to Poland and visits the daughter of Helena and Jan Kosiba, Michalina Wozniak, and her husband, Antoni Wozniak (1991).

Lena and Jacques in Ottawa (1994)

During her first visit to Pope John Paul II, Lena reads
to him "Golden-silverish," the poem about her life.

Monsignor Stanislaw Dziwisz and Lena (1996)

A private meeting with Pope John Paul II

An audience with Pope John Paul II.
Archbishop Dziwisz is standing behind the Pope.

Pope John Paul II, Lena and Michel with his two children,
Sigmond and Betty

Lena, her grandson Loren (Michel's youngest son), and her niece Elise Herzig (Adam's daughter) meet with Pope John Paul II

Lena and her granddaughter Amanda (Jacques' daughter) meet with Pope John Paul II in 2002.

Lena presents the first edition of *Building Bridges*
to Pope John Paul II while her son Jacques looks on.

Lena with her students, builders of the future,
in her classroom in Philadelphia

In Nomine Dei

June 13, 1996

Today, Rome is bright, sunny, and smiling at passers-by. Some of the passers-by are running – too preoccupied with time running faster than they are. In the big city, time and people compete to catch each other.

I am standing on the balcony of the Hotel Michelangelo, looking at the Cupola of St. Peter's Basilica. The Cupola of Michelangelo, the hotel name, Michelangelo, and la Pieta at the entrance to St. Peter's remind me of artists who tried to bring faith, through the splendour of beauty, into the souls of humankind throughout the ages.

My heart is beating faster than normal, not because of Michelangelo, but because at seven o'clock this evening I will meet Pope John Paul II. With me is my younger son, Jacques, a lawyer, born in Canada. We both know that our expectations are different. My son was born in freedom and lives in freedom. I survived the war in Poland, and I know what it means to have to fight for survival.

So many years had passed. I live in freedom now, and I try to use this freedom with an appreciation for the air I breathe, with a prayer without words, when I lift my eyes to the sky and thank the Almighty for the shining light trying to dance among the clouds, changing the scenery according to the time of day. Yes – how many times I pray, without words, my eyes lifted to the sky.

The Vatican is within walking distance, but we take a taxi, knowing that we have to pass through the side entrance and be directed to the private quarters of the Holy Father. We are greeted by a young Polish priest, Father Mieczyslaw Mokrzycki. We take the elevator together. We follow a long corridor, and come to the room in which the audience is to take place. It is a rather large room with one long table and chairs around it. From the middle of the high ceiling a magnificent chandelier casts its brilliant light. On one of the walls is a very beautiful picture – a modern picture of Christ with both arms stretched out, like on the cross. The painter expresses not the passivity of this man on the cross, but rather his gesture of wanting to join his hands with others. In the picture on both sides of Christ are two silhouettes: one of a man who is kneeling, another who is sitting. For me the painting represents Christ of the twentieth century during the Second World War. Beneath the painting is a very beautiful small crucifix and a few small sculptures.

Monsignor Stanislaw Dziwisz, with whom I had exchanged letters and telephone calls, enters a few minutes later and greets us very warmly in Polish. Our conversations are entirely in Polish, which Jacques also speaks. Monsignor Dziwisz tells us that the Holy Father will arrive in a few minutes. Then the door opens. The Holy Father shakes hands with us. Monsignor Dziwisz leaves. We sit close together: the pope, Jacques, and me.

Pope John Paul II knows about my family, my books, my poems. I had started corresponding with him immediately after he was elected in 1978. My three books, which I had sent him, are displayed on the table. The Holy Father asks us a few questions. The atmosphere is relaxed and friendly. Here we are, sitting in front of a great man, who treats us as friends from the start. The Holy Father asks me a few questions. I am very moved. Here I sit, a Jewish woman from Poland who decided one day in her youth in Poland during the war that, if she survived the war, she would try to spread understanding among people of different religions, ethnic groups, races, and cultures. That was in Poland in April or May 1943 on a sunny day. Now, here I am in Rome in 1996, in front of a man whom I admire very much. Pope John Paul II not only knew about my pain – he also understood it. We talk about my work as a professor in Philadelphia, about the interdisciplinary courses I have developed that link art with history and the conscience of humankind. The pope also asks me about my visit to Poland and about the performance of my cantata-play, *The Little Shoes*, by the Polish Theatre Eljiot in Auschwitz.

After a few minutes I ask the Holy Father if I could read to him some excerpts from a long poem which I wrote in Polish because of him, some fifty years after I left Poland in 1946. That poem, "Golden-silverish," contains the saga of my life.

The Holy Father agrees, and listens very attentively to my thoughts and words. In this poem I also express my thoughts about Christ crying, feeling abandoned during the Second World War, witnessing the crimes against innocent people.

After I read the poem we speak of anti-Semitism throughout the ages, and at one point I ask what can be done to change this attitude. The Holy Father looks at me. In his eyes are compassion and understanding. Slowly he says, "What about Vatican II?" I do not know where my answer comes from, but I say, "It is not enough." I cry.

Jacques looks at the Holy Father and asks, "Do you know why my mother is so moved and cries? Because she has waited for this moment for fifty years." My son is right, so right. I had been waiting for this meeting with the shepherd of millions of Catholics. Yes. We are talking of hate and love.

The Holy Father speaks with Jacques for a long while with sensitivity and warmth, asking him about his family: his wife and three daughters. The pope knows that Jacques had lost his father at the age of eleven. He understands my son because he himself lost his mother at the age of nine. The pope knows what it is like to be brought up by only one parent.

At the end of our conversation there is a moment that I will never forget. The pope takes Jacques in his arms, embraces him very warmly, and then, with his two hands, he holds Jacques' head and kisses his forehead. I knew the Holy Father was trying to give my son some warmth.

The audience lasts forty-five minutes. Except for a few minutes with the photographer, we are alone in the room.

The Holy Father leaves. Monsignor Dziwisz brings us to the elevator and we part.

My son is silent.

As we leave the Vatican, after a while Jacques says, "This man is only goodness." These are his first words. I knew what he meant. The kiss on his forehead remained with him.

II

An hour after the audience, we go to a small restaurant near the hotel, where we eat outside. We talk very little. Each of us is absorbed in our own thoughts. At one moment Jacques says, "You have to write an article. The title of the article should be 'Building Bridges.' Do it. You can do it."

At the table mother and son sit, contemplating one hour of time, a victory of understanding of two different worlds coming together in mutual respect and belief in a better tomorrow.

III

Before my departure from Rome I write a letter to the Holy Father. In this letter I write about how impressed and grateful I am for our conversation. I also describe the thoughts that came to me that Sunday morning. I had gone to the top of the Cupola of Michelangelo and walked up the narrow, winding steps, high, high, high – and there, while standing above Rome and observing the city below, I understood that even the tallest cupola in the world could not be as close to God as anyone could be, if we possessed true humanity, true humaneness and understanding for another human being.

It seems to me that in his understanding of others, Pope John Paul II is nearer to God, nearer than the highest tower in the world.

A few days later in Philadelphia, I received a letter from the Holy Father. He appreciated my thoughts and encouraged me to be always myself. I thanked God.

In July 1996, I wrote one of many letters to the Holy Father. In this one I included a poem written on June 30 on the train from Philadelphia to Washington:

The Encounter

June 13 in Rome
was breathing in the early
summer.
On the streets reigned motion,
cars, bicycles, people
united in one rhythm.

Time!
without mercy, impossible
to attain –
eternal time
unreachable.
Time, whose Creator
is
the omnipotent God –
time
for some a treasure
for others a curse –
time
whose kiss
can make love sacred –
time
who in the split
of a second
can destroy
a city.
Time!

How many times
in our prayers to God
Who was the Creator of time
we beg
that time
slow its pace
even for a while,
that would allow someone

whom we love
to remain
another few minutes
on the earth.

How many times
in our prayers
we ask time
to run faster
at night,
some lonely night
when we are waiting
for the dawn
and the night
seems to be cruel.

How many times
in our prayers
we pray
that the half an hour
of an encounter
lingers on
a little longer
because every second
of this encounter
brings a balm
for wounds
that do not heal.

In the room
was the Holy Father
the woman and her son.
The woman and her son
came from far away.

The Holy Father, the shepherd

of the souls
of millions of Christians
met a woman
who believes in God
and in the goodness
of the Holy Father.

In the touch of two hands
the hand of the Holy Father
and the woman
was warmth,
the warmth of this sun
of the youth
maybe from Wadowice
or maybe from Jaslo,
maybe from Krakow
or from Zakopane –
on this unforgettable day
in June,
when the dreams were floating
like the delicate blue waves
of the air,
there in Poland.

The wounds
in the heart of the woman
were not healed
but the balm of consolation
was created
in the touch
of the Holy Father's hand
who understood the tears
transparent and sincere
from the bottom of her heart
full of love
for God and men
beyond the borders
of religions.

Two prayers
unexpressed in words
met there
in Rome
and left a mark
of understanding.
Dear Holy Father,
Thank you.

And after came a dream
beautiful, never forgotten.

This was not in Rome.

In Tatra in Zakopane
two people
were sitting on a rock –
in silence they looked
at the shining surface
of the Morskie Oko.[1]

This was the Holy Father
and I.
Such a wonderful encounter
in the dream of a dream.

In this encounter
the youth came back,
the Holy Father and I
were celebrating
the vacation of dreams.

We were young again
and we believed
that one day will come
when people
will join hands together

and ... there will be no more war
and ... no more hate
and the children will repeat
the words of the prophet Isaiah
about the wolf and the lamb.

For very dear beloved Holy Father.

A few days later I received a reply from the Holy Father with very warm words, in response to my poem which I wrote, as the Holy Father notes, in the train between Philadelphia and Washington. His words continue to mean a lot to me. They are the foundations of a very special bridge between a remarkable Catholic priest and this Jewish woman, both from Poland. His words and his encouragement lie at the heart of this book, written during the final years of the one century and the first few years of the next.

IV

The last century – the century of progress and of violence, of science unleashed for the well-being of humanity as well as for its destruction; the century of advanced technology allowing the world to replace human beings with highly intelligent robots; the century which brought the darkness of two world wars, where people not only died on the battlefields and in the cities, bombed from the skies above, but were burnt in gas chambers – there appeared a pontiff, a man humble before God, a man strong in front of people. This man had decided to convey the mission of hope with a strong conviction, that the history of humankind depends on building bridges between people of different religions, different races, different backgrounds, different ethnic groups, and different cultures.

From simple bridges of rope and wood we progressed to the works of skilled bridge builders in stone and steel. Who provided the blueprint, the plan for the structures?

Can we build bridges between people of different religions, races, ethnic groups, backgrounds, and cultures? What would be the basis of such a bridge? For Karol Wojylta, there existed and still exists only one basis: his love of all humankind. If such a love is a blessing from God, suddenly this love becomes a manifestation of strength. This is not the strength of power, abolishing by force and often by law the freedom of choice in shaping individual convictions. No, this strength comes from the eagerness to explain the role of differences as the constructive parts of the bridge, which could be built in a very beautiful way and would not disturb the lines of God's horizon.

When I think of His Holiness John Paul II, I recall a poem that he wrote in 1939, in Krakow, Poland.

Over this your white grave
the flowers of life in white –
so many years without you –
how many have passed out of sight?

Over this your white grave
covered for years, there is the stir,
in the air, something uplifting
and, like death, beyond comprehension.

Over this your white grave
oh, Mother, can such loving cease?
for all his filial adoration
a prayer:
Give her eternal peace –[2]

Humanity is the family of all people through all time. And if humanity represents this fragile family, then the strongest bond responsible for its continuation is love – and who better than a mother to implant this miracle, the strongest light able to penetrate even the darkest night of life? Pope John Paul II loved his mother. It was his mother, whom he lost at a very tender age, who endowed him with the spirituality of love beyond human comprehension. She brought her child to the idea of searching, searching love beyond human comprehension in God, in Christ, and in the Virgin Mary.

In his poem "The Negro," John Paul writes:

My dear brother, it's you, an immense land I feel
where rivers dry up suddenly – and the sun

burns the body as the foundry burns ore.
I feel your thoughts like mine;
if they diverge the balance is the same;
in the scales truth and error.
There is joy in weighing thoughts on the
same scales,
thoughts that differently flicker in your
eyes and mine
though their substance is the same.[3]

Yes, the substance is indeed the same. At one and the same time, the family is a personal one and a more abstract one that links us to all humankind. Our challenge is to keep building bridges of trust and hope and possibility at a time when ignorance and fear and suspicion threaten to divide our world.

The Snowflakes of November

The snowflakes were falling on November 17. The world was white, shining, and beautiful. The snowflakes were falling from somewhere high above, and they covered the entire city of Krakow.

When I think of snowflakes I hear the sound of the words: *platki sniegu* in Polish; "snowflakes" in English; *flocons de neige* in French; *Schneeflocken* in German; *flocchi di neve* in Italian; *sniezynka* in Russian. I hear music. When I see snowflakes I think they kiss the earth, the trees. The earth is so naked in winter. The trees without leaves look abandoned, lonely, and then the snowflakes come, kissing the soil and caressing the trees.

On November 17, the trees looked majestic in their new attire, an exquisite white brocade embroidered with diamonds.

This was the world into which the little girl was born. In the "House of Health," a clinic-hospital, a young woman gave birth to her first child. With her was her aunt, Klara Wurzel, who lived in Krakow. She had promised the woman's husband, who worked in another city, that she would take care of his wife during the delivery. The young woman was disappointed. She had hoped for a boy and had not hidden her feelings. Knowing this, her aunt said, "Yes, she is a girl, but she looks like an intelligent girl." This girl was me. Years later, when I repeated this story to my mother, she always said, "Forget it. I was happy to have you."

I always laughed, but my mother felt compelled to reassure me that I had indeed been welcome. I knew for sure that my father was thrilled to have a little girl. Since my early childhood, my father and I had a very special relationship; we understood each other without words, and he was the greatest guide that destiny could have provided me with. I loved my mother. She was the best mother in the world for me, but with my father I felt a magic touch. We were poets who went through life working and dreaming, dreaming and striving, dreaming and believing in the beauty of life.

Could Krakow have known that after so many years that little girl, who is so very much grown-up now, would describe snowflakes coming from the sky, feeling a certain nostalgia for them, and for the country of her birth as well as all the other countries she had ever lived in? So many cultures have touched her over the years. Yes, I will always remember Poland, but for each country in which I have lived and for the country in which I now live, I also have respect. I have respect for the soil on which I walk. And whenever I watch the sky I feel a oneness with the world and the Creator.

I call to mind the river Vistula, the queen of rivers for everyone in Poland. Were the Vistula's quiet waters covered with snowflakes when I was born? I believe that the Vistula sang a lullaby for all the children born that day in Poland, though lullabies do not make any difference – all children are the same. We are all little beings who come into the world innocent and pure, wanting to live, to love and to have parents and a country to care for us and provide a warm home, especially when it is snowing outside.

My mother, Laura (everybody called her Lusia), was short, tiny in fact, with light hazel brown eyes, light brown hair. Her maiden name was Goldman. She married my father in 1921. My mother spent the war years with her family in Vienna. The family had had to leave their estate. Her father was in the Austrian Army with one of his sons, who was a medical doctor. During the war the Russians destroyed their big, beautiful home and rose garden in Kalne. When the family returned in 1918 after the war, her father built a small house.

In the story of my life I believe I should tell the story of my grandfather, my mother's father, who loved God and all people, and who lived up to his convictions throughout his life. My mother adored him. She always admired him, this modern Jew, who took care of the Ukrainians in his village and who always spoke Polish, who loved the country where he lived, and who taught his children not only to love God and all people but also to take responsibility for their own actions.

My mother came from a family of eight children, four boys and four girls. One of her sisters had died at the age of sixteen. My mother loved her very much. Her father had an estate in Podolia in eastern Poland. The boys were sent to Lwow to be educated. The girls had two governesses who taught them. Each year the girls passed their exams with ease at the Lycee in Lwow. The governesses taught them various subjects, including philosophy, French, and music.

My mother's father loved people and took care of the village of Kalne, where he lived. There, in the years before the First World War, he built a school and a church. He believed that people should be educated and should have faith. Abraham Goldman earned a very good name in this part of the country. He was a practicing Jew with modern ideas. (Here in Philadelphia, where I live now, a young man arrived a few months ago from Kalne, which is in Russia now, and told my nephew, a lawyer here in Philadelphia, that his grandparents remembered the school and the church.)

My grandfather died after contracting typhoid from a refugee who had asked for shelter for the night. Even in 1920, many refugees from the First World War were wandering around Europe in the hope of returning to their original homes. An employee in charge of the estate said that they already had too many fugitives and could not shelter any more people. Apparently my grandfather overheard this and invited the woman into the family home. That night she fell ill and my grandfather and one of his daughters also contracted the same disease. When the doctor came he immediately diagnosed typhoid but had medicine for only one patient. My grandfather told him to give this medication to the stranger. My mother took care of my grandfather and her sister. My grandfather died shortly after; my aunt and the stranger survived.

My mother's mother came from Jaslo, in southeastern Poland. Her family, the Rubels, were also estate owners. Newly widowed, she decided to take care of the estate. It was a struggle because against the advice of many, she decided not to sell even a part of the estate, maintaining that she was attached to this soil which her husband had loved so much.

My father, Jakub Herzig (his family called him Kuba), was of medium height, with brown eyes and dark brown hair. I remember him with grey hair on his temples. He was born and lived in Stryj, in eastern

Poland. His father, Jozef Herzig, was an educated man from Sanok, in southwestern Poland. He had a small business in iron, but at one point in his life he had invested some money on the advice of one of his relatives and had lost everything. My father's mother was a very well-educated woman. She was the mother of four children, three boys and one girl. When her husband lost their money, she decided to take in out-of-town students, giving them a place to live and cooking meals for them. She wanted to help her husband at the moment of crisis. She succeeded in certain ways, as my father said, but she became consumed by the amount of work she had taken on. The only time she had to read books was on Saturday afternoons, when she was not working in the household. After my grandmother died very suddenly at the age of 42 after a miscarriage, my grandfather was never able to console himself. The youngest girl was taken in by her aunt, who promised to care of her. Two older brothers were already in Lwow studying law at the university, and my father, at the age of thirteen, started to earn money by tutoring his colleagues in high school. He often told me that his favourite time was during the summer vacation, when he was invited to stay with the students whom he taught. He was much appreciated as a tutor. The names Skole or Tatarow always come to my mind because my father enjoyed nature, and the countryside in these summer resorts was beautiful.

My father was a very good student. He also wrote poetry and loved to sing. He had a very beautiful, strong voice. After finishing high school he went to university in Lwow to study law, but he continued to go to Stryj often to see his father and continue his tutoring. A self-made man, he was very proud and very honest, when he met my mother. Neither had any money. Even so, years later in Montreal, I met a man from Brzezany (the city near Kalne) who described to me a party given in 1913 in my grandparents' rose garden to celebrate the high school graduation of one of my mother's brothers.

There was no money when my mother married my father – they had started their life together with nothing material but with a lot of love. This love was the greatest wealth my parents would later bestow on my younger brother and me. My father worked very hard and did not even dare to lose a day from his job as a young lawyer in Frysztak. The fact that I was born not in the small city but in Krakow also shows that my father cared very much for my mother and the child who was to be born. Years later, my mother showed me a beautiful love letter that my father wrote to her after I was born. He loved me even without seeing me because I was his daughter, the child of the woman he loved.

As I write this book, I imagine a scale holding my thoughts and I look closely at the balance. On one side are my memories, the past, and on the other my longings and expectations for the future. The balance keeps shifting. With each chapter of my life story, I realize that throughout my life, no matter my age at the time, my longings and my expectations for the future seem to prevail over my sense of the past. Yet I am aware that it is the past and my experiences that allow me to move forward. Together, they enable me to believe in my own contribution to the future, without thinking of the fragility and time limits of my own life.

From far away in my imagination I see snowflakes dancing on the streets of Krakow. Did these frozen flakes bring to mind memories and longings, a sense of being blessed from on high when I was born? I believe that they did – and therefore I am writing this book.

The Window

I n Poland the jasmine blooms in May. Delicate white petals of flowers with tiny hearts of sun appear at the surface of the world and breathe the warmth of spring. In the evening, the docile breeze brings the kiss of the stars. The spring sings a hymn of love. The sound of the bells from the churches calls Polish Christians to evening devotions to the Blessed Virgin. Perhaps the sound tells all the people who live in Poland about the love of one's neighbour. All people belong to one family, the human family, and we are linked to each other through our dreams, our suffering, our struggle with destiny, and our struggle for a better tomorrow.

On May 18, 1920, in a small bedroom in Wadowice, not too far from Krakow, Karol Jozef Wojtyla was born. The waters of the Vistula flowed quietly through Krakow, telling the history of Poland to the streets and to the trees – and maybe one drop of water told the world that in Wadowice, Karol Wojtyla, the future poet and pope, was born.

Who is this man who prays and thinks, who works, who speaks with God, with Christ, with the Virgin Mary, and with people? Who is this man, who uses words in many languages, this man who searches for understanding, teaches love, and prays for the peace of the world? He is the builder, the architect of peace in the world, the teacher of people, the shepherd of millions, and the defender of those who suffer.

One day, visibly moved, Pope John Paul II was reminiscing about his early life. When Karol came into the world, his mother's first wish was that the midwife should lift the curtains in the window of the bedroom and open the window. A ray of sun entered the room. The church bell and the hymns to the Virgin Mary were the first resounding echoes of the world that the baby heard. Life greeted the future pope with the melody of prayer.

The greeting of light, the Holy Mass, with the church bells on this day in May perhaps became a symbol for this one whose destiny was to be a shepherd to millions of souls. Perhaps his mother's poetic gesture brought spirituality to the child, tuning the strings of his heart to become an armour against evil – the strings of the heart: love and strength.

This delicate woman offered her son something beyond words. Did she offer her son poetry in the form of an action or deed? Does the poetry of a deed actually exist? Do the deeds of humanity, our strivings and behaviour, have something in common with poetry? Is not the source of each action only one thought, one single thought accompanying the steps forward or making it difficult to make decisions, to take part in the pulsating current of life? What is this poetry of the deed? Is it the awareness of the sense of belonging to the trees, to the golden heads of wheat which give us daily bread? What is this poetry of action? Is it the gaze of people who look at the world created by God to discover each day the revelation of the sun and the stars and try to retain in their eyes the flickering breath of eternity? What is this poetry of the deed? Is it a sense of responsibility for the beauty and the justice of humankind? And what is this beauty of humankind? The beauty is freedom, the power to breathe freedom. And what is the justice of humankind? It is based on reverence for God and respect for all, created as we are in the image of God. We are born and we die the same way.

Through the window open to the world, one ray of sun brought light to the room on the second floor of a small apartment house. Ever since his birth, this ray of sun has accompanied Pope John Paul II on his wanderings, from Wadowice to Krakow and from Krakow to the Vatican, and from there to the rest of the world. The window with the sun's ray shows the horizon of the world. That open window in Wadowice provides vistas of the rivers and the oceans, and the streets of Calcutta, of Nairobi, of New York and Rio de Janeiro, the alleys full of trees in Australia, the forests of Peru and the streets and the pathways and rivers, flowing through the whole world.

On the Piazza San Pietro under the giant Cupola of Michelangelo, John Paul II calls on the world to love and understand one another.

Those who listen to the words resounding in that space can grasp the resonance of the strings of the heart.

His wanderings started in Wadowice. Before the child could distinguish the echoes of the world and take his first steps, his mother, very weak and delicate, offered in her humble and sincere prayer the most beautiful benediction – love and strength – and . . . an open window.

Love Truth as Pure as Crystal

I remember one evening in winter. In my diary, which I received as a gift for my birthday, my father wrote this:

Love truth as pure as crystal –
a radiant, bright eternal mistress,
although lying
sometimes pays more
the most precious is
not what enriches your pocket
but what enriches your soul.

I eventually lost that diary, yet the words of my father still live in my heart.

As my parents later told me, I started to walk and talk very early. I think about my first words that I can remember saying: *tatus* and *mamusia* (daddy and mommy). Even today, when speaking French or English, when I talk about my parents I often say *tatus* and *mamusia*. That first language is engraved deep within me. Polish was my mother tongue. Poland was my country. How often later in life have I heard, "You are Jewish, you are not Polish." I was a Polish Jew with my rights to my country, and I could not understand that someone dared to contest my sense of belonging. One day when I was a few years old my father said to me, "I know that you love Poland, but before someone has to remind you who you are, don't forget that you are Jewish, and be proud of who you are." These words will remain with me forever.

Very often I think about how wrong it is to tell people who were born on a certain soil that they do not belong to the country of their birth because of their ethnic group or religion. After living in several countries, and having taught in the United States for more than twenty years, I often discuss this topic with my students. Everyone wants to have their place under the sun – the trees, the mountains and the waters, the familiar surroundings – and no one has the right to take away the blessing of feeling at home. The features of the face, the colour of the skin should not become the criteria of judgment or verdict. I also believe that the same should apply to all immigrants who, in their search for freedom or a better future, decide to put down roots in their country of adoption. Some immigrants appreciate their country of adoption even more than those who have lived quietly for many generations on the same soil.

After I left Poland many people asked me if I ever spoke the Jewish language, Yiddish. My parents did not speak Yiddish, and the only grandmother I knew spoke Polish. This part of Poland where my grandparents were born had belonged to the Austro-Hungarian Empire before Poland became independent in 1918. There were many Jews like my parents and their families. They were committed Jews but at the same time, Poland was their country, and many of them fought for Polish independence. Jews had lived in Poland for many, many centuries. However, my father believed in the importance of the Hebrew language, and later on I was taught Hebrew by a teacher who came once or twice a week to our home. My father also believed that one day Jews would be able to live in the land of their ancestors if they chose to do so.

We went to the synagogue only three times during the year: on Rosh Hashanah (New Year), on Kol Nidrei night (the eve of the Day of Atonement), and on Yom Kippur (the Day of Atonement). When I pray today I can read Hebrew, but I do not understand everything, and therefore I read some of the prayers and the psalms in English translation. I did not pray every day until I lived in Paris. But this is to advance my story, beyond my memories of childhood.

I often think about my early years. My parents moved from Frysztak to Jaslo when I was eighteen months old. I remember only vaguely our first apartment in Jaslo, but I remember vividly the sound of the city's electrical power plant. The sound of this plant was very distinct and accompanied me during our stay in Jaslo until the outbreak of the Second World War.

One evening, in our first apartment, I remember seeing my uncle Herman, my father's brother, lying on the sofa. Later I found out that my uncle, who had a high position in the Polish government as a director of finance in Gdansk, on the Baltic Sea, had died of pneumonia, there in our home. My parents took care of him after he became sick. I mention this because I still remember the sadness. When, after forty-three years away from Poland, I went back to Jaslo and visited the destroyed Jewish cemetery, the only grave that it was possible to recognize (although the marble on which his name was engraved was broken into pieces) was that of my uncle.

When I was almost three years old, we moved to an apartment at 14 Staszica Street. This was a two-storey building. The owners of the house, Mr. Rybak and his wife, lived on one side of the house. On the other side was my father's office and our living quarters: the bedroom, and the dining room. The dining room was a very large room with windows facing the big park and the courthouse. It was convenient for my father, and my parents decided to move there even though the apartment was very small.

The most joyful event of my childhood was the birth of my brother, Adam. He was born at home when I was two years and nine months old. My mother's cousin, Dr. Kormel, was present. I was in the dining room sleeping on the sofa with my teenaged aunt, Rozia, my mother's youngest sister, when I heard the cry of a newborn baby. At first my aunt did not tell me what it was, but then I found out that I had a brother. I think this was my happiest moment. I had a brother, my little brother. Also, when my mother asked if this was a boy or a girl, I heard my mother's aunt, Karolcia Rubel, say, "Lusia, my word of honour, it is a boy." From the day my brother was born, he became the most important one in our family. I never minded it a bit. Certainly he was smaller; he was little, I was big. My brother was named Adam Hendryk, and I was named Teresa.

Everything had to be for Adam, especially as I was strong (I loved to eat) and he was always very skinny (he did not like to eat). My love for my brother continues to this day. Then, I always took care of him. Today I realize that he wants to take care of me, sometimes more than I want.

Yes, in our home we were taught how to love, how to care. I was never jealous. I remember once when he had chicken pox, since it was very contagious, I had to sleep at the home of our beloved Aunt Karolcia and Uncle Robert. How I loved them! But I was so worried about my brother I could not sleep.

I recall the view from the windows in our dining room. The chestnut trees in the park, their white flowers in the spring – and the chestnuts waiting for me in autumn. The birds, the sparrows, a few pigeons, accompany me in my search for words. The beggar Morela smiles at me.

Were the sparrows important? Were the pigeons important? The chestnut trees? And the beggar? Yes they were – and the lilac trees in the gardens, white and purple, and the dahlias planted by Mrs. Rybak, and the owners' daughter-in-law – these were all my friends. They smiled at me, they called me in the morning announcing each new day of life, announcing happy days. There was always someone kissing me "good night." I knew I was loved, just for myself. The small apartment, the park, the country – these enter my room here in Philadelphia where I write, reminding me that even now they are still in me, awakening all my emotions.

My diary was lost during the war, but the words of my father, my guide, remained with me as I wandered from one country to another. They crossed the Atlantic Ocean, where they continue to live and where they have not lost any of their strength.

In 1956, my father died in Montreal. I could not attend his funeral because I was pregnant with my younger son and the doctor had advised me to stay in bed, so I wrote a farewell note for my *tatus*. This note included the words about love and truth that he had written in my diary. The letter was read during the funeral and after, as I had asked, it was put in his coffin.

Yes, my father gave me the strength to love truth, "the radiant mistress," and to be always faithful to the voice of the soul. My conscience is never silent. The voice of my conscience enriches my soul, as it has done since my earliest childhood. To write out these experiences and memories is to accept the challenge of forgotten and unforgotten events. There are people whose smile has never disappeared from my memory. And there are tears that I must not shed in public.

The art of writing autobiography sometimes stops being an act of memory, with descriptions of days and nights passed by, and becomes instead a testimony to human triumphs and defeats, to visions and dreams that came true or never occurred. The words we write are mere fragments of time, which by passing too fast took away the kiss, the feeling of being held in loving arms, leaving only a memory of happiness. This memory of happiness becomes a never-exhausted well. My never-exhausted well was and remains my childhood.

Tempus Fugit – Aeternitas Manet

I n the quiet apartment at No. 2 Rynkowa Street, a little boy is playing. From time to time the child looks at the holy images on the walls, the sundial in the church, the clock he sees through the window. On the sundial is an inscription. The little boy does not know what is written there, and once he asks, "*Mamusia* ("Mummy" in Polish), what does it say? Please read it to me." "This is written in Latin," says the mother, "and the words are '*tempus fugit – aeternitas manet.*'"

"And what does it mean?" asks the child.

"It means," the mother says, "that time flies and eternity remains."

"I know what time is," says Karol. "Time is that there is two o'clock in the afternoon and three o'clock in the afternoon – and father is working – but what is eternity?"

The mother thinks for a while and then says, "Eternity is something that exists forever." Maybe she says something more. Karol does not remember the rest of the conversation. The child is silent – he only looks at the picture of Jesus and the Virgin Mary, and thinks: Christ will always be here, and the Virgin Mary, and God.

At night in the darkness, in his memory, the words come back: "Time flies, eternity remains." He tries to explain to himself how time runs. He thinks he understands it. Time runs, it flies. It means that in a few years I will grow up. I will be as big as my brother Edmund. And eternity? Eternity – I would like *mamusia* to live forever.

* * *

Why was Karol thinking about his mother? His mother was often ill, but she never complained. He knew that *mamusia* was weak, not like other mothers – and *mamusia* was sad. Was it because she had lost a little girl, Olga, before he was born? *Tatus* (Daddy) helped at home; he took care of the apartment, cooked the meals.

The room was dark, but Karol could not sleep. Mother came in. "Lolus, why are you not sleeping?" she asked. Mother was always calling him "Lolus." "Karol" was too serious for a little boy; "Lolek" or "Lolus" implied warmth, a caress. Yes, Mother gave him a lot of warmth – even when she came to ask him why he was not sleeping. She kissed his forehead and hugged him and then covered him with a quilt and a blanket to keep him warm. Yes, Lolek wanted his mother to stay alive always. He liked it so much when his mother read him fairy tales. He loved his mother's voice.

The home of the Wojtyla family had a religious atmosphere. At the entrance of their apartment was a majolica urn filled with holy water, in which Lolek would dip his fingers and cross himself whenever he entered or left the apartment. His parents taught him to be religious. Sometimes in the evening his parents read the Bible aloud. While listening to the stories, Lolek thought that religion is this *aeternitas manet*. The family also repeated prayers with the rosary beads.

Once he heard his mother say, "Oh, maybe Lolek will be a priest." On another occasion she said, "Lolek will be a great man." A great man – what is this "great man?"thought Karol. He never asked. He did not know what his mother thought about when she repeated these words. It was true, he wanted his parents to be proud of him – because he was proud of them. Everyone called his father "Lieutenant." Karol's father always wore the uniform of an officer; he was a professional soldier, first in the Austrian Army and later in the Polish Legions. When the little boy thought about the Polish Legions he always stood straight with pride. The Polish Legions had successfully fought for the independence of Poland. In his home he often heard conversations about independent Poland and how, after years of bondage, Poland was breathing freedom.

Karol often observed his father praying and kneeling at a prie-dieu in the apartment and thought that during his prayers his father also was thinking of the independence of Poland. The Wojtyla household was characterized by a sense of dignity, respect, love, and faith. The future pope grew up in these surroundings.

The years passed. Karol learned about life. As a boy he travelled from time to time to Krakow to visit his mother's three sisters and his brother Edmund, who was fourteen years older than he. Edmund was studying medicine. During one of these visits Karol entered the cathedral at Wawel for the first time. There he attended Mass during Holy Week, the week before Easter. In Wawel Cathedral, Karol saw for the first time Count Adam Sapieha, Archbishop of Krakow. The image of the cathedral and the archbishop remained engraved in the child's memory. The majesty, the liturgy, the reciting of the psalms, and the flickering candles left their mark in the thoughts of the future pope.

There at Wawel, according to his childhood memories, the child, Karol Wojtyla, understood for the first time that this magnificent cathedral with the majesty of the liturgy, with the archbishop and the flickering candles, was offering him a second home. This second home was the house of God, of Christ. The child was enchanted with the splendour of the church and the moment. Perhaps at the same time he felt that this house of God was his home, like the home of his family, the home with the sundial that he could see through the window, on which was written *tempus fugit – aeternitas manet*.

In his book *Crossing the Threshold of Hope*, Pope John Paul II writes,

> Much has been written about prayer, and further, prayer has been widely experienced in the history of humankind, especially in the history of Israel and Christianity. Man achieves the fullness of prayer not when he expresses himself, but when he lets God be most fully present in prayer.[4]

When is God present in prayer? God is present in prayer when we search for and find God, God's nearness, God's arm, God's warmth. This can take place only when we find a way not to think about ourselves in our prayers.

After many years of praying, the priest-poet wrote the poem "A Conversation with God Begins":

> The human body in history dies more often and earlier than the tree.
> Man endures beyond the doors of death in catacombs and crypts,
> Man who departs endures in those who follow.
> Man who follows endures in those departed.
> Man endures beyond all coming and going
> in himself
> and in you.

The history of men, such as I, always looks for the body
you will give them.
Each man in history loses his body and goes towards you.
In the moment of departure
each is greater than history
although but a part
(a fragment of a century or two,
merged into one life).[5]

Yes – within the life of Pope John Paul II we can find a "fragment of a century or two," perhaps in the form of his deeds and his poetry, as a gift to the world? This pope-poet remembers – in his prayers, in his encyclicals, in his writings and poems – people, trees, and birds.

In the atmosphere of the twenty-first century wander the words of the prophets of Israel, the words of St. Francis of Assisi. These words join a melody of hope and the blessing of faith of Pope John Paul II, who respects each person on earth. These words and this melody accompany the astronauts in their search for new discoveries when they pray for a successful journey far away from the earth, when they feel that they want to be nearer to God. They know that humanity is a mere grain of dust vibrating in the air and that the presence of God is the light, which sometimes reveals only a small particle of eternity.

In 1997 John Paul II visited Sarajevo. There he officiated at Holy Mass in an open field. The crowds listened; they prayed with the man who did not forget the lesson of his childhood and home. Millions of snowflakes danced with the wind, but undaunted, Pope Paul John II continued the prayer. In the crowd there were old people, young people, and children. Sarajevo, the battlefield. Sarajevo, which had seen the cruelty of so much hate, listened to the words. Sarajevo witnessed a prayer for peace.

Sarajevo, the snowflakes, and the soil become a part of the prayer, long before, when in his childhood apartment, Pope John Paul II saw through the window the sundial with the Latin inscription. *Tempus fugit – aeternitas manet.* "Time flies, eternity remains."

The snowflakes melted on the ground, but the words, the dreams about peace, about love of fellow human being, permeated the soil of Sarajevo in Bosnia-Herzegovina. Perhaps there in the crowd was a child who connected the silhouette of the pope with faith and religion – and a prayer to God for all people. Perhaps within this one child, present during this Holy Mass said in spite of the snowflakes and the wind, there remains an echo of the prayer, and maybe this child will one day transmit the prayer for peace in the world to his child many, many years from now. *Tempus fugit — aeternitas manet.*

"O Sole Mio" and the Nightingales in the Park

Whenever I think of my childhood I hear sounds: lullabies and operas, and the concerts of nightingales in the park. There are sounds of the winds, a strong wind that accompanied the snowstorms and the delicate breeze caressing the far-away wheat fields. There are songs of love, gypsy romances, and Italian songs from Sorrento. And behind our windows during the years spent in Jaslo, there was also the sound of the electric plant, interrupted sometimes by the whistle of a passing steam train.

These songs of yesterday have never disappeared from my inner being; they express in me all the feelings I had, feelings without words or sometimes illustrated by libretto or text written by a stranger who became a mentor in showing the colours of feelings. Years later I read that in Sanskrit the word for feelings and colours is the same. I interrupted my reading to admire this centuries-old fusion of colours and feelings.

Did my feelings enter the feelings of my older son, Michel, who a few years ago wrote a book of poems, *I Hear Music in Every Psalm*? Are genes in some way responsible for feelings in people? Why is it so important for me to write about music in my life? Or is this perhaps one of the most important features of my being?

Do the waves in the sea bring a melody? Do the waters in the streams in the forest touch the trees around with a quiet symphony, changing according to the seasons?

* * *

Our home was a reflection of my parents' life. There, in a small city in Poland, we found out about La Scala in Milan, there in my home Chopin became my friend, a friend like Janka or Wanda in school. Chopin, played by my mother, visited us very often. Sometimes I thought about Moniuszko, a Polish composer who wrote "The Woman Weaver." Today I think that music was interwoven in my thoughts just as today are my prayers are also interwoven. But interwoven does not mean a patchwork – interwoven means that the different threads come together thanks to skilled hands who do not hesitate to give their time in order to create an original work. Yes – the weaver was my destiny, but the threads, these were provided by my parents and their guidance for searching the threads – feelings – colours in nature.

As a child, I remember my mother accompanying my father on a baby grand piano in our dining room. My father sang operas, songs, parts of operettas and musicals, often in different languages. He would sing "Santa Lucia" in Italian, and "O Sole Mio" in Polish. "O Sole Mio" became "Moje Slonce." I remember every word of the main aria of *Rigoletto* with the Polish text. I remember *Tosca* and *La Traviata*. I will never forget the aria from Leoncavallo's *Pagliacci*. Through the text I understood the nature of every clown and his "columbine." I remember when my *tatus* explained to me when I was five or six years old that often when a clown amuses people, he smiles through tears. Yes – this was a lesson for life. It was the first time I heard about the concept "smiling through tears." It was the first time I encountered the meaning of suffering and the mask of happiness covering the inner tragedy.

Years later, when I admired Velazquez's *Las Meninas* (The Maids of Honour), I did not see the beautiful dress of the Infanta Margarita, but I saw the dwarf, the jester, dressed in his magnificent velvet attire – I looked at his face with his eyes penetrating the eyes of the viewer. Suffering was illustrated through the eyes of the jester of the Spanish court, while at the same time, he tried to face the world with the wisdom of knowledge – the real meaning of life. Again, years later, I learned that the great Indian poet and composer Rabindranath Tagore composed lyrical tunes to his own Bengali words that were so colourful and full of feeling like the romantic ballads. In an article entitled "The Meaning of Art," Tagore says, "Our immediate consciousness of reality as an end to its self gives us joy and this joy has its expression in arts." He points out that "in Sanskrit there is a word which means emotions as well as colour. Emotion gives colour to our consciousness, we see ourselves strongly when our mind is excited by any feeling."

"O Sole Mio" of Italy shone in the evening in our small apartment. My father's strong voice also sang the aria from *La Juive* by J.I.F. Halevy. There were operettas from Vienna: *The Merry Widow*, *Der Zigeuner Baron* (The Gypsy Baron), the waltzes of Strauss, and "Wien, Wien nur du allein." There were Russian songs in Polish, the romances.

I remember one Polish song about a *montagnard* who has to leave his mountains in search of a livelihood. The song expresses the sadness of someone whose heart will remain in the mountains forever. And there was a song from the time of the war of independence, the time of the Polish Legion under the leadership of Jozef Pilsudski, in which white roses bloom and bring to mind lives lost on the battlefields – lost for the freedom of those who come after them.

In my home I also heard my father singing Yiddish lullabies. I remember the melodies – their sweet nostalgia. I asked my father to translate the words for me. In one of them, written by Morris Rosenfeld, a Jewish poet who emigrated from Europe to New York, a father sings a song for his son. He says that whenever he sees him, his son is sleeping because he leaves early in the morning to work in a sweat shop. When he comes home at night after a long day's work, again his son is sleeping. When I first heard the song I did not know anything about the hardship experienced by people emigrating to the United States. This was also the first time that through song I encountered social history.

One evening in our home my father introduced us to jazz and to gospel music. I had not known about gospel music before, about songs that gave black people hope, courage, and strength during their time of slavery. I remember when I saw a black man for the first time in 1946 in Berlin, a tall, handsome American soldier, that evening of gospel songs came flooding back.

One time at home my father discussed an American book translated into Polish. The book was written by a Jewish musician who played in a jazz band made up of African-Americans. The musician was arrested and while in jail he wrote the book. It became a bestseller in the late 1920s. I do not recall the name of the author, but I remember that my father read us one page describing the similarities between the experiences of a black mother and a Jewish mother. Both tried to take care of their children but could not save them from discrimination.

Today, I think about this very often. A black mother and a Jewish mother can shelter their sons inside their homes, but on the street so often, the black child is called "a bloody nigger" and the Jewish child "the dirty Jew."

I have attended many universities in my life, but none of them has given me better lessons for understanding my fellow human beings than those I received in my own home. When I was very young, my favourite song was a Polish one, "Bajki" (Fairy Tales). The lyrics were written by Julian Tuwim, a great Polish poet and a Jew, who later made a very great personal impression on me. This song is about a nanny who tells fairy tales to the little boy she cares for. When the child becomes an adult, he asks the girl he loves to tell him the same fairy tales. We need fairy tales in life.

As I write today about it, I find myself once again in our dining room in Jaslo. My children know about the song. My father would sing it to my older son, Michel. And my younger son, Jacques, who is named for my father (who died five months before Jacques was born), asked me more than once to sing the song for him. Even his three daughters recognize the tune. They love it.

"O Sole Mio" and the nightingales met in our home. The world of music opened for me a window on the universe where language becomes secondary and feelings play a role in getting to know people and their cultures. The feelings and the colours are one.

The Sky and the Earth

I n Genesis we read, "In the beginning God created the heavens and the earth." Does humanity start its dialogue with God when we first come into the world? Is the new life of every human created in the image of God enriched with a gift, a gift of heaven, when we open our eyes and look above? What is life? Is the life of each person an experience of waiting for a ray of sun? Is the life of each person a reflection of the rainbow? Does the life of each person mirror day and night? Bright day or dark night, or the night full of stars, fireflies of heaven? Is this new life, the life of everyone from the beginning of their existence, endowed with the gift of the earth, this earth on which they will tread when they learn how to walk?

And what is love? Feeling? Is feeling the revelation of a miracle, a sense of happiness that someone has found another human being and together they can discover a new planet or the cosmos when the depth of feeling knows no borders? What is poetry? The words eternalized in the book, the song, the letter or the scrap of paper, the words expressing the echo of beauty or chaos, the echo of the angels or the echo of the fight with the devil? And what is music? The music of crickets on a summer day or the song of the nightingales at night accompanied by the strings of a harp?

Yes, we have dialogue with God when we gaze at the sky. We have dialogue with God as we touch the surface of the ocean with our lips or when we think about God who created the sky and the earth.

What is dialogue with God? We talk with God if we are able to take part in creating history, which God began. God is the creator of heaven and earth, this earth which is a tiny planet in the universe. But we don't know what the cosmos is, and in our inability to penetrate the mystery we accept our powerlessness, or rather, we accept our weakness. Very often, the greatest physicists develop a feeling of wonder as they face the puzzle of the phenomena of nature. We know that we don't understand, and in the awareness of our humility, our admiration is linked with fear. We admire God as creator. After meditation we pray for God's care.

And who is the child? This child that we love as a mother, a father, or a stranger, who in the eyes of the child discovers the greatness of God. And how does the poet comprehend the world? Does a person see the whole world in the mirror of his or her being? Does a person in his breath or in her touching the surface of water feel the pulse of life? The water in the stream is different from the water in the ocean; the water in the waterfalls disappears before the touch of our hand. Our tears have the taste of salt like the waves of the sea, and this taste remains on the lips of humans beings when they immerse themselves in water or swim. It is touch, the breath, the taste of life, the revelation of the existence of God and the revelation of the existence of man.

What does the poet see through his pupils when he has a dialogue with God? John Paul II writes,

> As long as you receive the sea,
> those waving circles of the sea
> into your open eyes,
> you feel all depth, every frontier
> drowning in you.

> But your foot touches a wave
> and you think: it is the sea
> that dwelt in me,
> spreading such calm around, such cool
> . . .

> Oh, to drown! to be drowned, first leaning out,
> then slowly slipping –
> you can't feel steps in the ebb,
> trembling you rush down.
> A soul, only a human soul sunk in a tiny drop,
> the soul snatched into the current.[6]

The poet sees and feels the soul, this soul immersed in one drop of water, this soul "snatched into the current."

The pope-poet can create a sanctuary under the open sky in the presence of a crowd, and this crowd looks with astonishment on this man who comes into contact with God in different parts of the world – under the sky of Peru, or Paris or Philadelphia. During his encounters with the crowds, this pope-poet is able to retain the essence of his being. At the same time, with his soul he strives to reach the family of humankind – people of different race, language, and religion. The greatest bond of communication is the soul – the motor that drives and the light that illumines our deeds – the soul and the commandments of God engraved on the tablet of the conscience.

On April 13, 1929, Karol's mother died at the age of forty-five. After the funeral, Karol and Edmund went with their father to Kalwaria Zebrzydowska to pray for the soul of their deceased mother. In his despair, the father of the future pope looked for support for his sons and for himself. The father believed that in the sanctuary of the Mother of Christ, his pain would find consolation in faith. Years afterward, Pope Paul John II said that, for him, Kalwaria Zebrzydowska was the reservoir of faith. Pilgrims come to this sanctuary during Easter and the Feast of the Assumption. Like the Holy Virgin in Czestochowa (the Black Madonna), the Madonna of Kalwaria Zebrzydowska occupies a special place in the hearts of Polish Christians. At Kalwaria Zebrzydowska, after the death of his mother, in his suffering the pope of today perhaps asked the Virgin Mary to take him under her care. The nine-year-old child, who was deprived early on of his mother's care, found the Mother of Christ, and he prayed ardently that she would help him overcome his loneliness and guide his steps.

Who is the Virgin Mary? For Karol this was not an abstract image of a mother from faraway Jerusalem. She was a mother who had suffered and understood the sufferings of all mothers who suffered before her and after her in the history of mankind. This mother – *Mater Dolorosa* – became a symbol of mothers and children seeking consolation in their faith.

The poet-pope never forgot the suffering of the orphan. He longed to have his mother with him. But he could not scream, he could not express his pain. He only prayed that the Holy Mother would give him the spirituality and the strength – the grace – to lift up the hem of eternity for a while, to reveal the sun and send him a tiny ray of light.

This adoration for the Blessed Mother perhaps started there, when the nine-year-old boy stood or knelt beside his father and his older brother and prayed with his own words. Maybe at this time he said, "Holy Mother, don't leave my father, my brother, and me."

The Blesed Mother and prayer helped him become a man, a righteous man with heart and mind, with a good, sincere heart, a great open mind, and a fully formed conscience.

In the encyclical *Dominum et Vivificantum*, about the Holy Spirit in the Church and in the World, John Paul II says this about conscience:

> The conscience therefore is not an independent and exclusive capacity to decide what is good and what is evil. Rather there is profoundly imprinted upon it a principle of obedience vis-à-vis the objective norm which establishes and conditions the correspondence of its decisions with the commands and prohibitions which are at the basis of human behaviour, as from the passage of the Book of Genesis which we have already considered. Precisely in this sense the conscience is the "secret sanctuary" in which "God's voice echoes." The conscience is "the voice of God," even when man recognizes in it nothing more than the principle of the moral order which it is not humanly possible to doubt, even without any direct reference to the Creator. It is precisely in reference to this that the conscience always finds its foundation and justification.[7]

In Pope John Paul II's modest room in the Vatican there is a picture of the Blessed Mother, the Black Madonna from Czestochowa, whom the Polish nation crowned in the seventeenth century. Perhaps there in the Vatican memories return – memories of childhood and memories of the Holy Mother who offered her care to the nine-year-old boy and helped him to grow up to be a true, noble man. Maybe there in the Vatican the Holy Father thinks and prays that the children who are born can live in a world where the love of one individual for all humanity reigns.

And maybe, during the war, the Holy Father, the Messenger of the Church, thought about the Mother of Christ when Jewish mothers cried in Krakow as Jewish children were killed without mercy.

Maybe through building bridges, Pope John Paul II tries to ease the sufferings of all mothers and children, and especially those who are persecuted.

The ABCs of Life

What does the ABC of life mean? Is it only the first lesson in school? What is this ABC of life? Is it searching in the world around you for the keys to understanding life? Or is this the revelation of your first discoveries in your own being and at the same time putting to the test your own longing? Is this the exploration of your own dreams, which were not taught but were formed within you at the moment you came into the world and started to breathe on your own? Do we encounter the first miracle of life as the power of inhaling air into our small lungs? Do we encounter the second miracle by distinguishing people around our bed and feeling arms taking us and giving us the kiss of love?

There are millions of different ABCs of life, and thinking about that makes us wonder about all the possibilities that life offers to us on a gold tray, asking: "Try me? Taste me?" – Life is worth testing. The ABCs of life offer us the taste of life – rich, fascinating, sometimes acting as a strong drug or caressing, giving us the sweetest dreams. We taste life through our feelings. First they overwhelm our emotional being, and later they invade every part of our organism, acting as a stimulant in every particle of our physical being.

I remember one summer on my grandmother's estate when I learned one of the many ABCs of life. I am perhaps six years old. My parents, my brother, and I are spending a few weeks' vacation there. Even though she is struggling to hold on to it, my grandmother does not want to sell a single acre of her estate. Even so, there are magnificent horses in the stable. Her two sons, Leon and Ben (Benio), who help her manage the estate, love horses as their late father had.

For several days I observe my father always riding the same horse, The Count. I loved to watch him riding fast. He had ridden horses since he was young at the homes of his students during summer vacations. One day after my father came back from his ride, I go to the stable and ask the man in charge to put the saddle on the horse that my father had ridden a short while before.

Riding was to become just one of the innumerable ABCs of my life, those ABCs of life that make us wonder about all the possibilities that life offers to us on a gold or platinum tray, asking: try me, taste me – life is worth testing. These ABCs of life offer us a taste of life, rich, fascinating, sometimes acting as a strong drug or as gentle as a caress, giving us the sweetest of dreams. We taste the ABCs of life through our feelings.

I tell the man in the stable, Petro, a young Ukrainian who spoke Polish, that my father has allowed me to go to the stable and I ask him to prepare The Count for me. I also tell him, after he had saddled the horse, to lift me up. I tell him I know how to ride.

I start to ride. I will never forget the taste of speed. I hold the reins tightly as I start to gallop. I experience joy. I am not afraid. I go far through the fields and suddenly I realize that I do not know how to turn the horse. The Count is still galloping when we come to the fields where people are working. I know how to stop the horse, so I do, and ask what I have to do to turn the horse round. Someone advises me to pull the reins left or right. I do. I succeed and I come back to the stable very happy.

My parents, of course, had a very different experience of this memory. I had disappeared for quite a long time, and they had started to look for me. Petro had told them that I asked him to put me up on the saddle of The Count and said I had told him that my father had given me permission to ride.

Meanwhile, somewhere in the fields a worker had found one of the fancy little combs that I used to keep my hair in place. My parents became even more worried. Everyone was anxious to see me back. I was reprimanded, but eventually allowed to ride again. My father said to me, "Be careful, and tell your mother or me when you want to ride." My father's attitude was typical of the way I was treated – "Be careful." I think that he enjoyed my courage, certainly more than my mother did.

The vacation was great. During our stay on the estate my two cousins arrived: Albin and Jerzy. Albin was my age and Jerzy was eight years older. Jerzy was a very good-looking boy. For me he was the best looking boy in the world. He had blue eyes, blond hair and was very tall and slim. Years later, when I was a teenager, I thought he was a very handsome man and I did not try to hide my feelings. Even today, after so many years, he remains my good-looking cousin.

Albin started to ride horses with me and Jerzy took pictures. He was very proud of his camera. He also developed his pictures alone in the cellar, in his darkroom. Albin and I were not allowed to enter there. Albin was the best friend I ever had until the end of his life. Albin was the son of my mother's older sister, Hania. She was married to a lawyer, Maximilian Schiff. They lived in Rymanow, just 40 kilometres from Jaslo, and my parents visited them often. Although Albin forgave me, he was always reminding me that because of me he had broken his nose. He was referring to an accident that happened when we were three years old. One day after Albin had received a gift of a wooden horse, I told him that we should ride this horse together. While riding, I pushed Albin, he fell and broke his nose. I was very, very sorry, but my sympathy could not straighten his nose.

We loved to visit Aunt Hania. She had a good sense of humour. She also played the piano. She loved me because she did not have a daughter, something she often she complained about. My uncle was very serious, very educated, a great scholar, always studying. As a child I could not understand why he seemed to love a big set of encyclopaedias best.

During our childhood we store memories. When it comes to my own outlook on life, I think I never stopped storing memories. Certain events in my life left a mark and contributed to my understanding of nature and of people. I always look for common ground when I meet people, and this allows me to create links of understanding beyond the surface of things and events.

There is another childhood reminiscence which has left in me a never-changing fascination with nature. This feeling of the presence of nature is another gift of life. During our next vacation, my parents, my brother, and I travelled by train to the Baltic Sea. The journey from Jaslo to Sopoty (Sobot, today) took more than nine hours. We were very excited. For Adam and me that was our longest trip. On European trains it was possible to open the windows in the compartments and on the adjoining corridors. I remember when my father took me from the compartment in which we were sitting and brought me to the window in the corridor. He opened the window and showed me the sunset. It was magnificent, with millions of colours, at first not moving and later disappearing in the sky. It was a miracle unfolding itself as my father explained to me in a most poetic way the splendour of nature. This enchantment with nature has never left me. One day when I read the poet Byron's question, "Are we a part of nature, is nature a part of us?" I understood that both Byron and I had grasped the link between nature and humanity.

After obtaining my Ph.D. in Philadelphia, I was awarded a fellowship at the University of Pennsylvania in 1980. My philosophy research project on the meaning of life was accepted. As part of my research, I prepared 72 questions designed to investigate people's understanding of the meaning of life. I interviewed psychiatrists, psychologists, and social workers in the Philadelphia area. The university provided me with a list of people to interview. One question was this: "Do you remember any sunset in your life?" I posed this simple question to different people, yet for some it was astonishing. They would ask, "Is it important? Does it have anything relevant to the meaning of life?" After a while, even if they declined to answer the first question, some were anxious to come back to it and said "Maybe, maybe, remembering a sunset does have something to do with the meaning of life."

One of the social workers was very interested in my question. Her reaction was spontaneous. She exclaimed with enthusiasm, "Yes, yes, I remember! It is not a sunset but a dark night with many, many stars," she said. She continued, "I am from Montana. My father was a farmer. One winter night when we had a lot of snow, we could not get the car near the farm. My father decided to park quite far from home. He took me on his shoulders and at one point he told me to look at the sky. I was three, four, or five years old. My father talked to me about the sky, the stars. And this evening never disappeared from my being." I was in Philadelphia, interviewing a woman who grew up in Montana, and I saw that the social worker's father and my father were alike. These fathers, one from Montana and one from Poland, had offered their daughters a great lesson, the ABCs, as it were, of life with nature.

I was very young when I went to elementary school. I was always the youngest in the class because the principal of the Maria Konopnicka School, Mrs. Alfreda Breitmeier, was a friend of my parents (her husband was from Stryj and had been a classmate of my father's), and she thought I would enjoy learning. She was right. I loved school and my first teacher, Mrs. Orlowska (I am so sorry I have forgotten her first name). Mrs. Orlowska was middle-aged, with long braids around her head. She was a widow, was very kind, and she made me love school. She did not mind my sense of humour and wrote many kind words in my diary "to the smiling pupil."

I was fascinated with my teacher, and with learning. I always walked to school with my friend Janka Mordawska, a daughter of two teachers, who also knew my parents well. I sat near Janka during my twelve years of schooling – we were always together, and after 43 years when we met again, we had not changed our idea of a great relationship, and each year at Christmas we wrote to each other.

I was in this elementary school for four years. I loved stories, songs, and counting. I loved everything. Janka and I found a shortcut going to school, so we were always very early. The shortcut led us past a big bakery where we enjoyed the smell of fresh bread every day. The people working in this bakery always smiled and laughed with us as we walked by.

In elementary school I learned to appreciate Poland, her history, her fight for independence, and the beautiful landscape and nature of Poland. I remember Jan Kasprowicz's poems in the collection *Krzak dzikiej rozy* (A Wild Rose Bush), written in 1898, about the beauty of the Tatra mountains.

When I was in the fourth grade, the Marshal of Poland, Jozef Pilsudski, who created the Legions and fought with these legions for independence during the Second World War, went on vacation to the island of Madeira. School children were encouraged to write him a letter or postcard. I was very excited when my teacher singled out my letter and said it was beautiful. I do not remember what I said there, but I was very proud of having written it. It was true I was proud of my words, but my handwriting was certainly not beautiful. I tried to imitate Janka, whose handwriting was exquisite, and is to this day beautiful. But I did not succeed.

I had many friends in school. I admired one of my first grade classmates, Janina (Dzidzia) Czelusniak, for her beauty. She was really a beautiful girl and always wore nice clothes. I remember one day I saw her wearing an embroidered light-green sweater. I had never seen anything as beautiful as this sweater, but it did not enter my mind to ask my parents to buy me something similar. I never envied anything and I think this was also implanted in me by my parents. We knew that certain people had more money, or less, but money was not considered the most important factor in having a happy life. However, many years later in Philadelphia I bought myself a very inexpensive sweater because it was similar to Janina Czelusniak's.

But why do I write about a sweater? This is also part of the ABCs of life – seeing, liking, and paying attention to everything. Mindfulness, as it is called in Buddhist philosophy.

To know about the beauty of the Tatra mountains teaches us to look at our surroundings, and to admire a sweater that we like teaches us about everyday pleasures. We often forget how children form their tastes in childhood.

One day during my elementary school career I was shocked into sadness and disbelief. It was my introduction to animosity toward Jews as it was presented in a Christmas play. Several schools presented a play about Christmas in the Sokol Theatre, the biggest auditorium in Jaslo. I attended this play with my father. I remember we sat near the front, in the third or fourth row. At one point a teenage boy actor said, "And the Judases, the Jews, I will not spare." My father got up, took my hand and with his strong loud voice said, "I did not come here to listen to anti-Semitic remarks." There was consternation among the audience which lasted a few minutes. My father had made his point for the people present there and for me, and we left.

Later, during the war, my parents, Adam, and I were forced to live as Christians with forged documents. We had many friends who worked for the underground, and I was connected all the time with them, sometimes providing them with useful information since I worked as a secretary in the sawmill and was at the switchboard. My German director had many conversations with the police authorities and on my telephone line. I was able to gather information about what was going on in the vicinity.

One Sunday afternoon in the spring of 1944, a few weeks before this part of Poland was liberated by the Russian forces, a friend brought a colleague of his to our home. This particular friend visited us very often but this was the first time we had seen his colleague, an educated young man who was active in the underground. Naturally, we were discussing politics and the present situation. Suddenly, at one point the man said, "Frankly speaking, I have to admit that I hate Germans, but I hate Jews even more. Even now, knowing that the German occupation seems to be at an end, if I knew where any Jew was hiding, I would denounce him or her to the Germans." I will never forget my father's reaction. He calmly asked a simple question: "Why do you hate Jews so much?" And the answer was, "My father hates them. And my grandfather does, too." I will never forget this conversation because my father said this not only for him but also for the benefit of Adam and me. He wanted to show us that in spite of our dangerous way of living, he still had not lost his courage and dignity. Here we were, four Jews, the whole family. If our friend's colleague had suspected us for one moment, I would certainly not be writing this book.

This was the end of our conversation. The two men left. We had in our hands a powerful clandestine paper informing us of the fight that was taking place in the forests and in the cities.

We have to weigh in the balance these remarks: hate on the one side and the actions of people who did not stop being human beings on the other.

The Street

Some streets seem to retain the breath of people who live on them. Some streets seem to preserve the memory of the steps of every passer-by. Some streets smile. Others cry. Some streets are bland and inexpressive, while the truly memorable ones possess a soul.

On a narrow street in Barcelona is a small museum devoted to Pablo Picasso. The entrance to this museum opens directly onto the street, and the street lives with Picasso. Raynouard Street in the sixteenth arrondissement of Paris, not far from the Place Trocadero and the Eiffel Tower, retains the memory of the great novelist Balzac, the connoisseur of human characters. Certain streets in Jerusalem remember the words of the prophet Isaiah and the words of Christ, and their thoughts seem to vibrate in the air.

In Wadowice, there is the street on which little Lolek took his first steps in the city that would leave its mark on the future pope, the shepherd of one billion Catholics, who sees people as people in spite of their different religions. Many people – Catholics as well as Jews – walked on the streets of Wadowice. (In this part of the country there were not many Protestants or Orthodox Christians.)

Catholicism is bound up with the history of Poland, a country whose geographic location has ensured it an important role in the history of Europe. Two neighbouring powers, Russia and Germany, have left their traces on the shape of Polish history, with their constant challenge to Poland to be ready to defend her political independence and to defend the Catholic Church. Poland was often called the rampart of Christianity.

One in ten Poles were Jewish. The sense of belonging to Poland was deeply rooted in the Jews who chose to live there, and in 1939 they numbered 3,300,000. How did these Jews reach Poland? Where did they come from? Who were these Jews? Like Jews anywhere in the world, Polish Jews belonged to many different groups. Some were rich, some were poor; some were very poor indeed. Some possessed deep knowledge of Judaism and religion, some possessed deep knowledge of science, culture, or history, while some were not educated at all. Some were pious and went to the synagogue every Saturday. Some were assimilated; only their identification papers reminded them that they were Jews. Others were assimilated but still remembered that they had Jewish ancestry. Some were great scholars recognized not only in Poland but across Europe as well. Among the Jews of Poland were famous poets, writers, composers, pianists, violinists, and singers. Some knew Yiddish, while others were not familiar with it at all and spoke only Polish. Many were farmers, shoemakers, merchants, and tailors. They lived in the cities, in the villages, and in small settlements. Carpathia and the Tatra Mountains were theirs. The Baltic Sea was theirs. Poland was their homeland. They did not know any other soil. A Jewish child, eyes open for the first time, saw the Polish sky and the Polish earth.

Not surprisingly, many legends have been passed down about the history of Jews in Poland. One tells the story of the first Jew who came to Gniezno, long before the Poles had accepted the Christian faith. At that time the inhabitants of Poland congregated in Gniezno to choose a leader who could govern the country. The meeting was long, but still the Poles could neither decide, nor agree among themselves. Finally, one of them proposed offering the position of ruler to the first newcomer to arrive in Gniezno. The next day a foreigner, a Jew, arrived and the Poles offered him the crown. The foreigner said that he must think it over and asked for three days to reflect before he made a decision. In the group awaiting the answer was a certain strong and courageous man named Piast. After the first day of waiting, without paying attention to the people around, Piast opened the door to the room where the Jew was staying and requested an immediate decision. The Jew quietly answered, "I cannot accept the Polish crown and become your king, but I can offer you a king. His name is Piast. Piast, the only one who had courage to open the door and come in without any hesitation, knowing that the country needed a ruler."

This Jew was Abraham Prochownik. Through the legend we get to know something of the spirit of the people, along with the name of the first Polish Jew, who, like Abraham in the Bible, was received in a foreign country. For the first time in the promised land, Melchizedek, the King of Salem (today's Jerusalem) met Patriarch Abraham. Melchizedek, whose name means "just king," greeted Abraham with bread and wine and offered him his blessings. We read about it in Chapter 7 of the Letter to the Hebrews.

> This "Melchizedek, king of Salem and priest of God Most High," "met Abraham as he returned from his defeat of the kings" and "blessed him." And Abraham apportioned to him "a tenth of everything." His name first means righteous king, and he was also "king of Salem," that is, king of peace. Without father, mother, or ancestry, without beginning of days or end of life, thus made to resemble the Son of God, he remains a priest forever.
>
> (Hebrews 7:1-3)

Abraham Prochownik, like his ancestor Abraham, met people who received him with all their heart. The legend is a living one, and in every century someone adds a few words, a description, an expression of admiration or astonishment. In this way the legend cannot be erased from memory.

Somewhere in Wielkopolska, near Gniezno, an old man would tell his grandson the story of a Jew whose name was Abraham Prochownik. Years passed. Many years passed. What happened to Abraham Prochownik, no one knows. His name also has its meaning. The Polish word *proch* means "dust" in English. The grains of dust of the first few Jews mingled with the grains of dust of the Polish soil. There near Gniezno on this soil walked Catholic and Jewish children near one another. Their homeland was Poland. They did not know any other soil.

In all the schools in Poland, children learned by heart a poem that begins with these words:

Who are you, little Pole?

What is your sign?

The white eagle –

In Polish schools, the Catholic and Jewish children learned, side by side, how to be Poles. For Jews it was not difficult to learn how to be Polish. In all the countries where Jews lived it was possible to be loyal to the country and contribute to its history and culture. If Jews all over the world showed these characteristics, they could be seen as the outcome of the teachings of the prophet Jeremiah and his letter sent to the inhabitants of Judea after they were exiled to Babylon. This letter became a testament of Jeremiah and a guiding thought for all the Jews dispersed in the world.

> Thus says the LORD of hosts, the God of Israel, to all the exiles whom I exiled from Jerusalem to Babylon: Build houses to dwell in; plant gardens, and eat their fruits. Take wives and beget sons and daughters; find wives for your sons and give your daughters husbands, so that they may bear sons and daughters. There you must increase in number, not decrease. Promote the welfare of the city to which I have exiled you; pray to the LORD, for upon its welfare depends your own. . . .
>
> Thus says the LORD: Only after seventy years have elapsed for Babylon will I visit you and fulfill for you my promise to bring you back to this place. For I know well the plans I have in mind for you, says the LORD, plans for your welfare, not for woe! plans to give you a future full of hope. When you call me, when you go to pray to me, I will listen to you. When you look for me, you will find me. Yes, when you seek me with all your heart, you will find me with you, says the LORD, and I will change your lot; I will gather you together from all the nations and all the places to which I have banished you, says the LORD, and bring you back to the place from which I have exiled you.
>
> (Jeremiah 29:4-14)

The Jews who heard Jeremiah understood that they should not listen to the false prophets who were promising them a return to Judea after a short time. According to Jeremiah they had to build houses, cultivate vineyards, and work and pray for the prosperity of the country in which they lived. From generation to generation they continued their traditions and customs and tried to live according to the rules of their religion. Maybe they were not even thinking about Jeremiah's letter. But this letter was the foundation of their sense of belonging to faraway Jerusalem.

In Ethiopia, Jews lived in complete seclusion from other Jews for a thousand years, and they survived as Jews. In many places in China it is possible to meet Chinese Jews whose ancestors came from far away.

In the same way, the Polish soil was the country of Jews, and not only in poetry. The Polish soil offered them a home. A home cannot be between the sky and the earth. Home must be built on the soil, and the soil becomes dear for the one who lives in this home. The church was near the synagogue, the synagogue was near the church, and prayers from both mingled high in space above the Polish sky.

In *Crossing the Threshold of Hope*, Pope John Paul II recalls a conversation with Victorio Nossori about his childhood and youth in Wadowice.

> Nossori: At this point it is natural to assume that Your Holiness intends to speak of Judaism.

> Pope John Paul II: That is right. Through the amazing plurality of religions, arranged as it were in concentric circles, we come to the religion that is closest to our own – that of the people of God of the Old Testament.

> The words from the Declaration *Nostra Aetate* represent a turning point. The Council says: ". . . . The Church, then, can forget neither that it received the revelation of the Old Testament through that people with whom God, in His ineffable mercy, made the Ancient Covenant, nor can the Church forget that it draws sustenance from the root of that good olive tree onto which have been grafted the wild shoots, the Gentiles. . . . Therefore, since the spiritual patrimony common to Christians and Jews is so great, this Sacred Council recommends and promotes a mutual understanding and respect, which can be obtained above all through biblical study and fraternal discussion" (4).

> The words of the Council's Declaration reflect the experience of many people, both Jews and Christians. They reflect my personal experience as well, from the very first years of my life in my hometown. I remember, above all, the Wadowice elementary school, where at least a fourth of the pupils in my class were Jewish. I should mention my friendship at school

with one of them, Jerzy Kluger – a friendship that has lasted from my school days to the present. I can vividly remember the Jews who gathered every Saturday at the synagogue behind our school. Both religious groups, Catholics and Jews, were united, I presume, by the awareness that they prayed to the same God. Despite their different languages, prayers in the church and in the synagogue were based to a considerable degree on the same texts.[8]

The prayers John Paul II refers to were expressed in Latin, in Polish, in Hebrew, and often in Hebrew translated in Poland, but they reached the same God.

The Minuet of Ignacy Paderewski and "Janko the Musician" of Henryk Sienkiewicz

I remember as a child listening to my mother as she played the piano alone, not accompanying my father. One day as I listened I asked the name of the piece she played. "This is a waltz of Chopin," she said simply and then explained that Chopin was a great composer who had composed many waltzes. Thus the name of Chopin entered my memory. Later, when I played "Valse Brilliante," Opus 34, No. 3, I remembered my first encounter with this music many years before. I wanted to play like my mother.

I started taking piano lessons at the age of five and a half. I wanted to play Chopin. I told this to my first music teacher, Mr. Mirski. I forget his first name. He was quite old, maybe 45 or 50 years old. He came to Jaslo every week from the city of Rzeszow, and was considered the best teacher in the area. He asked me to do exercises – scales up and down the keys. He was very strict, and after the first six months he told my parents that I would never play in my lifetime because I didn't practise. "She wants to play Chopin without knowing how to read music properly," he said. My mother thanked him, and a month later I had a new teacher, Mrs. Dollard. She was the former wife of Mr. Mirski, and lived in Jaslo with her second husband. She had three children. She taught me piano and ballet combined with rhythmic exercises. There were only six or seven girls in the dancing group. Mrs. Dollard was beautiful and charming, and she treated her pupils like her own children.

My mother watched my progress very attentively. She always said that she could teach me piano, but she believed that I needed the guidance of someone who was not involved in my everyday life. My mother sat with me almost every day and listened. She corrected my mistakes, often playing for me and encouraging me to aspire to play well.

I don't exactly remember when I took part in a piano recital for the first time, but I was maybe seven or eight years old. I had to play a minuet by Ignacy Paderewski. I was very proud since I knew a lot about the composer. He was famous as a pianist and a composer, and had also played an important role in Polish history. It was Paderewski who, in the name of Poland, signed the Treaty of Versailles when Poland regained her independence. In 1919 he became Prime Minister. Although he served in this capacity for only a few months, he earned respect in Poland and elsewhere, where his fame as a pianist and composer preceded his involvement in politics.

I looked forward with great anticipation to my piano recital. The minuet was not too difficult, and I thought it would be fun to play in front of an audience. Just after I began playing, I realized that I had forgotten one part of the minuet so I skipped this part and immediately continued without stopping. Only people who were well acquainted with this minuet would know what I had missed. It was true, I had forgotten a few measures, but I did not panic. That recital taught me something. I knew that in life we must always go forward. When I think about it today, I realize that events that occur in childhood can provoke our immediate reaction and become constructive or destructive forces years later. I also understood that we can learn from our mistakes. I was better prepared for my later recitals, and there would be many. Each time, I remembered that minuet of Paderewski.

History and culture began to shape my character in my childhood. My admiration for Chopin and for Paderewski left a very great impression on me. Polish culture and Polish history entered the atmosphere of learning every day at home and in school.

My parents also believed in the value of sports. I remember when I started skating and skiing. One time, I was skating on a rink in the park. In my memory, I see always my mother wearing her Persian lamb coat and a little mink hat, standing beside the skating rink, shivering. Each time I fell she tried to reassure me that after two or three times around the rink, I would skate better. When I complained that I was cold, she told me not to be afraid to skate faster. Later, whenever I skated in different parts of the world, I thought about my first skating rink and my mother beside it. Many years later in Montreal, I was happy when one of my sons told me that he was proud of me when I took part in the evening skating and that I was one of only three parents on the rink. When I came to Philadelphia I tried to skate with my cousin Albin in the Marriott near the City Line. We were quite often together and had many opportunities to talk about our childhood.

The idea of swimming came to me when I was at the Baltic Sea for the first time. One day it was cool but I insisted on going into the water. I was the only one; the shore was deserted, except for my mother waiting for me. Suddenly a young lady came, and started to speak to her. Apparently she asked why my mother had let me go into the water on such a cold day. After I came out of the water the young woman started to talk to me, but since she did not speak Polish (she was German) I asked my mother to translate. My mother spoke German very well. The woman invited me to come to an open-air performance by the Berlin Opera, in which she was singing. My parents already had tickets, and although Adam was very young, they decided to bring both of us along. This was the first time that I experienced theatre in the open air. The whole opera was like a fairy-tale story for me. I did not understand very much, but the voices were wonderful and I watched not only the stage but the also the sea, far off in the distance, illuminated by the lights.

The summer after that, when I was six or seven, I decided I had to teach myself how to swim. So many other people could swim, so why not me? I worked hard, trying to imitate those other people. I did not want to take lessons since I thought it must be easy to swim. And I succeeded one morning in one of the three rivers flowing near Jaslo (Jasiolka, Wisloka, and Ropa). I do not remember which beach I was on when I started to swim. I called this the first time "swimming by myself." Very often I had a good partner in Albin, who spent a lot of his vacation time in our home. His father was ill, and his mother travelled with her husband to consult with different medical doctors in Poland and even beyond. Eventually his father improved. During the Second World War, he died in the Soviet Union after the family was deported by the Russians.

When I think of my life in Jaslo, I try to imagine life in Wadowice at around the same time. Karol Wojtyla was in a school very similar to mine, and like me, he was brought up in a home atmosphere where loving parents tried to give the best they could offer. I also like to think that Chopin and Paderewski entered his mind during his childhood as well. This was our Polish culture planted in our thoughts.

I know that Karol Wojtyla liked music and also liked sports. Ours was the first generation born in an independent Poland, and at the same time we were taught about the history which preceded us. We loved Poland, we loved life, and we loved freedom. We appreciated this freedom and we were always aware that Poland was situated between two giants – Germany and Russia. Although the majority of Poles were Catholics, their neighbours had different religions and cultures. I was Jewish but I did not love Poland any less than Janka, who was Catholic. Church bells were familiar; they were equally a part of her childhood and of mine.

In our schools we were introduced to the world through Polish literature, as well as to world literature in Polish translation. In my fourth grade, one of the stories that impressed me was Henryk Sienkiewicz's *Janko muzykant* (Janko the Musician), in which Sienkiewicz describes a young boy who lived in a village and loved music. I remember the teacher told us to write about "Janko the Musician" for our homework. We were to think about him and music. My thoughts were preoccupied with the youngster who, in spite of his difficulties and poverty, dreamt about becoming a musician. I was very moved by the story, and I started with the sentence: "Music is an international language." I no longer remember what I said after that, but it was at this time that I began to understand children who were poor and whose life was very different from mine. Like all other children, they too had dreams. My teacher liked my composition very much and asked me to read it aloud to my class. After bringing the composition home I went to show it to my father. He was not in his office, but the apprentice lawyer who worked for him read my assignment and said, "You will be a good lawyer." I did not become a lawyer, but I was proud after hearing his opinion of my work. Many years later I still think about how Janko the Musician often faced suffering and humiliation but did not give up on his dreams.

The second work of Sienkiewicz that I read during my early childhood was *W pustyni i w puszczy* (In Desert and Wilderness). In these adventures of an English girl and Polish boy I learned to admire faraway places and the courage and heroism of the main characters. The historical books by Sienkiewicz that I read later on were strongly connected with Christianity. These novels illustrate Polish culture, where history and the Christian faith intermingle. *The Knights of the Teutonic Order (Krzyzacy)* was the best addition to the history classes showing the complicated relationships and fights between the Poles and the Teutonic Order. Sienkiewicz's famous novel *Quo Vadis*, about the beginnings of Christianity, the cruelty of Nero, and the persecution of the first Christians, has always remained in my memory. I read it with my whole being. Years later I went to see the movie *Quo Vadis* with my older son Michel in Montreal, and I cried. Michel tried to console me, saying, "Mummy, this is only a movie. Don't cry." I realized that I was crying just as I had cried the first time I read the book.

We do not forget our childhood. I sometimes touch the keys of my piano now and play the beginning of Paderewski's minuet. Since that first recital I have forgotten more than one part of this composition, and my staccato has less rhythm and more nostalgia. I am transmitting the story of my life now in words which I write in English on American soil. "Who are you?" I ask myself. I try to answer, "You are the past and the present, and the beginning, if you only know how to dream."

Like Janko the Musician, I learned a lot in my childhood. I dare say that far away in the Vatican, the Holy Father, who read the same books as I read, knows that to continue to dream is one of life's greatest gifts.

Father and Son

K arol was thirteen years old when his brother Edmund died. For the second time, death looked into the eyes of this young boy and in silence took his brother, of whom Karol was so proud. He was as proud as his father, knowing that his son was a medical doctor. Edmund died in Bielsko, where he contracted scarlet fever from a patient and did not survive the illness. An acquaintance who witnessed Karol getting the news related that Karol uttered only one sentence: "This was the will of God."

Without a doubt, the death of his brother was a great blow to Karol's father and to Karol, who recalled on countless occasions the moments he had spent with Edmund. During Karol's visits, Edmund, his doctor brother, had tried to re-introduce him to his life and to his work. In the hospital Karol accompanied Edmund and often talked to the patients. Often this cheerful young boy brought smiles to the sick people. Karol met the suffering of strangers and tried to bring them just a little joy. Perhaps already at this time Karol's nature and his outlook on life were directing him toward helping those who were suffering.

The brother left forever. In the Wojtyla family, only the father and son remained, and the son understood that he had to accept destiny and the will of God with faith.

Karol's father loved him very much and wanted to instill in him moral and physical strength. He knew that the conditions of life could vary and he tried to fortify Karol by different means. Sometimes Karol had to stay in an unheated room for long periods. But he was accustomed to discipline and never complained. He believed that what his father was doing was right. Along with his demands, Karol's father gave him much love and warmth. He instilled in him the meaning of faith and brought up his son as a religious person. At the same time, through his own behaviour and example, he always emphasized that people should be treated with understanding and respect regardless of who they were or what they believed. This respect for God and all people was important guidance for his son.

At the same time Karol's father also fostered in him a love of life. He tried to take the place of Karol's mother and to make sure his son had a home. He took care of Karol, and focused all his attention on his upbringing. He taught Karol to take care of his appearance and always to dress neatly. He helped Karol do his homework. He prepared meals and tried to see that his son ate regularly. Sometimes father and son would go to small restaurants. In the evening they would go for walks. During these walks their friendship deepened. Their conversations and discussions covered a range of topics.

Without a doubt, the memories the Holy Father has today go back not only to his experiences as a student and later as a professor in the Catholic University in Lublin, but also to the lessons his father gave him in the course of their conversations during those long walks.

All of us develop our own philosophy of life. But who helps to lead us to those philosophies? Not only our teachers and professors in schools and universities, but also the members of our family, and all those we meet in the course of our lives, who influence our outlook on the world. These are the people who try to help young minds and, later, adults, get to the source of goodness and evil.

Our character is shaped in our childhood and our youth. Some of the shaping of character attributes and features are the outcome of our combat with ourselves in the moment that we realize that we could be whoever we are supposed to be. The German poet Johann Wolfgang von Goethe wrote:

If we take man as he is
we make him worse,
if we take him as he ought to be
we help him to become one.

Students who study the works of famous philosophers may sometimes reflect, in their own lives and thoughts, ideas that were implanted in their childhood and youth. As a professor at the Catholic

University in Lublin, Karol Wojtyla likely thought about his father while giving lectures on Aristotle and his concept of the "good." It is true that the philosophy of life of the young Karol started there in Wadowice, before he studied the *Nicomachean Ethics* and the fragment about the virtues and weaknesses of man. The world of Aristotle and his student may have contained all the seeds that were planted in Karol by his father.

When Karol started to serve Holy Mass in 1930, he was ten years old. The church brought to this motherless child the spiritual outlook that allowed him to remain a cheerful boy and live peacefully with the people who surrounded him. This particular period, from 1930 to 1938, was without doubt a very important one in the pope's life.

In the Gospel according to Matthew is a passage that is often quoted by Christians in answer to the question "Why did you help the Jews who were in danger during the war and not hesitate to risk your own life?" In Chapter 25 we read these word of Jesus:

"For I was hungry and you gave me food, I was thirsty and you gave me something to drink, I was a stranger and you welcomed me, I was naked and you gave me clothing, I was sick and you took care of me, I was in prison and you visited me." Then the righteous will answer him, "Lord, when was it that we saw you hungry and gave you food, or thirsty and gave you something to drink? And when was it that we saw you a stranger and welcomed you, or naked and gave you clothing? And when was it that we saw you sick or in prison and visited you?" And the king will answer them, "Truly I tell you, just as you did it to one of the least of these who are members of my family, you did it to me."

(Matthew 25:35-40)

Perhaps the father of Pope John Paul II recited his Psalms aloud, and perhaps their words remained in the memory of the son, who was raised by his father to grow up as a good man. Psalm 146 describes the kind of trust in God that Karol's father instilled in him as a child:

Trust in God the Creator and Redeemer
Hallelujah!
Praise the Lord, my soul;
I shall praise the Lord all my life,

sing praise to my God while I live.
Put no trust in princes,
in mere mortals powerless to save.
Where they breathe their last, they return to the earth;
that day all their planning comes to nothing.
Happy those whose help is Jacob's God,
whose hope is the Lord, their God,
The maker of heaven and earth,
the seas and all that is in them.
Who keeps faith forever,
secures justice for the oppressed,
gives food to the hungry.
The Lord sets prisoners free;
the Lord gives sight to the blind.
The Lord raises up those who are bowed down;
the Lord loves the righteous.
The Lord protects the stranger,
maintains the orphan and the widow,
but thwarts the way of the wicked.
The Lord shall reign forever,
your God, Zion, through all generations!
Hallelujah!

The father may have directed his son's attention to the verse "God gives sight to the blind." Many people possess excellent eyesight, but they have no spiritual vision and they do not see God. Others, through the grace of God, are able to see what is not visible. There exist also those who neither see the visible, nor are able to feel God.

Years later, the pope-poet would write "The Song of the Hidden God."

What does it mean that I see that much
in seeing nothing?
When the last bird sinks below the horizon,
and the wave hides it in its glass,
still lower I fall, plunging with the bird
into the tide of cool glass.
The more I strain my sight, the less I see.
Water bends over the sun to bring the reflection nearer,

the farther the shadow divides
the water from the sun,
the farther it divides the sun from my life.
For in the dark there is much light
as there is life in the open rose,
as there is God descending from the heights
to the shores of the soul.[9]

When the Holy Father was born, his mother asked that the window be opened in the room in their apartment in Wadowice. Through this open window, the mother showed her child the world, and the father introduced a guide for him to fulfill the assignment given to him by Heaven, in the land of God "descending from the heights to the shores of the soul."

The Painting of Vlastimil Hoffman and the Wild Pink Roses

S o often we remember the dates of births, of weddings, of events which were recorded in official papers and statistics, but I believe that there are certain days and places which for an individual, especially for a child, leave more than great, important records of the steps of life. There can be a painting, a flower, even a blanket which was already torn, but we cared for it when we were small.

I recently invited my sixteen-year-old granddaughter, Emily, to see a play on Broadway. We stayed in a hotel, and she brought the small, old teddy bear I remembered she cherished when she was two or three years old. This teddy bear is still with her today. I looked at the teddy bear lying near her when she slept. Although Emily is no longer a little child, her attachment to her childhood treasure had not diminished. What did it represent, this teddy bear? It was her security blanket. I realized that I too have a security blanket, only mine is composed of my memories, and I am grateful for them.

Not too long ago in my classroom, I sat at the piano, and as part of a lecture on appreciating the gift of life, I sang one of my songs, "I Never Ask Why." The words perhaps illustrate my personality. When I sing, "I never ask why / I never ask why / Why do I never ask why?" my memories of distant yesterdays become my security blanket. I am grateful for what I had, for people I loved, for people who loved me. My respect for God is in the song when I sing, "A kiss of long ago left me a taste of life," and when I say at the end, "How lucky I am / I never ask why / because I tasted life." When I sing it, initially it is with a very strong voice, and afterwards, as emotions soften my voice, even with tears in my eyes, I thank God for what I had.

For some people, the dates recorded in official documents are most important. For me, a reminiscence of a painting I saw long ago or a touch of the petals of wild pink roses is more significant and contributes more to my understanding of life. It shows I tasted life and I feel it in my perception of every day. I marvel at the mystery of the sunset at Key West, in Florida, and the mystery of the sunset in Venice or in Stockholm. I hear it. It is stored in my being. I sit at the piano, and with the touch of my fingers I give an illustration of the setting sun, because it is a part of my being and therefore I can play the melody – my melody – on the piano. Again I wonder – I marvel – at how my piano responds. I realize in one moment that my inanimate piano receives from me the gift presented by my soul.

I had not had a baby grand piano since my childhood. My pianos after the war, in Krakow, Paris, Montreal, and Philadelphia, were always small upright pianos. I appreciated them, but I still dreamt of having a piano like the one at my parents' home in Jaslo.

I wrote once in a poem that the piano of my childhood was taken away to Germany during the war, and that maybe someone is playing it in Munich or in Frankfurt. But into this piano of my childhood and youth I poured out my feelings and my dreams, when I dreamt in Jaslo about various distant lands.

When I was nine, we moved from Staszica Street to an apartment inside another apartment. My father needed more than one room for his office so he used three of the rooms which we had occupied before as our living quarters. My parents rented these rooms on Kosciuszki Street, not too far from Staszica Street. We no longer had the view of the park – I regretted not seeing the trees and the sparrows.

We lived on the second floor of the tallest building in Jaslo (three floors), which was owned by the Propper family. There, for the first time, Adam and I had our own room. We loved it.

It had lilac wallpaper and there were angels on it. I loved to look at them as I was falling asleep. Adam and I could no longer see the park, but at least we had angels all around us – another "security blanket." We also had beautiful white furniture that my parents bought in Krakow.

This was the first time we had nice furniture at home. On one of the armoires were sculptured flowers in baskets. In these new living quarters we were thrilled to meet our neighbours, the family of Jan and Helena Kosiba. They had six children, with the seventh child born a few months later. Three of the children – Bolek, Irka, and Misia – were almost the same ages as Adam and me. We became very friendly with them, and our parents became friends with Mr. and Mrs. Kosiba too.

Since my childhood I remember each of the paintings, drawings, and other pictures in our first apartment and in my father's office. In our new apartment we had even more walls, so my father started buying more pictures. One day after a trip to Krakow he brought back a beautiful painting of two children by Vlastimil Hoffman. Against a blue background with a sky above were a boy and a girl. This painting became important for me in a psychological sense. I remember my mother once said to somebody who visited us and who admired the painting, "I see here the strength and courage of the boy and the loving, sweet face of the girl, who with her head on the boy's shoulder shows her dependence on him. We don't know if he is her friend or her brother." I looked at the painting again and again, this painting that now gave me a new meaning and had become a source of my reflection. Who were these two blond children with blue eyes? Who was Hoffman, the painter? This painting started me on a journey into all the art displayed on the walls of our apartment, which everyone who visited said looked like an art gallery, as there were so many paintings. I did not know about Eugène Delacroix at the time, but I later learned that he said, *"la peinture est le pont entre les âmes"* … "Painting is the bridge between souls." And thus I began to build bridges into almost all the paintings and drawings hanging on our walls.

The next painting that caught my attention was a very good reproduction of *The Angelus* by Jean-François Millet. Two French peasants stop their work in the fields when they hear the bells from the nearby church, and they pray. The viewer does not see their faces because they are leaning slightly forward, but the painting reveals the serenity of their prayer.

The third painting to remain with me was *The Street Sweeper*, painted by a painter from Lwow. I remember only his last name, Erb. The silhouette of the man on the street has something pathetic about him. The colours are green – dull green – and yellow, enveloping the street sweeper, with his head bent toward the ground, and his movement. The street and the street sweeper are one – united – in a certain manner.

I also remember the painter Wodynski (I think his first name was Stanislaw) from Jaslo, who painted a portrait of me when I was six or seven years old. I am standing near the piano wearing a white organdie dress. In my hair is a white bow. I had to pose every day for one hour or more for seven or eight days, but I did not mind at all.

During the war, Mr. and Mrs. Kosiba tried to hide and save a few paintings from the more than a hundred that we had accumulated by then. They helped us in the most critical moments during the war and never forgot the importance of art in my father's life. During the last German offensive in 1944, Jaslo was destroyed. The one painting that was saved with their help was that of the boy and girl by Vlastimil Hoffman. This painting accompanied my parents on all their wanderings, from Poland to France, and from France to Canada. After my parents died, Adam brought it to Philadelphia, where it is proudly displayed in his living room. I often look at the painting. The boy and girl remind me of Adam and me; I rely on Adam and I often try to put my head on his shoulder. This thought came to me while describing the story of the wandering of the painting and our own wanderings.

As Dr. Albert Schweitzer wrote, "Life is thought and action." I think about these words very, very often. Thoughts nourish the child, the youngster, and later on while acting in life leave a touch of warmth or coldness, a touch of a breeze during one unforgettable summer or a touch of love or understanding between two human brings.

Almost every Sunday afternoon in spring, my father would take me fishing in a pond some distance from our home. This pond belonged to my mother's grandfather's estate, and later belonged to my mother's uncle, who lived in Jaslo. My father and I loved to walk together. We always went first through the streets of the city and then to what we called "our path" near the Ursuline convent on the outskirts of Jaslo. The sisters were highly respected by everyone in the vicinity. Besides their daily occupations, they also taught embroidery to girls who were interested in handicrafts. They were also known to teach Jewish girls who wanted to acquire the skills of embroidering lingerie for brides.

On our walks my father often told me stories. Among my favourites were the *Iliad* and *Odyssey* by Homer. I knew a lot about the blind poet, and I especially enjoyed it when my father quoted him in ancient Greek.

(He had received his high school education in a classical *gymnasium*, where he had been taught ancient Greek as well as Latin.) My father also introduced me to the world of two Polish poets, Stanislaw Wyspianski and Cyprian Norwid, long before I heard about them in my classes on Polish literature. Stanislaw Wyspianski, who was born in Krakow, made a great impression on my father. I listened and listened to the excerpts of the drama *Wesele* (Wedding), recreating the characters in a time of history of struggle and dreams. I also tried to imagine the stained glass windows of Kosciol Franciszkanow, the Franciscan church in Krakow. At this time I first heard the story of St. Francis and his love for nature. During these afternoons, Cyprian Norwid came alive for me with his courage to present Prometheus in his own way. I also remember that it was my father who told me of Norwid's respect for the Jews.

One day near the Ursuline convent I discovered a row of magnificent wild pink roses. I remember delicately touching, then bringing my cheek to, their soft pink petals. They were like velvet caressed by the sun. I never forgot it. When, after 43 years of absence from Poland, I came to visit Jaslo, I asked the taxi driver to take me to the convent. He was curious – why did I want to go there? I did not answer. I went to look for the wild pink roses, but they were no longer there and I was sad. I asked myself over and over why the sisters had not saved the pink wild roses with the velvet touch.

One day in Jerusalem when I visited Yad Vashem, the world-renowned centre for documentation on the Holocaust, I was very moved by the room commemorating the one and a half million Jewish children who were killed during the war. The room was dark. On the ceiling were lights presented as stars. And then, I don't know why, I thought about the children whose faces were as soft as the petals of the wild roses. I asked myself why these children perished during the war like the pink roses near the Ursuline convent in Jaslo.

School and Conscience

In his work on ethics, the Italian idealist and philosopher Benedetto Croce writes that there are two forms of knowledge: intuitive knowledge, which we obtain through our imagination, and intellectual knowledge, which we obtain through our intellect. Individual or universal knowledge depends on whether we take into consideration the images engraved in our imagination or the concepts that result from our reasoning.

Sometimes intuitive knowledge cannot be replaced. One who possesses this knowledge can be endowed with an experience in which there is not even a shadow of intellectual knowledge. A painter observing the moon, or someone listening to music and in the melody feeling joy or nostalgia, sadness or triumph, has an experience that is available only to that person. There are moments in which every one of us becomes a poet or a painter, because in our thoughts appear words and images that are the expressions of never-before-experienced emotions. The view of the sky, the sunset, the shape of a cloud becomes a source of admiration for the Creator. Never before have we seen this beauty, and if we are able to reflect on this extraordinary experience and can give a form to it, then we become artists. If we can create and can make these feelings accessible to others, we can offer to the world what we experience.

Michelangelo believed that a painter does not paint with the hand but with the mind. Leonardo da Vinci related that the prior of the convent of Santa Maria della Grazie in Milan could not understand why Leonardo often spent whole days in the refectory looking at his painting *The Last Supper* without touching a brush. According to

Leonardo, the minds of great geniuses act best when they are not performing any physical work. In his fresco, Leonardo tried to see what others did not. Later on, after contemplating his painting, he continued his work according to his observations and his intuition. This way he was able to make changes to the unfinished painting.

The artist possesses emotion, but only when emotion and reason collaborate can artists achieve their goal and express their experiences in a form that can be understood by the audience.

The Poet-Pope John Paul II is endowed with deep intuition. From the very early years of his life, that intuition has allowed him to see certain truths that are not easy to understand. Questions to which he could not give answers brought young Karol to philosophical inquiry. Intuitive knowledge combined with a philosophy of life shaped the man whose poetry and philosophy would, in turn, allow him to shake the walls of history. We must also not forget that the basis of his observations and thoughts was his deep religious sense.

Kant, the German philosopher for whom the goal of moral theory is to answer questions – such as: What is morality? Where is the base for this morality? What is the difference between moral and immoral acts? – became a source of interest for Karol, whose way of thinking, always connected with faith in God, was very receptive to this search for the truth of life.

Kant introduced the concept of the human conscience as a tribunal before which every one of us is responsible for our own behaviour. Is the conscience the judge of our being? Does the conscience play a role as a guide to our deeds? Do we direct our behaviour according to our sense of responsibility, or is our behaviour an outcome of our moral posture? These questions fascinated the teenage Karol. Later in his philosophical studies he came to his own interpretations of will and obligation to moral behaviour and deeds connected with the problems of everyday life. In his lectures in Lublin as a young professor, Karol Wojtyla tried to introduce his students to the works of Immanuel Kant, Max Scheler, and St. Thomas Aquinas to work out a foundation for Christian ethics, and for the elements governing everyday decisions.

This nourishing conscience which was always present, this conscience that was so often discussed in the philosophy of Kant, was very sensitive to the injustice described in detail on the pages of history. As the pope, Karol Wojtyla does not hesitate to bow his head and ask for forgiveness in the face of injustice that others accept in silence or indifference. Pope John Paul II believes that silence and indifference do not have any right to exist if we realize that we were created in the image of God.

In Psalm 8 we read:

What are humans that you are mindful of them,
mere mortals that you care for them?
Yet you have made them little less than a god,
crowned them with glory and honour.

We therefore stand only one step lower than the angels, and we should be aware of the role designed for us by God.

Dante Alighieri, in his epic poem *Paradiso*, Canto 31, describes the angels he saw. He says that each angel possesses a special lightning and each is different from the others.

In the thirteenth century, St. Thomas Aquinas stated with the precision of a philosopher that an angel does not have any physical form. However, when we think about good people we often compare them to angels. The human imagination gives us the form. We say that a good man or woman is like an angel because their behaviour, their ethical demands, show that they have a conscience and that in this conscience is a spark of God. Their deeds prove the existence of conscience in just and courageous people.

Pope John Paul II, who certainly read the Bible during his childhood and his youth, remembers the words of Christ about illusion – about how often people do not know how to interpret God's commandments. In the Gospel of St. Matthew, we read the words of Christ:

"Not everyone who says to me, 'Lord, Lord,' will enter the kingdom of heaven, but only the one who does the will of my Father in heaven. On that day many will say to me, 'Lord, Lord, did we not prophesy in your name, and cast out demons in your name, and do many deeds of power in your name?' Then I will declare to them, 'I never knew you; go away from me, you evildoers.'"

(Matthew 7:21-23)

This sense of morality, this atmosphere of love in the Bible, are visible in the behaviour of the caretaker of the souls of millions of Catholics. During his pilgrimages he does not hesitate to bow his head, and in his humility asks the forgiveness of those who were persecuted. Who were they, and who are they still, these people who are persecuted in the different parts of the world? The pope meets them, he thinks about them, and he looks into their eyes, which often show the cruelty and injustice they have suffered. He talks to them, he understands their pain.

Before the arrival of Pope John Paul II, the First Nations people of Yellowknife, in the Northwest Territories of Canada, rarely heard words from non-Natives that could give them hope, that could help them believe that good people, no matter their religion or the colour of their skin, would have the courage to ask for the forgiveness of their sins. Yet, there in Yellowknife, on September 18, 1984, these First Nations and Inuit people listened to the words of the Holy Father and no doubt understood that this man was not only the spiritual guide of the Catholics, but a caretaker of souls.

Who are these First Nations people, living in Canada between the Atlantic and Pacific Oceans, in North, South, and Central America? These people who were killed without pity only because they were in the way of the Europeans?

In today's literature we discover that Canada's First Nations people often had a greater sense of morality than those who came to seize their land, telling them they had no rights to it. We look at the faces of these people and we discover features engraved by the wind. We look at Aboriginal, Native or Inuit art and admire the skill of the movements and the hands of artists who have chiselled the history and the beliefs of their tribes in wood, in bone, and in stone. In one of the tales we find a history of a soul of a man who after death comes to "another world," to "the land of big hunting" and "the great hunter." The soul is asked whether its owner made even one man happy during his or her own life. If only the people who were killing in the name of "faith" had known this legend.

In his book *A New Image of Man*, Ardis Whitman quotes a story told by Fulton Oursler about a Native man who studied at a university and became a lawyer. For many years he did not visit the place of his birth and his childhood. In middle age, he decided to return and spend the summer in the forest of his childhood. During this vacation he caught fish and hunted. He had a guide who always accompanied him. Every day at sunset the lawyer disappeared for several hours and left the guide alone. One day the guide decided to follow and observe the lawyer. He tried to keep at a distance because he did not want the lawyer to see him. At one point he stopped. At a distance of a few steps, he saw that the lawyer had started a fire and put a wooden log on two stones for a seat. At this moment the lawyer spotted the guide and in silence gave him a sign that he should approach. He showed him a place on the log to sit on as if it were a bench. Opposite it, on the other side of the fire, the lawyer put another log on two stones and left this log empty. The lawyer sat beside the guide. Silence reigned. After half an hour the lawyer started to talk. He told the guide that during his childhood, every day before evening his mother would go outside and sit in a quiet place, inviting the Great Spirit to visit her. This mother introduced spirituality to her son. She wanted to make contact with this invisible Great Spirit, and she wanted her son to have the awareness that this Spirit existed and that he could invite the Spirit and exchange thoughts and feelings with him. For her this meant the strength of life.

The lawyer said that during his stay at the university and in the city he never thought about his mother, but that when he came back after so many years to the forest of the tall trees, he found that he longed for the Great Spirit once more.

The story has parallels to the pope who seeks to build bridges. Like the lawyer, Pope John Paul II seeks to bring together his intellectual and intuitive sides, his respect for religions, and his love for others, to promote understanding of the nobility and dignity of each human being.

His upbringing in Poland had its influence. In Polish schools, children were taught about the Teutonic Knights. The Teutonic order very often killed Poles in the name of faith. The novel *The Teutonic Knights*, by the famous Polish writer Henryk Sienkiewicz, was on the required reading list in schools. The book describes the methods used in converting Poles to the Christian faith.

When I read the pope's statements, I see the messenger of God who has always tried to understand humankind with his feelings, with his reasoning, and with his conscience. In Yellowknife, speaking to the Inuit and First Nations people, Pope John Paul II acknowledged with repentance that they were the victims of the newcomers who in their ignorance considered Native culture lesser than their own. The pope said that the time had come for forgiveness and a new beginning, for building relationships based on the Biblical commandments of brotherly love, which call for justice and an acknowledgment of the rights and freedom of all peoples. In this proclamation of freedom the pope wished to remedy the errors of the past that had taken so many victims. In Yellowknife on September 18, 1984, his words vibrated in the air, over the place where, centuries before, first contact between Native peoples and Europeans had resulted in such tragic circumstances.

John Paul II returned to this same theme when he spoke in Alice Springs, Australia, in November 1986. With sincere feelings of sorrow, he talked about Christians of goodwill who knew that the Aborigines in Australia were being treated badly. He recalled that although they had inhabited the land for thousands of years, when the white man arrived they were relocated to reservations. Many families were divided, and children became orphans, and the original inhabitants of Australia were forced into exile in their own land, a strange land of exile. Luigi Accattoli writes about this visit in *When a Pope Asks Forgiveness: The Mea Culpa's of John Paul II.*

Grieving Christians

The message that Pope Wojtyla gave to the Aborigines of Australia in November 1986 brought the denunciation up to date as regards the insensibility of so many Christians to the drama of the natives:

"Christian people of good will are saddened to realize – many of them only recently – for how long a time Aboriginal people were transported from their homelands into small areas or reserves where families were broken up, tribes split apart, children orphaned and people forced to live like exiles in a foreign country."

Learning from the Errors of the Past

With the following text we are in the United States, where perhaps the insensibility to the sufferings of the North American Indians has been more pervasive and the responsibility of Catholics has been less acknowledged. But by this time the pope is not making such distinctions. When he speaks of the responsibility of Christians, he means all Christians. He is willing to carry blame for the sins of those who do not even consider him as their representative:

"The early encounter between your traditional cultures and the European way of life was an event of such significance and change that it profoundly affects your collective life even today. That encounter was a harsh and painful reality for your peoples. The cultural oppression, the injustices, the disruption of your life and of your traditional societies must be acknowledged. . . . Unfortunately, not all the members of the Church lived up to their Christian responsibilities. But let us not dwell excessively on mistakes and wrongs, even as we commit ourselves to overcoming their present effects. . . . Now, we are called to learn from the mistakes of the past and we must work together for reconciliation and healing, as brothers and sisters in Christ."[10]

I went to Australia recently, where I visited the Art Gallery of New South Wales in Sydney. As a result of this visit I will always remember the art of the Aborigines. According to their beliefs, when a person dies, the bones are put in a hollowed-out log; on the bark is painted the history of the life of the deceased. In one museum gallery I saw a row of these decorated columns, where, with the help of painting and chiselling, the Aborigine artists expressed a deeply held belief in the spirit of humanity. The images on the bark were impressive. In the same museum I bought a video about this art, entitled *The Dreamings*. It shows contemporary Aboriginal artists talking about dreams that have endured through the ages and about the art that is transmitted from one generation to another. One of the painters recalls with great emotion how her father taught her to paint and sculpt.

In a park just across from the gallery stands a gigantic, powerful tree that is considered one of the oldest trees in the world. Looking at the tree, I thought of the ancient tree bark painting and of the images in the video. The art endures, and the dreams will always exist in spite of the centuries of persecution. Our dreams of a better world are possible if we are able to ask for forgiveness.

This old tree, not far from the ocean, has witnessed different chapters in the history of Australia, a history that flows like the tides of the ocean. Even though one wave may threaten the shore, it may be followed by one that kisses and heals the ravaged shores. And, perhaps, the tree thinks about the pope – a poet.

The pope, like this tree, has witnessed many different chapters in history, and through the influence of his father, learned key values and subjects from his youth that would serve him first as a man, then later as pope. These include honesty, intuition, philosophy, religion, knowledge, the meaning of responsibility, the role of conscience, confidence, a modest way of life, and respect for his teachers. All of these formed young Karol's character.

The death of his brother certainly left a very great impression on Karol, but it did not take away his enthusiasm for life. Karol loved life. He liked sports and he was a very good student. While he had time for entertainment, he was also very religious. For him the church was a place in which contact with God allowed him to understand the people and the world around him: at school, in his daily life, his interaction with colleagues, or on the field where he sometimes played soccer. Karol's eyes were open to everything around him.

At this time, Karol met every day with Father Kazimierz Figlewicz, the vicar and catechist in Wadowice.

Karol did not forget Father Figlewicz, and in his conversation with [his biographer] André Frossard he expressed his recognition for the priest who certainly remained in his memory: "I owe a lot to the priests, especially one who is today in his old age and who still in my early youth with his simplicity and goodness brought me nearer to Christ, and who also knew later on in which moment as a confessor to say 'Christ shows you the road to the priesthood.'"[11]

The whole life of an individual is formed during childhood and youth. It is based on the awareness of who we are, who we wish to become, and how we choose to live. If we consider it our responsibility to take part even in the smallest way in the building of the world, then we realize that with each step, history depends on each one of us. This awareness can become constructive or indifferent, destroying goodness or fighting for this goodness. Benedetto Croce gives the example of the painter acquiring knowledge by looking at the sunset. The beauty of the sunset strengthens our awareness of the beauty of the world and helps us understand that through admiration for nature, we grasp the greatness of the Creator. This recognition of the omnipotence of the Creator allows us to search for the sense of our being. If we know what we really want and have a sense of responsibility, then we are able to comprehend the meaning of universal goodness. Yes, if we know what is good in each of us, and if our faith teaches us to love our fellow brothers and sisters, then we will treat people with the same respect we demand for ourselves.

We learn from teachers and from nature, and our school becomes other people, the sun, the sky, the trees, and the enchanted land, that invites us to love what nature offered us on the day of our birth. Teachers get their information from schools and universities, according to their own comprehension of the subjects, presented to them in lectures. It depends on the students to work out for themselves which information they should deepen and which they should erase. The books teachers use can teach laughter and hatred, traditions and prejudices engraved deep in the mythology of some nations that demand absolute obedience or the abolition of the truths of honesty. At this moment comes the personal choice of which road to follow: the path of the sun or the path of ruin? Or perhaps even the road without end, directing people who choose this path wherever the wind blows.

There in the church of Wadowice as a ministrant, young Karol, perhaps returning out of breath, exhausted after a soccer match, or very impressed with school, was able to find a place for conversations with God. These conversations with God started there after physical effort, after kicking the soccer ball or skiing. There on the mountain, skiing with the wind lashing his face, feeling the force of the wind, admiring the penetrating beauty of shimmering white snow, the young Karol perhaps composed a prayer of thankfulness. He thanked God in his prayer for the world, for the power of God, for his life, and for his own being, his comprehension, and his intuition.

Perhaps while he was praying "The Gift and Mystery" in church, a deep feeling of the existence of God made such an impression that the future pope discovered the greatness of seeing through the eyes of his soul.

Years later the pope wrote "The Song of the Hidden God":

For long
Someone was leaning over me –
on the line of my eyebrows
his shadow had no weight.
Like a light filled with green,
like green with no shade,
an ineffable green that rests
on drops of blood.

That leaning gesture, both cool and hot,
slides into me, yet stays overhead,
it passes close by, yet turns to faith
and fullness.

That gesture, both cool and hot,
a silent reciprocity.

Locked in such an embrace,
a gentle touch against my face:
then amazement falls,
and silence, the silence without a word,
which comprehends nothing, and the balance is nil.
And in this silence I lift
God's leaning gesture
above me still.[12]

The unique green of the Polish grass and the distinctive green of an old tree in a park in Australia meet in the phrase "God's leaning gesture." Only a poet reaching a deep mystical spirituality can see the light full of greenery:

Like a light filled with green,
like green with no shade,
an ineffable green that rests
on drops of blood.

What is this greenery? Does this spring come every year? Maybe this spring without shade is the spring reborn in everyone who feels God in the pulse, and in the blood, flowing through the veins, straight to the heart. Who can feel this greenery of life? Only someone who possesses the feeling of a "leaning" of God can feel this – good, delicate, full of freshness, and at the same time warm. This "leaning" of God allows us to feel, to see, to retain this meeting with God, maybe in one drop of blood, which circulates through all the veins on the journey to the heart.

I Remember Krakow

Each child first lives in a small universe. This universe is the home. It can be a small apartment, a villa, a cottage, or a hut. In every one of these living quarters are windows and doors through which the child encounters the sky above. Outside are trees or streets, stones on the pavement or flowers in a garden. The environment can be happy or violent. Voices and words enter this small universe. The first voices and words remain in a child's memory and teach them how to speak, how to use this voice which becomes the instrument of communication with the universe that appears through the window. Language enters existence with very special sounds indicating courage or despair, joy or complaint, and different sounds that help the child discover that different languages also exist in the world. The child's curiosity is awakened. The universe from behind the window grows and becomes a fascinating puzzle in its complexity, and at the same time invites exploration of every piece of the puzzle. The child catches the names of streets, of different cities, the names of rivers and oceans, in conversation, and after becoming acquainted with these names tries to imagine the distant places.

Later on, the universe becomes larger. School enters the field of knowledge and provides triumphs and downfalls of the child's comprehension. The world appears in all its glory and mystery. Again the child explores everything with his or her own eyes, but at the same time this world is also presented through the eyes of the child's teachers, filtered through different books and lectures. This time the future unfolds its possibilities almost without limits. Imagination adds splendour to the unknown, distant vistas in space and time. All this, together with nature, becomes a background of life. Each sunrise and each sunset plays a role in the pursuit of knowledge. Knowledge is acquired through intellectual comprehension. Besides intellectual comprehension, feelings are involved. Seeing and feeling are important additions to the mere facts of a subject. There are those who deliberately try to exclude their feelings, and as a result they become indifferent to many facets of life. I dare say that even in science, if feelings are involved, the individual is harnessed in their assessment to never forgetting the dangers concerning human endurance. I see it especially when we use progress without weighing the consequences of our choices on the environment and the quality of life.

Why, then, while writing about my life, do these thoughts enter my eagerness to reflect on my memories? Why does the present take part in reflection of my memories? It is because my formative years created my being as I am and the events of my life often called for me to make my own judgments before I could channel my actions? The actions I took reflected my upbringing.

I was born between two wars. I spent my childhood and my early youth before the outbreak of the Second World War. I was taught certain moral values, and I survived the war. After surviving the war I decided not to stay on the margins of history. I tried to add a small voice in the name of my moral upbringing. When I first began to describe the life of Karol Wojtyla, many times I stopped and whispered, "My God, I was brought up like him, the future pope, although our religions were different." Intellectual knowledge and intuitional knowledge meet in verbal and written expression. Certain words enrich our vocabulary with courage and faith, while others introduce fear and doubts in our own opinions, frustrating our ability to analyze our conscious and even subconscious behaviour.

Karol Wojtyla and I were lucky to live in homes where our parents' love reigned. We were also lucky that in our elementary schools such values as courage and honesty were emphasized. They provided us with confidence in our own comprehension, and led us to respect those who were our guides.

One very memorable event of my childhood was my first trip to Krakow. (Years later, when I was doing research for this book, I discovered that the young Karol was also fascinated with his first trip to Krakow.)

I was eight years old and Adam was around five when our parents took us by train to the city, which I knew from legends, tales, and songs. We stayed in a hotel for two days. From the windows of our room we could see the Planty, the park of Krakow surrounding the city. I remember especially the first day. At noon, right after our arrival, I saw a bugler on top of the Kosciol Mariacki (St. Mary's Church), and I heard a sound – a bugle-call that suddenly stopped in mid-note. I knew the sound from the radio. Afterwards we went for lunch. It was my first meal in a restaurant. I even remember what I chose from the menu; it was my favourite, a delicious beet soup.

My parents told us their plans. They wanted to show us a few places, especially the Wawel, the Royal Castle and the National Museum. They also told us about the famous altar of Wit Stwosz, a sculptor who came to Krakow from Nürnberg at the end of the fifteenth century. His altar in the Mariacki Church is one of the most important masterpieces in the city.

We walked along Grodzka and Stradom Streets, leading to *Wawel* Castle. We admired the works of art in the castle, and to this day I remember some of the paintings. The first one to capture my attention was *Portrait of a Man*, painted by the Dutch painter Govaert Flinck. I later learned that he was one of Rembrandt's pupils. Each time I give my course on Rembrandt, I recall that before I knew anything about Rembrandt, I was familiar with the name of Govaert Flinck because I had seen his painting in my childhood.

The second painting that caught my attention was *Portrait of a Boy on Grey Horse* by the Polish painter Juliusz Kossak. My father told us that several famous Polish painters were members of the Kossak family. The third painting that made an impression on me was by one of the greatest painters in Poland, Jan Matejko, who left a great legacy of masterpieces celebrating historical events. The painting I remember was *Sobieski in Vienna*. Jan Sobieski was the king of Poland who led the Christian Alliance against the Turkish Army, which he defeated in 1683 near the gates of Vienna. He was called the Saviour of Christianity, Vienna, and western European civilization.

A few other memories from Krakow are still very vivid. In the National Museum we admired a drawing by Stanislaw Wyspianski entitled *Motherhood*. My father had introduced me to the writings of Stanislaw Wyspianski at a very early age, and he remarked to us that although Wyspianski's life was very short (he died at 38), he provided his native city with many treasures.

I cannot remember where exactly, but in one of the museums in Krakow we saw an exhibit of a few paintings by Maurycy Gottlieb, a student of Jan Matejko. Maurycy Gottlieb was a Jew who, although he died at the age of 23, left his mark on the history of Polish painting. He began to study art at 13 in Lwow, and later went to Vienna, but his most important teacher was Jan Matejko, who believed in the talent of his young student and foretold a great future for him. Among the paintings of Gottlieb, we saw *Jews Praying on the Day of Atonement.* (This painting contains a self-portrait.) He was considered an excellent portrait artist who knew how to recreate the inner psychological being of his models. Many years later I found out that he was often subjected to anti-Semitic remarks.

A few years ago, here in Philadelphia, I was invited to speak at Bet Am, a Philadelphia synagogue. The topic was "The Meaning of Life." Before entering the auditorium, Rabbi Robert Leib invited me to his office, and there on the wall I saw a reproduction of Gottlieb's painting *Jews Praying on the Day of Atonement.* It made a tremendous impression on me: here was the picture that I saw during my first visit to Krakow. My past came back and with this memory came back the now-vanished world of the Polish Jews. I was very moved. I asked the rabbi where he had bought the reproduction. He replied that before coming to Philadelphia from his native South Africa, he visited an art gallery in Cape Town, and there he saw this reproduction. He liked it, bought it, and decided to bring it with him to Philadelphia.

Those praying Jews in the painting survived, if only on the canvas.

When I think of our first visit to Krakow, I realize that my parents were introducing my brother and me to the treasures of Polish culture by showing us this historical city. At the same time, my father told us of the very active life of Jews in Krakow. In the part of the city called Kazimierz was the oldest synagogue, built centuries ago. We walked long hours through the streets, admiring the monuments, the architecture of certain churches and buildings. Naturally we bought some souvenirs in Sukiennice, a indoor mall with many stands selling popular souvenirs, jewellery, paintings, and the costumes of the region.

In one of the small galleries my father bought a set of interesting drawings depicting the streets of Krakow in different seasons. I especially loved the picture of Krakow covered in snow.

I also remember that near the hotel where we stayed was a very elegant store selling children's clothing. A sky-blue coat was displayed in the window. I told my parents that I loved this coat and asked them to buy it for me. My mother checked the price and said, "This coat is too expensive for us, but I promise to buy fabric, and in Jaslo the dressmaker will make you a coat similar to this one." The blue colour of the sky became important. I got a blue coat, and to this day blue is my favourite colour.

I have been in Krakow many times since then, but this first encounter left a very strong impression of the city where I was born, the city that I loved.

I returned to Krakow under very different circumstances during the war. One day, the German director of the wood mill where I worked sent me there to deliver some papers concerning speeding up the delivery of wood. It was very convenient for me because although my parents, Adam, and I had identity papers, they were "not the best" documents, and it was during this time that we were required to hand to the mayor of Surochow, where we lived, our birth certificates for the so-called *Kennkarte*, a kind of passport issued to all Poles by the German authorities.

Using this opportunity, I decided to visit a member of the underground whom I knew and who occasionally provided baptismal certificates. I had the address, 24 Krupnicza Street, on the second floor, and when I arrived I saw the door was open. I went in and there stood two men: one in a Gestapo uniform, the other in civilian clothes. The man in uniform brought me into the kitchen. In the meantime the second man opened the door to one of the rooms, where six, seven or eight people were sitting. The owner of the apartment was absent. I understood that something was wrong. The Gestapo man asked me to sit down near the table.

"Why did you come to this apartment?" he asked. I answered that I had met Mr. Mucha a few weeks before on the train and he had promised me a piece of fabric for a spring suit. I smiled and added that I liked nice clothes. The Gestapo man looked at me and asked for my identification papers. In my purse I had the three certificates that had been issued just an hour before. When I arrived at the office to deliver the letters from my director, I was met by a young German employee, and I had an idea – it would be great to have an official piece of paper from the Krakow office responsible for the wood mill in Surochow. I asked the employee if he could issue three such official papers from the head office in Krakow stating that we worked in the wood mill in Surochow. And he agreed. One had Adam's name, one had mine, and the other had the name of a fugitive from Auschwitz, a Pole who worked as a bookkeeper in Surochow. I carried these three papers in my purse. I handed the Gestapo man my certificate. He watched me very closely. I was wearing a little hat of my mother's which I sometimes wore when I travelled. I took off this hat, put it on the table and said, "Now you can see me better. I have problems with my eyes. They are inflamed." Right away, I asked him if by any chance he knew a good eye specialist. It was true that I had eye problems but to this day I cannot understand why I switched the topic of conversation. He looked at me again, took a piece of paper, wrote an address, and asked me to meet him there. He promised to give me the name of a specialist, then he let me out. I walked downstairs still not believing that I was free. The janitor saw me leaving and said, "I wanted to warn you that Mr. Mucha's apartment was the 'kettle'," which meant that everyone who went there was arrested and interrogated. Mr. Mucha, who held an important position in the underground movement, had been warned of the danger and had fled from Krakow. Later that evening, I took the train to Jaroslaw and from Jaroslaw to Surochow.

Many times I have been asked to tell my life story. I hesitate because the more I tell it the more difficult it is to believe that certain events took place. In the back of my mind was the thought that no one would believe me. This is the first time that I have put down on paper the description of my visit to Krakow in May 1943.

When I think about that second visit to Krakow, suddenly I see Karol Wojtyla living and working there. He, too, was struggling with danger and difficulties. And certainly this time in his life became engraved in his being. Whoever tried to listen to their conscience during these dark days faced decisions that could jeopardize their convictions. As I write this book, I picture him in my imagination working in the quarry, surrounded by people who were suffering. I see him issuing false papers for those in need. I see him praying, asking God to have mercy on the homeless, the hungry, and those without shelter.

The years that followed the war were never able to erase the painful past. Maybe the Holy Father, in his actions, is trying to implant in people a sense of responsibility for the fate of humankind, in the light of those dark events of the last century.

Krakow, I will not forget you.

Cornflowers, Poppies, and my Country

When I think my Country –
I express what I am, anchoring my roots.
And this is what the heart tells,
as if a hidden frontier ran from me to others,
embracing us all within a past
older than each of us;
and from this past I emerge
when I think my Country,
I take her into me as a treasure,
constantly wondering how to increase it,
how to give a wider measure to that space
it fills withal.[13]

In the Polish fields, filled with golden sunlight, the flowers bloom: dark blue cornflowers and red poppies smile and sing a hymn of love for the earth in which they grow. The wheat and rye pray to God to allow them to ripen in the sun and offer the inhabitants of this land in which they grow bread, the tasty bread of freedom. Bread and flowers: the mysterious beauty of gifts from God delicately interwoven into the bouquet of life.

In Poland, bread, in China, rice – nourishment, the appeasement of hunger. As flowers bring joy, they smile on life – the blooming cherry flowers in Japan, in Washington, and in the Polish orchards.

When, as children, we take our first step on the soil, at first we are not too sure of ourselves. Later on, we walk, run, rush through the wide streets or narrow paths, climb mountains or swim in lakes, streams, rivers, or oceans. Sometimes, we will stop, bend over, and touch the surface of the earth, this earth on which each of us is born, the soil on which some of us find ourselves after destiny has exiled us from the place of our birth. Sometimes we will take a grain of this soil and kiss it, this one grain, as a sign of our sense of belonging and attachment. This morsel of earth becomes "our" earth because we were born on it, or because we later adopted it. This earth is our earth; we are part of it. And it is this same earth to which we give our feelings that we will also give the dust of mortal remains after our death, when we will become a grain of the earth. Humanity knows how to love or to fall in love with the soil on which each of us walks.

Poland is golden fields and cornflowers and poppies, the homeland for those born there and those who fell in love with her. The country sings with the rustling of trees and splashes of water in the mountain streams. The land cries when the pitiless hail hits the ground or the storm lashes the helpless fields with wind. The land laughs when freedom dances in the air we breathe, where the earth at our feet contains a mix of the grains from the fields and the blood of battles where wheat once grew. These fields of battle and these fields of grain exist side by side – as do people of all perspectives who love this, their native land.

Karol Wojtyla, John Paul II, loves Poland as he loved his mother. He was taught to love his land, and he knows what this land represents for its inhabitants. When we read the series of poems he wrote about his native land, we understand the boundless love he has for it, a love that helps one person to toil with a plough and another to fight for each inch of this land:

Thinking My Country I Return to the Tree

1
The tree of knowledge of good and evil
grew on the riverbanks of our land.
Together with us it grew over the centuries;
it grew into the Church through the roots of our conscience.

We carried the fruits, heavy but enriching.
We felt the tree spreading,
but its growing roots remained deep in one patch of earth.
History lays down events over the struggles of conscience.
Victories throb inside this layer, and defeats.
History does not cover them: it makes them stand out.
Can history ever flow against the current of conscience?

2

In which direction did the tree branch out?
Which direction does conscience follow?
In which direction grows our land's history?
The tree of knowledge knows no frontiers.
The only frontier is the Coming which will join into one Body the
struggles of conscience and the mysteries of history:
it will change the tree of knowledge
into the Spring of Life, ever surging.
But every day so far
has brought the same division in each thought and act,
and in this division the Church of conscience grows at history's
roots.

3

May we never lose that clarity before our eyes,
in which events appear, lost in the immeasurable tower
where man yet knows whither he is going.
Love alone balances fate.
Let us not increase the shadow's measure.
A ray of light – let it fall into the hearts and shine through the
darkness of generations. Let a stream of light penetrate our weakness.
We must not consent to weakness.[14]

In these words is the seed of attachment that will remain forever.
What is this seed? Is it love, or is it responsibility? This land provides
those who feel a sense of belonging to it a source of confidence in
themselves. We gain freedom every day if we know how to behave
within the limits of this freedom and respect the boundaries of our
own dignity and the dignity of others.

We are all searching for the road. Sometimes the road is steep and we must climb. But it is an act of will not to stop, or stumble, or fall. Each step towards the ideal of the common good is directed by our unbent will.

When he was still able, Pope John Paul II, in his voyages, would kneel and kiss the soil of each country he visited. Only those who feel strongly about their own land can also show their respect for foreign lands and soil, countries with their own inhabitants.

Polish cornflowers and poppies – cornflowers with the colour of the sky before the sunset and red poppies like the blood flowing in our veins.

Only those who love their country can feel the pulse of the country. There, high above, is the omnipotent God who kisses the earth with the warmth of the sun, and some chosen people feel the kiss of God in their pulse. Who are these people chosen by God? Good people who listen to the voice of their conscience. Is it true that millions of people in the course of human history listened to their conscience? How many have ordered their conscience to "be silent"? Can history ever flow against the current of conscience? These words bring back memories of the Second World War, and with them these questions: Why were so many consciences silent? Why did so many people perish?

People perished *because* consciences were silent. Karol Wojtyla is right when he says that history cannot flow against the current of conscience.

Is this part of love of God, the awareness that conscience is the highest judge guiding our actions? Is it possible to love our own religion and traditions but at the same time to have respect for all people and for all the fields of wheat and plantations of sugar and rice? Different religions, different plantations, different trees, and different workers – but one humanity created in the image of God.

In the first chapter of Genesis we read:

God created man in his image: in the divine image he created him; male and female he created them. God blessed them, saying: "Be fertile and multiply; fill the earth and subdue it. Have dominion over the fish of the sea, the birds of the air, and all the living things that move on the earth." God also said: "See, I give you every seed-bearing plant all over the earth and every tree that has seed-bearing fruit on it to be your food; and to all the animals of the land, all the birds of the air, and all the living creatures that crawl on the ground, I give all the green plants for food." And so it happened. God looked at everything he had made and he found it very good. Evening came, and morning followed – the sixth day.

(Genesis 1:27-31)

"Have dominion" over the earth. These words make us responsible for our country, our own behaviour, and the behaviour of those groups to which we belong. How do we search for God in the blades of wheat in order to give people nourishment? How do we search for God on the faraway shores of the oceans before finding God in ourselves, in our conscience? Can we search for God on foreign soil before we have met and understood people in our small villages or bustling cities, before we are fully acquainted with our own country? Our surroundings, the literature of childhood and youth, and our experience of history have a very significant meaning that will affect how we approach others.

Michelangelo was right when he said in one of his poems that a thought not endowed with the grace of lifting us to Heaven is empty. Without the blessing of God, thought does not have any value. Can this grace of thought lifted up to the skies express with the strength of its feelings the present and future? Was the thought of Michelangelo, who painted the ceiling of the Sistine Chapel, blessed? On this ceiling we see God giving life to the first man.

Karol Wojtyla wrote, "Earth, you will always be part of our time." And the earth and humanity are part of our time. The work of Michelangelo represents the world in which he was born – the world of the Renaissance. Michelangelo was 33 when he started to paint his fresco, *Creation of the World*, in 1508; he finished it when he was 36. This painter, who all his life believed that he should work only as a sculptor, offered the world the expression of his sense of belonging to his time, the period we know as the Renaissance. After the Middle Ages, the Renaissance gave people the possibility to express themselves without the fear engendered by the culture of the Middle Ages.

St. Francis of Assisi left to history a great gift, "The Canticle to the Sun." This saint taught the Western world not only about charity among people, but also about love for nature, for the sun, for the stars. He opened the gates of free interpretation of the world for painters, writers, and philosophers.

In the "Canticle to the Sun" he writes:

Blessed be Thou, O God, for all thy creatures,
especially for our brother, the Sun,
who gives us the day, and by whom Thou lightest us.
He is beautiful; he beams with great splendour,
he is Thy symbol, O Thou Most-High.
Blessed be Thou, O God, for our sister,
the Moon, and for the stars,
which thou hast set in the sky
clear, precious and beautiful.[15]

In another work St. Francis wrote: "My mother bird – you are indebted to God." The ideas of St. Francis greatly influenced Christian culture. Painters started to paint more freely, writers started to think along different lines – freedom of thought and interpretation can be said to have started in the thirteenth century, and the rebirth of thought and culture of the Renaissance began. Giotto paved the road for Leonardo da Vinci, Raphael and Michelangelo. People started to look at the sun, at the stars, at humanity to see not only the darkness but also the beauty and greatness of the world.

The time in which children are brought up, the country in which they live, the surrounding culture, their native land, actively affect their behaviour. Later, conscience also plays a role. Sometimes this conscience does not agree with current thinking. People who are faithful to their conscience become the avant-garde of future generations. One such individual was Michelangelo. Born in Tuscany, he was fascinated from his earliest childhood by the marble in the vicinity of Carrara. Sculptures executed from this marble became treasures of humanity. The newly structured Italian language, the city of Florence, and the works of Giotto opened new vistas of creativity. The Christian world started to breathe new freedom, and the popes, especially Pope Julius II, wanted to make the Vatican strong. And beautiful. Julius understood that he should give the painter a free hand in interpreting beauty. Michelangelo searched for inspiration in God while painting silhouettes that recalled gods from the Greek Olympus.

Pope Julius II, who admired the fresco *Creation of the World*, did not live to see the part of the ceiling of the Sistine Chapel containing Michelangelo's *The Last Judgment*. This fresco is different; it does not resemble the *Creation of the World*. Michelangelo was older – *The Last Judgment* was painted between 1534 and 1551, and Michelangelo was 66 years old when he finished it. Michelangelo had matured. Beside the beauty of the world of antiquity emerged another beauty, the beauty of maturity, the thought connected with the destiny of humanity and of faith. Dante Alighieri came back with all his strength in "The Inferno," the section of *The Divine Comedy* that addresses Hell. In his sermons, the Dominican Savonarola criticized the time of the Renaissance. Both these works found resonance with *The Last Judgment* fresco. Savonarola was burned as a heretic, but his words lingered in the air of Florence. It is true that the Christ of Michelangelo, judging the world, is presented in a manner only a Greek sculptor could imagine. But centuries later, this painting continues to be a warning to the conscience of all.

But why am I, in writing a book about a pope who builds bridges, reminiscing about the frescoes of Michelangelo in the Sistine Chapel during the Renaissance?

John Paul II is a product of his country, of the history and literature of his country, and of the people he encountered, as I am. And just as the Renaissance allowed people to breathe freely after years of fear during the Middle Ages, Pope John Paul II, after the years of his native land being enslaved, was able to breathe freely in an independent Poland. Yet, at the same time, he did not forget that this freedom was obtained through the suffering of many others. Michelangelo absorbed the philosophy of his time by listening to the philosopher Ficino in the Medici Palace. Similarly, this philosopher-pope has tried to combine Greek philosophy, especially Plato, with Christian philosophy, and to reconcile the philosophy of Christianity with the philosophy of the twentieth century, the century of progress and the age of gas chambers.

Michelangelo built bridges through his art. Pope John Paul II builds them with his words and actions. He is the shepherd of souls, a guide to one billion Catholics. He is also a poet, whose poems, plays, and sermons are reminders of human destiny, in his country and beyond in the world. Like the tension between the two frescoes of Michelangelo – the hopeful *Creation of the World* and the sombre *Last Judgement* – so John Paul II seeks to build bridges of understanding between people of peace and cultures of violence. He does this in his prayers and sermons, and travels, fully aware that at this moment in history, humanity is confronted with the great task of the future. The existence of this future depends on the conscience of all humanity, not of one man but of millions. In the Church of St. Peter in Chains, in Rome, there is a magnificent sculpture, also by Michaelangelo: *Moses and the Ten Commandments*. It reminds us that there, high above, is God, and between God and each one of us is our conscience.

Karol Wojtyla remembers the Polish fields, the cornflowers, the poppies, the country. But the horizon of his thoughts today embraces the whole world as humanity waits for the blessing of God.

Marie Antoinette and *The Heart* of Edmundo de Amicis

I n my childhood and youth, one of my favourite places was my father's office. When he was away I would look through the window and observe the park and wonder about the changing seasons. I admired the trees, accepting their nakedness in winter and smiling with spring. Sometimes I would look at his library, at the books behind the glass. My father insisted that we should not read certain books while we were too young to understand them. This is why I did not open the glass door to take books out. According to my father, I was to wait for my eighteenth birthday to have access to his library, and I never objected. Sadly, our plan was interrupted, and I ended up reading very few of these books. The war started before my eighteenth birthday. The library was abandoned with the rest of our furniture during the war. We never got back a single book.

My parents believed that children should learn foreign languages at an early age, so I started to learn French very early, when I was five or six years old. My teacher was a cousin of my mother's who had studied in Paris for several years. Pola Rubel was beautiful, very delicate and elegant. She had short black hair, and she looked to me like a movie star. I loved her looks and I loved her way of teaching. I enjoyed French very much. We spent many lessons just talking about Paris. Pola described la Place de la Concorde, l'Avenue des Champs Elysées, la Tour Eiffel, l'Arc de Triomphe, and the gardens of the Tuileries. She talked about the Opera and the River Seine.

I repeated the names often, and at night I dreamed about being there. After Krakow, I wanted to see Warsaw and then Paris. I would make itineraries for my future trips. I would sit in my father's chair near his desk and think about Paris. Once, while dreaming of France, my eyes stopped at a miniature of Marie Antoinette in a beautiful frame. Beside Marie Antoinette was a picture of my parents with Adam and me, and two small photographs near each other. One was a photograph of Adam on a horse which my cousin Jerzy took during our vacation in Kalne, and the other was of me dressed in a Columbine costume. I acted once in a children's theatre production. I appeared on stage with a clown and we had a short dialogue about people in the circus. I was proud that the role of Columbine was given to me, and my costume in blue and white was exquisite.

I sat for a while and concentrated on the miniature of Marie Antoinette. One day many months earlier, when I asked if the Queen of France was happy, my father answered that she was very unhappy. I looked at the face of the beautiful young woman and thought about our happiness. I felt so happy. I loved my life. I loved people. I loved my school, my friends.

One afternoon after finishing a French lesson, I remember I went to my father's office because I wanted to look at a book on Paris. When my father came in he greeted me with a smile. I held the miniature of Marie Antoinette in my hand. "Tell me," I asked my father, "why you said a short time ago that this beautiful queen of France was unhappy." My father sat down beside me and for the first time I heard about the French Revolution and the beautiful young woman who died at the age of thirty-eight. My father said that before being sentenced to death, Marie Antoinette begged the mothers of France to spare her life. She was not successful and was executed on the guillotine.

The French Revolution became connected in my imagination with the face of the beautiful queen who died young. Many times I came back to this lesson about the history of France. Many times I thought about the cruelty of war, cruelty often replacing justice. Was this late-afternoon conversation with my father the source of my later thoughts? I often thought about mothers who give life to their children but are never able to shelter them when war takes place. I often reflected that mothers do not have any power, any influence on politicians who decide to solve conflict by declaring war.

Later that day, my father opened his large, glass-covered bookcase and showed me for the first time a book on Paris. I saw la Tour Eiffel, l'Arc de Triomphe and l'Avenue des Champs Elysées. I decided to go there one day when I grew up.

My interest in Marie Antoinette never diminished. When as a teenager I read the novel *Marie Antoinette* by the Austrian writer Stefan Zweig, I was fascinated by the way he brought the queen of France to life on the pages of his book. After *Marie Antoinette* I read many of his other books. I especially enjoyed his biographical studies such as *Magellan*. Through Zweig I was introduced to Balzac, Dickens, and Dostoyevsky in his *Drei Meister* (Three Masters), and to one of the greatest writers in France, Romain Rolland, an ardent pacifist and a Nobel Prize winner. Stefan Zweig became one of my beloved authors. When I think about it again I realize how many different ways lead to the world's cultures. After the war I found out that this famous essayist, playwright, and biographer had committed suicide with his wife in 1942 in Brazil. After Hitler came to power, Zweig, a Jew, had had to leave his beloved country, and he suffered badly as a result. In exile he wrote his last book, *Die Welt vom Gestern* (The World of Yesterday). I read his book in German. Here was a Jew who did not want to accept that his beloved Austria was no longer the "Austria of Yesterday," of his dreams, of his longings, and of all the values that were dear to him. How many Jews experienced this same pain when they were expelled from their homeland, their *Vaterland?* Stefan Zweig was one of those great Europeans who influenced my own perspective on life.

Many years later I was in Salzburg with my younger son, Jacques. While taking a tour, I asked the guide to show us the villa where Zweig lived. At first, the guide, a young girl who was very knowledgeable about the history of Salzburg, seemed astonished, but then she said she would show us the villa. The only sentence that she uttered was, "He committed suicide in Brazil."

As I write these words, I go back in time to the evening when Marie Antoinette and Paris became present to me so vividly. My father showed me the book on Paris. It was a beautifully illustrated book, and I learned a lot. Many times while studying in Paris, Montreal, and Philadelphia, I would think of other books of my father's which were on the same shelf as the book about Paris. There on the shelf were poems by Rabinranath Tagore, *The Wedding* by Stanislaw Wyspianski, a beautiful edition of *Das Buch der Lieder* (Book of Songs) by Heinrich Heine. Near Heinrich Heine's book was the book of poems by Cyprian Norwid, one of my father's favourites. Norwid left a rich legacy of deep thoughts about Poland, the human condition, and history.

I remember that near Heine's book was Friedrich Nietzsche's *Also Sprach Zarathustra* (Thus Spake Zarathustra). When I teach courses on the Holocaust and the war, I always mention Nietzsche. Hitler used Nietzsche when he proclaimed his theory of the *Übermensch* (Superman). Hitler disputed the equality of people, and believed that some races are superior to others. Nietzsche, speaking about the death of God, says, "Dead are Gods, now we will that *Übermensch* live ... I teach you Superman." Nietzsche also says, "What can be loved in man is that he is a transition and destruction."[16]

There in my father's office, I knew nothing about Nietzsche's philosophy. Nietzsche's book was placed on the same shelf as the poems of Juliusz Slowacki (one of the leading Polish poets) and the poems of Heinrich Heine. Later, during my studies at McGill University, I was fascinated by the philosophy of Immanuel Kant and eventually wrote my master's thesis on ethics and aesthetics in Kant. I compared the two German philosophers: one trying to implant the seeds of ethics, and the other planting the seeds of hate and destruction. How was it possible that the seeds of destruction and hate found a fertile ground in people who gave the world Immanuel Kant?

My father's library had two books near each other, the poems of humanity and teachings of cruelty and hate. Maybe the most important thing for every human being is the freedom of choice. Each one of us, at different times in our lives, becomes a fertile ground for goodness or evil.

Is every child susceptible to the teachings of his or her family, environment, and school? Is the philosophy of life taught by inspiring and encouraging certain actions and sometimes by weighing on the scale feelings and practical thinking? Is the art of living presented only by examples of famous heroes and of those who are successful, no matter how high the price? Don't we have to recognize also the honest people who were never renowned but who showed by their behaviour that they followed the principles of ethics, and who struggled just to maintain fellowship in their own noble way?

* * *

My relationship with my brother was very special, and I would often consider myself almost grown-up during our conversations. I admired his loyalty to his friends, and sometimes I was astonished when I observed his reactions to everyday activities. We often played together, especially when we were with the Kosiba family. He helped me whenever he could. We fought sometimes, but in my brother I have always had my best friend. While we played games together, Adam displayed a great sense of humour and when we quarrelled he could turn a disagreement into a joke. I was stubborn. I wanted to have my way and constantly reminded him that he was my younger brother. I scolded him when he biked too fast, especially when he competed against older children. He was very fast. Adam was skinny. I envied him. I was never skinny. Adam was delicate. My parents had to plead with him to eat. My mother would bake him the best chocolate cake, which he had to consume every afternoon with a glass of milk. I do not remember anyone telling me I had to eat. He was a good pupil but missed a lot of school because he often had a cold or a fever. I was very proud that he played the violin, and his teacher, Mrs. Rybarski, enjoyed him as a pupil. Because of the war Adam abandoned the violin, but he learned to play the harmonica, and to this day he still plays it when he is surrounded by his family and a few close friends.

When I think about Adam, I remember one evening when he rose greatly in my esteem. After my father came from his office he told my mother that Mr. Jozef Mordawski, Adam's teacher, came to see him and said, "You should be proud of your son." (Mr. Mordawski was a family friend, and Janka, his daughter, was my best friend.) He told my father that during recess he overheard the conversation that Adam had with one of his classmates. This classmate came from a very affluent home and brought oranges to school every day. In Poland oranges were very expensive, and he used to eat the oranges and give the skins to the pupils around him. One morning Adam approached the boy and told him never again to bring oranges to school. Adam said, "If you want to eat them, eat them at home, not here." This was the day that I understood how good my brother was. I respected him.

I write very often about moments of my childhood, and I realize that certain characteristics don't disappear in later years. Adam was always a realist. I was a dreamer.

* * *

I remember a very special birthday when I was ten years old. Mrs. Helena Kosiba came to my mother and said, "We should celebrate Renia's (Teresa's) birthday." And she added, "Lusia, I will help you. I will bake the cakes and cookies."

Mrs. Kosiba loved Adam and me. We spent a lot of time in the Kosibas' apartment and we were treated almost like their own children. Our parents also became very good friends with Jan and Helena. When Jan had difficulties with his properties, my father tried to help him and was always ready to cheer him up with his advice. Helena gave us different herbs when we were sick, and when my father had kidney problems she helped him more than the doctor. Helena had had a very difficult childhood. She had lost her parents at a very early age. She married at sixteen and was always ready to give her love to people around her. We always spent the Christmas holidays with the Kosiba family, and after Passover, when we would eat matzah for eight days in a row, she always sent us a tray with different delicacies.

My tenth birthday was very memorable. Many of my friends came, and we had a great time. I remember Mrs. Kosiba's cookies to this day. I received many gifts and a few books, three of which widened my horizon of dreams. The first one was Eliza Orzeszkowa's *Nad Niemnem* (On the Niemen River). The story about Polish people living in Lithuania was depicted with a woman's sensitivity. It was possible to feel the attachment to the soil and the readiness to pay the price of freedom. There was also the admiration for working people who wanted to keep the old traditions and retain their dignity during the difficult times, under threat from the Tsarist policies. Eliza Orzeszkowa taught patriotism in a most beautiful way. When I read her book I did not know that she also wrote novels about Jews. In *Eli Makower* and *Meir Ezofowicz*, she depicted Jewish life in the Jewish quarters and at the same time introduced to Polish readers the old traditions and the changes which were occurring within the lives of young Jews. She was also able to present in her books the humanistic traditions in Jewish culture.

The second book was *Dick dziecko Kina* (Dick, the Child of Cinema). I do not remember the name of the author, but this book offered me an image of Hollywood and the story brought me a breeze from California. The third book was *Serce* (The Heart), translated from the Italian *Il Cuore*. I was very impressed with this book by de Amicis. A few months later I discovered that the book was not on the shelf with my other books. I cried. My father asked me why I was crying, and I said "I lost 'The Heart.'" He laughed. He did not understand at first. I explained. Two days later I got another copy. The typist from my father's office made a beautiful cover from shiny paper, and in the middle he drew a heart in red ink.

There in my little Polish town, Jaslo, I saw for the first time an Italian city. De Amicis showed me Turin chestnuts, Turin high school boys, and Turin was no longer foreign to me. In one of the stories, "The Little Scribe from Florence," the father of a family earned his money copying by hand books that were later printed. The father worked very hard at this. His son, a high school student, wanted to help his father, and one day he decided that after his father fell asleep at night he would continue his father's work until dawn so the work would go faster. He developed the same style of handwriting, but after several weeks, he became so exhausted that he was late for school. His marks began to suffer. His father shouted at him every day, asking why he had changed. His son's writing was so perfect that it never occurred to the father that he was being helped in the copying of his books. He just thought he had been working faster and better. The son endured humiliation for many months, continuing to help, until one night he fell asleep while writing. The next morning his father found him sleeping at the desk. Suddenly he understood that his son had endured the humiliation and shouting only because he wanted to help.

This story, and other stories by de Amicis, influenced my life and strengthened me. As a child I understood it, especially since I loved my father very much. Years later, in 1971, I was in Turin. From the Hotel Palace I looked at the chestnut trees outside the windows. They were familiar to me for they had grown for me in Poland, in Jaslo, in my imagination. The little scribe from Florence still lived for me. Here is an example of the influence of the written word, one powerful book. Choosing a certain pattern to satisfy our ethics, even if this ethical approach is not recognized, demands determination. Determination also helps in communicating with other people. This book taught me the value of making choices that allow us to become what we want to be.[17]

Are We Members of the Same Human Family?

Sometimes it happens in conversation: we stand
facing the truth and lack the words,
have no gesture, no sign:
and yet – we feel – no word, no gesture
or sign would convey the whole image
that we must enter alone and face alone, like Jacob.
This isn't merely wrestling with images
carried in our thoughts;
we fight with the likeness of all things
that inwardly constitute man.
But when we act can our deeds surrender
the ultimate truths we presume to ponder?[18]

In *I and Thou*, the Jewish philosopher Martin Buber says that our whole life is based on dialogue: dialogue with nature, dialogue with humankind, and dialogue with God. Dialogue between people can be based on equality, when we treat the other person exactly as we treat ourselves, or on inequality, when we treat this other person as an object or consider them inferior to ourselves. (The dialogue with nature is beyond the form of conversation expressed in words, but rather on the border of conversation.) Dialogue with God is different. We turn to God in our thoughts and words, and later we feel that God is answering us. The omnipotent God is this great "Thou" present in each of our dialogues. Is this what we feel when it seems to us that God addresses us? Is this the flicker of God in our conscience? Does this flicker of

God allow our prayer and our thoughts to touch the hem of eternity? When we make choices that take into consideration the dignity of the other, those with whom we are in contact, does this consideration influence our behaviour? Should we treat other people as we treat ourselves? Do we consider the dignity of the other person when we make choices? Do we search for the presence of God in our decisions? Or do we listen to those who try to influence and advise us to treat some people as objects and thus take away their dignity, the dignity given to each person by God?

In countries where people of different nationalities or religions live side by side, very often children and young people have to make their own decisions. Often children are forbidden to play with other children who are said to be "different." Young people often accept the influence of their peers or the political climate of the country in which they live in directing their decisions. These young people do not realize the dilemma of moral nature; they submit to the will of others and they give up their right to choose. As they mature, their character and their nature have no opportunity to form themselves. This submission to the influences of the environment is not temporary. As adults they let themselves be influenced by their environment, and these influences become a foundation for their behaviour in the rest of their lives, in their relationships with people, with their country, and even with God. Youth is like soil that needs to be planted with good seeds, and later people must learn how to cultivate these seeds and make them grow. One poem, one sentence printed in a novel, may awaken the resonance of compassion, if we allow the mind and heart to think and feel without interference.

In Poland before the Second World War, every tenth resident was a Jew. The Polish rulers' treatment of the Jews varied according to the time in history and to the people who influenced the country's internal policy. Often, this treatment depended on the Church.

This was the world into which Karol Wojtyla was born. He lived on the street near a Catholic church, and the church was near the synagogue. In the secondary school in Wadowice, Karol Wojtyla had to choose – to treat his Jewish peers as equals and make friendly relationships with them, or to treat them as many anti-Semites were treating them, as newcomers, as foreigners. Although many Jews took part in the uprisings that ultimately led to independence, and although many Jews fought in the Pilsudski's Legions and shed their own blood to defend Polish soil, there were many anti-Semites in Poland. Karol Wojtyla had to choose between Polish writers who respected or hated Jews. Also very important was the atmosphere in Christian homes, where sometimes Jews were considered human beings and the Old Testament a part of Christian faith, and sometimes Jews were considered as Christ killers and nothing more.

After Hitler came to power in Germany, the atmosphere in Poland was permeated with hate propaganda against Jews. After the death of Marshal Pilsudski, who never forgot the part Jews played in the fight for Poland's independence, the situation worsened.

Who are the writers who formed young Karol Wojtyla's character? Though the words of nationalists and politicians who hated the Jews were ever present, there were also the great Polish authors: Adam Mickiewicz, Juliusz Slowacki, Cyprian Norwid, Stanislaw Wyspianski, and Leopold Staff. Karol Wojtyla, whose life was formed not only in school but also at home and in the church, was a reflection of their inspiring thoughts.

In 1952, in his cycle of poems, *Thought – Strange Space*, he writes about searching for words while "facing the truths." Although the poems were written in the decade following a world war, we can see in them the thinking and behaviour of Karol Wojtyla, the priest, the bishop, the cardinal, and later the pope. We see the input of feeling that allows him to reach deep truths, accessible only to one whose sensitivity participates in the search for these truths.

In this youthful, sincere poem-hymn, he asks his soul to "worship the glory of the Lord, Father of great Poetry – and so good." God, his Country, and the Slavic heritage were elements building the personality of young Karol Wojtyla. The young poet offered to God his sanctity, which is able to brighten the life of every person, and all that was most noble within himself.

We cannot forget the important influence of Polish literature in the education of the Polish youth, especially in an independent Poland. This literature was patriotic and an inspiration for the young minds of future politicians, representatives of Polish culture, philosophy, and the currents forming the independent country. Christianity was deeply rooted in Polish literature. The greatest Polish poets who lived during the nineteenth century and emigrated to Paris could freely express their thoughts. Adam Mickiewicz, Juliusz Slowacki, Zygmunt Krasinski, Cyprian Kamil Norwid and others left masterpieces of poetry and prose. During the first part of the nineteenth century, the Romantic literature of Europe and North America grew out of the thoughts of the generations that lived after the French Revolution. Without a doubt, this literature influenced political events such as the unification of Italy and the Polish Uprising of January 1863. The revolutionary ideas of this period inspired many to fight for freedom and justice. The Polish representatives of Romanticism, especially poets like Mickiewicz, who lived in Russian-annexed Polish territory under the surveillance of the police, knew very well that they were limited in expressing their free thoughts. Poets like the Russian Alexander Pushkin or the Ukrainian Taras Shevchenko also suffered under Russian surveillance, as did Cyprian Kamil Norwid, Wincenty Pol, Zygmunt Kaczkowski, and Richard Berwinski in the prisons of Polish territories annexed by Prussia and Austria. The Romantic poets endowed Polish history with rich thoughts and exerted a profound, pioneering influence after the First World War.

A professor of Polish literature, Kazimirz Forys, founded a theatre in Wadowice, where students from the local schools helped produce the works of Polish writers. Here Karol Wojtyla acted in and even helped produce the *Undivine Comedy* of Zygmunt Krasinski. Karol was an excellent actor with a good strong voice, and he liked to sing. At this time he met Mieczyslaw Kotlarczyk, who was fourteen years older and a doctor of philosophy. He worked as a professor in a grammar school (*gymnasium*) in the nearby city of Sosnowiec, and often visited Wadowice to organized evenings of music and recitation there. Audiences were very deeply moved by the presentation of *King – Spirit* by Juliusz Slowacki. The idea of founding the Rhapsodical Theatre came after this performance. To know about the origin of the Rhapsodical Theatre and the role that Karol Wojtyla played in its development is essential if we want to understand how literature and theatre shaped the character of the future pope.

In his book *John Paul II*, Tad Szulc describes some of the events that occurred during this period of the future pope's life.

> Wojtyla's horizons were not entirely confined to Wadowice during his high school years. Members of the Theatre Circle were often taken by their teachers to Krakow, never missing a

performance at Juliusz Slowacki Theatre there. And the circle put on performances of its own in many of the small towns surrounding Wadowice. All in all, Wojtyla was gaining a fine education and exposure to universal culture and ideas.

His leadership qualities were also being recognized. Not only was Karol a top student and the elected president of student organizations, but he was in constant demand as the spokesman for the high school on national occasions. He led the uniformed high school contingent in national holiday street parades, right behind the infantry regiment. On an anniversary of the 1791 Constitution, for example, seventeen-year-old Wojtyla was put in charge of a special performance of Slowacki's patriotic *Kordian*, directing it and playing the lead role. And when Archbishop Sapieha came down from Krakow to visit the Wadowice boys' high school on May 6, 1938, Karol greeted him on behalf of the student body.

This was another turning point in Wojtyla's life, though he could not have guessed it. The archbishop, sitting in a red leather armchair, was so impressed by the welcoming speech that he asked the Wadowice parish priest, Father Zacher, what plans Wojtyla had after graduating later that month. Was he thinking of entering the seminary? Zacher replied, "I'm not sure, but it will probably be the university." Karol then said, "If Your Excellency will allow me, I would like to answer for myself: I plan to take Polish philology at Jagiellonian University." The severe archbishop sighed, saying, "Too bad, too bad!" The topic came up again at the faculty dinner, and Father Zacher told Sapieha that "this young man has the theatre in his head." The archbishop said once more, "Too bad, too bad. . . . We could use him . . . ."[19]

The young Karol not only read Juliusz Slowacki but often reflected on the creativity of Adam Mickiewicz. During his stay in Paris, Mickiewicz met Andrzej Towianski, who cultivated a special reverence for Napoleon as a link between the earthly and the unearthly world. Mickiewicz was devoted to Towianski, and under his influence wrote *Books of the Polish Nation*. Some critics considered this book a national bible, with its ideals of activities towards liberation and its slogans in the Romantic spirit.

As a patriot, Mickiewicz dreamed, on Parisian pavement, of Poland. His *Ode to Youth* became a source of inspiration, and not only for Poland. The Poland he knew and loved, fighting for freedom, was always present in his thoughts. He depicted this Poland with a description of the life of the nobility and of Polish people against the background of customs and contemporary history in the epic poem *Master Thaddeus or The Last Foray in Lithuania*. In this masterpiece Mickiewicz displays dramatic dynamism in his description of history and the character of people from different levels of Polish society. In *Master Thaddeus* we see a portrait of a Jew who loves Poland. This portrait is engraved in the minds of Polish Jews, for whom "The Concert of Jankiel" reveals how this great national Polish poet understood the attachment of a Jew to Poland. In order to illustrate its importance to an understanding of Polish culture, here is a major scene from this work:

> For in the yard of the castle the officers and ladies, the privates and the village girls were already standing in couples: "The polonaise!" they all shouted with one breath. The officers were bringing up the army musicians, but the Judge whispered in the General's ear:

> "Pray give orders for the band to restrain itself for a while longer. You know that today sees the betrothal of my nephew, and it is the ancient custom of our family to celebrate betrothals and marriages with village music. Look, there stand the player of the dulcimer, the fiddler, and the bagpiper, all worthy musicians – already the fiddler is making mouths, and the bagpiper is bowing and begging with his eyes that I will have them begin – the poor fellows will weep. The common folk will not know how to skip to other music; so let them begin and let the folk have their fun; afterwards we will listen to your excellent band."

> He made a sign. The fiddler tucked up the sleeve of his coat, squeezed tightly the finger board, rested his chin on the tailpiece, and sent his bow over the fiddle like a race horse. At this signal, the bagpipers, who were standing close by, blew into their sacks and filled their cheeks with breath, making a quick motion with their arms as though flapping their wings;

you might have thought that the pair would fly off on the breeze, like the chubby children of Boreas. But there was no dulcimer.

There were many players of the dulcimer, but none of them dared to perform in Jankiel's presence. (Jankiel had been spending the whole winter no one knows where; now he had suddenly made his appearance along with the General Staff.) Everybody knew that no one could compare with him in playing that instrument, either in skill, taste, or talent. They begged him to play and offered him the dulcimer; the Jew refused, saying that his hands had grown stiff, that he was out of practice, that he did not dare to, that he was embarrassed by the men of high station; with many a bow he was stealing away. When Zosia saw this, she ran up, and with one white hand proffered him the hammers with which the master was wont to sound the strings; with the other hand she stroked the old man's greybeard, and said with a curtsy:

"Jankiel, be so good; you see this is my betrothal; play for me, Jankiel. Haven't you promised to play at my wedding?"

Jankiel, who was beyond measure fond of Zosia, nodded his beard as a sign that he did not refuse. So they led him into the centre of the company and put his instrument on his knees; he gazed on it with delight and pride, like a veteran called back to active service, when his grandsons take down from the wall his heavy sword: the old man laughs, though it is long since he has had a sword in his hand, for he feels that his hand will not yet betray the weapon.

Meanwhile two of his pupils were kneeling by the dulcimer, tuning the strings afresh and twanging them as a test of their work. Jankiel with half-closed eyes sat silent and held the hammers motionless in his fingers.

He lowered them, at first beating a triumphal measure; then he smote the strings more briskly, as with a torrent of rain: all were amazed, but that was only a test, for he suddenly broke off and lifted both hammers aloft.

He played anew; now the strings trembled with motions as light as though the wing of a fly were sounding on the string, giving forth a gentle, hardly audible buzzing. The master fixed his gaze on the sky, awaiting inspiration; he looked down and surveyed the instrument with a haughty eye, he raised his hands and lowered them together, and smote with both hammers at once; the auditors were amazed.

All at once from many strings there burst forth a sound as though a whole janissaries' band had become vocal with bells and cymbals and drums. The "Polonaise of the Third of May" thundered forth! The rippling notes breathed of joy, they poured joy into one's ears; the girls wanted to dance and the boys could not stand still – but the notes carried the thoughts of the old men back into the past, to those happy years when the Senate and the House of Deputies, after that great day of the Third of May, celebrated in the assembly hall the reconciliation of King and Nation; when they danced and sang, "Vivat our beloved King, vivat the Diet, vivat the people, vivat all classes!"

The master kept quickening the time and playing with greater power, but suddenly he struck a false chord like the hiss of a snake, like the grating of iron on glass – it sent a shudder through everyone, and mingled with the general gaiety an ill-omened foreboding. Disturbed and alarmed, the hearers wondered whether the instrument might not be out of tune, or the musician be making a blunder. Such a master had not blundered! He purposely kept touching that traitorous string and breaking up the melody, striking louder and louder that angry chord, confederated against the harmony of the tones; at last the Warden understood the master, covered his face in his hands, and cried, "I know, I know those notes; that is Targowica!" And suddenly the ill-omened string broke with a hiss; the musician rushed to the treble notes, broke up and confused the measure, abandoned the treble notes, and hurried his hammers to the bass strings.

One could hear louder and louder a thousand noises, measured marching, war, an attack, a storm; one could hear the reports of guns, the groans of children, the weeping of mothers. So finely did the wonderful master render the horrors of a storm that the village girls trembled, calling to mind with tears of grief the

Massacre of Praga, which they knew from song and story; they were glad when finally the master thundered with all the strings at once, and choked the outcries as though he had crushed them into the earth.

Hardly did the hearers have time to recover from their amazement, when once more the music changed: at first there were once more light and gentle hummings; a few thin strings complained together, like flies striving to free themselves from the spider's web. But more and more strings joined them; now the scattered tones were blended and legions of chords were united; now they advanced measuredly with harmonious notes, forming the mournful melody of that famous song of the wandering soldier who travels through woods and through forests, oft times fainting with woe and with hunger: at last he falls at the feet of his faithful steed, and the steed with his foot digs a grave for him. A poor old song, yet very dear to the Polish troops! The soldiers recognized it, and the privates crowded about the master; they hearkened, and they remembered that dreadful season when over the grave of their country they had sung this song and departed for the ends of the earth; they called to mind their long years of wandering, over lands and seas, over frosts and burning sands, amid foreign peoples, where often in camp they had been cheered and heartened by this folk song. So thinking, they sadly bowed their heads!

But they raised them straightway, for the master was playing stronger and higher notes; he changed his measure, and proclaimed something quite different from what had preceded. Once more he looked down and measured the strings with his eye; he joined his hands and smote with the two hammers in unison: the blow was so artistic, so powerful, that the strings rang like brazen trumpets, and from the trumpets a well-known song floated to the heavens, a triumphal march, "Poland has not yet perished; march, Dombrowski, to Poland!" – And all clapped their hands, and all shouted in chorus, "March, Dombrowski!"

The musician seemed amazed at his own song; he dropped the hammers from his hands and raised his arms aloft; his fox-skin cap dropped from his head to his shoulders; his uplifted beard waved majestically; his cheeks glowed with a strange flush; in his glance, full of spirit, shone the fire of youth. At last, when the old man turned his eyes on Dombrowski, he covered them with his hands, and from under his hands gushed a stream of tears.

"General," said he, "long has our Lithuania awaited thee – long, even as we Jews have awaited the Messiah; of thee in olden times minstrels prophesied among the folk; thy coming was heralded by a marvel in the sky. Live and wage war, O thou our – "

As he spoke, he sobbed; the honest Jew loved his country like a Pole! Dombrowski extended his hand to him and thanked him; Jankiel, doffing his cap, kissed the leader's hand.[20]

In every Polish *gymnasium* students would read and discuss the "Concert of Jankiel," and reflect on the issue of choice. What should they do? Should they think about Jews as portrayed by Jankiel in *Master Thaddeus*, selling fruit or shoelaces at a stand in the marketplace? Should they include the owner of the store or small shop in their reasoning, or listen to the anti-Semitic propaganda and boycott him? Among these students was Karol Wojtyla. What should he do? Should he listen to the voice of Roman Dmowski, who not only hated the Jews who peddled their goods, but also hated the excellent writers and talented poets who considered themselves Polish poets but who were Jews? The Polish language was their mother tongue. They did not know any other language. Roman Dmowski and the Polish nationalists took from the Jews their rights to Poland, their country, this Poland in which they were born.

Polish literature was a treasury of thoughts for Karol Wojtyla. In *Master Thaddeus*, Mickiewicz described the "Concert of Jankiel." There were also other writers who offered Karol Wojtyla a positive image of Jews and Israel. Stanislaw Wyspianski, in his drama *Acropolis*, described the modest shepherd boy David fighting with Goliath. He describes David, a harpist, and in the words of Wyspianski you can hear the sound of David's harp. In the words of the Polish writer you can hear the melodies of the Old Testament vibrating in the world. Leopold

Staff, in his poem "The Judgement of Solomon," admires the wisdom of the King of Jerusalem, who could choose the real mother of a child, over whom two mothers fought. Does Solomon help us to solve these kinds of dilemmas according to the ethical principles that were offered by God, far away on Mount Sinai? Thomas Merton, a monk, a Catholic thinker and author of many philosophical works, wrote in *Seeds of Contemplation*:

> Every moment and every event of every man's life on earth plants something in his soul.[21]

In a later version of the book Merton wrote:

> Souls are like wax waiting for a seal. By themselves they have no special identity. . . . The wax that has melted in God's will can easily receive the stamp of its identity, the truth of what it was meant to be.[22]

Karol Wojtyla, the future pope, met a variety of people in school, in the theatre, and in church in Wadowice. In the Bible, in Christ, and in the saints, he encountered the world of history and human problems which were also reflected in Polish literature.

There, in Wadowice, was a microcosm of this world, shaping the posture of this man and his role as a member of the human family.

Professor Jan Lisowski and Emperor Marcus Aurelius

I often think of teachers entering their classrooms in September. There they meet a group of students, each of whom is an individual. In a few years some of these students will become professionals in different fields. Some of them will become scientists, some will be successful or less successful business people, some will be artists, poets, dancers, doctors, explorers, or actors, some of them will be leaders of countries. Some of them will be curious to find the essence of their own life by going forward every day to challenge this essence. Some of them will be passive, never taking the opportunity to raise their voices and play a part in history. In existentialist philosophy, existence precedes essence. It is up to us to create this particular essence for our existence.

A teacher who enters the classroom in September observes and scrutinizes the students. And each of the students is scrutinizing the teacher. The teacher has been taught how to treat the students. Each of the students decides how he or she will treat this particular professor. Who will prevail in creating the atmosphere of the classroom?

There are some teachers who take part in shaping the character of youngsters. There are some teachers who will remember certain students – the ones who gave them new ideas and widened their horizons.

In my life there were those teachers who taught me how to think, those who encouraged me to dream, those who tried to change me, and those who helped me to raise my eyes to the sky and be grateful for life. Some became my friends, and I owe them my thanks and I also offer a prayer of gratitude to God that they appeared on the path of my life.

At the end of fourth grade I passed the entrance exam into *gymnasium* (high school), where I would spend the next eight years. I passed my entrance exam easily and was proud to be admitted to the High School of Blessed Jolanta, a private high school for girls (there was no public high school for girls in Jaslo).

From my first year there I had the feeling that I was almost grown-up. I was the youngest in the class, since I had entered elementary school early. As in elementary school, I sat beside Janka Mordawska, but I also became very friendly with a few other students. This circle of new friends included Wanda Ziemnowicz, Bella Braun, Irka Pronyszyn, and Irka Fafara. Later on I befriended Hala Welfeld, Renata Zuker, Niuna Boronska, Zosia Palica, Pola Grabschrift, and Danka Pawlowska. I was friendly with my whole class. They were all loyal and warm-hearted, and the atmosphere in my class was very pleasant. Since I had a sense of humour, my classmates appreciated me. However, some teachers were less enthusiastic since I often made the class laugh. Except for behaviour I had excellent marks on my report cards.

There were some professors who left a distinct imprint on me. The best professor I ever had was my history teacher for six years in the *gymnasium* and two years at the Lycee, Jan Lisowski. He opened my eyes to the history not only of Poland, but of the world. I attended many universities in different countries, but the lessons taught by Jan Lisowski gave me a foundation from which to understand political movements and the traditions and customs of different cultures. When Communism collapsed I remembered the words of my beloved professor. He had said that Russia was a colossus on legs of clay. I also remember his lecture on Egypt and the development of the alphabet. He taught me that one culture blends into another and that we all are the product of influences of mixed cultures.

As he taught me about Pericles, I tried to picture the Parthenon with *Athena Parthenos* inside, created by Phidias. I thought not only about Phidias' work, but also of his life and the power of the enemies of Pericles, who sent the great sculptor – maybe the greatest sculptor in the history of humanity – into exile. To this day we do not know if he died outside Athens or within the city as a political prisoner. The centuries follow one another, but the fate of many great people often depends on others who understand their creations or not, or who accept new ways of thinking, or who remain closed-minded out of envy, or whether they appreciate other people's talents or reject them. It was Phidias who created the life-sized statue of Zeus for the temple of Olympia. And though we know about Zeus, we know little of the struggles for political power in Greece. History is often obscure when it comes to the naked, human truth. It was from my professor at my school in Jaslo that I learned about the sculpture of Hermes by Praxiteles and the *Discobolus* (Discus Thrower) by Myron. Any time I look at the *Apollo Belvedere* in the Vatican Museum (a Roman copy probably of Greek origin of the late fourth or fifth century; no one is sure when this sculpture was made), I am transported back to that Polish classroom and those history lectures.

Aeschylus, Euripides, Sophocles, Socrates, Plato, Aristotle visited me in my Jaslo high school. Today I teach a course on the culture of the ancient world, and when I talk about Myron or Praxiteles, I remember the Greek notion of *kalokagathos*, beautiful and just. I see myself in the centre of the class discussing the idea of beauty and justice, not as separate issues, but connected one with the other.

I think it is important that I mention all these classes in my autobiography since all these thoughts have helped shape my way of understanding the world and people. It was Jan Lisowski who first taught me about Emperor Marcus Aurelius. I remember how I was interested in his *Meditations*, whose words I have retained through all these years:

> Men exist for the sake of one another. Teach them or bear with them.... He who does wrong, does wrong against himself. He who acts unjustly acts unjustly to himself, because he makes himself bad.[23]

I often repeated these words to myself during the oppressive days of the war, when injustice was spread among those who used their power and strength to abolish the rules of decency and humaneness.

Jan Lisowski also made me proud of my Polish history. Polish heroes were present in our classroom: Jan Sobieski fighting near Vienna, Tadeusz Kosciuszko fighting in America, and the fighters for Polish independence. We not only admired Marshal Jozef Pilsudski, who in 1918 led the Polish Legions to victory, but we revered him. I remember when I wrote a poem after his death, I cried because this was my beloved Marshal.

But, there were also moments where my feelings were deeply hurt at my beloved school. One day we were informed that a new director had been appointed. Her name was Idalia Grabianska, and she came from Warsaw. She was old, and she wore mostly purple dresses. She was often ridiculed by the students, who called her "the funny old lady." I do not know why, but I felt compassion for her, especially as she did not know anybody in Jaslo. She lived on the main floor of the school building.

At the beginning of her stay she did not know I was Jewish, since my first name was Teresa and this name was not often used by Jews. (I became Lena only after receiving false papers as a Christian during the war.) Apparently she was surprised to find out that I was Jewish, and I noticed that her attitude changed toward me.

One day "the funny old lady" came to teach Polish literature to our class and she gave us an assignment: we had thirty minutes to write about a winter day. I was very deep into my thoughts when suddenly I heard the words, "Mordawska [Janka Mordawska sat near me as always], are you not ashamed to copy from a foreigner!" It seems that Janka had taken a look at my paper. That day is engraved in my memory. How had I become a foreigner in my beloved country? I was shaken and hurt, but I did not cry. I left school earlier than usual and I walked home alone, not with my friends as usual. I did not walk on the street. I ran through the empty fields to my father's office. Somebody had inflicted pain on me, but I did not fight this time.

More than forty years later, when I went back to Poland for the first time, I finally spoke to Janka Mordawska about it, and she remembered the incident.

Teachers and professors leave a mark not only on students' report cards, but also on their memories. In my high school, there were other memorable professors besides Jan Lisowski. Some of them allowed me to strive, to be creative; some of them did not understand my drive to create. Most of my teachers were women. My Latin professor, Josefa Halucha-Mostranska, encouraged me to translate the poems of Ovid into rhyming Polish. I was very grateful for this challenge. Later, she sent one of my poems to a magazine which published it.

Marie Niekrasz, my Polish literature professor, knew how to present great writers and poets. She appreciated my essays, but she was very strict and did not like my behaviour. I remember one day when she said to me, "Remember, silence is golden," and I immediately responded, "We live in a time of depression. For me silver is enough." The students burst out laughing. I knew she would never forget this incident.

There was also Leon Krol, a professor from the boys' school, who taught us mathematics. He was a short man with a round face, very jovial and warm-hearted. One day he said to me, "Why do you even bother with mathematics? You are such a good writer." After that, I never applied myself to algebra or geometry even though I had been very interested in these subjects before. When I write a poem or compose a song, I often think to myself that we need mathematics to achieve proper rhythm and harmony.

Later, when I studied sociology at the University of Montreal, I thought about Professor Krol. I had difficulty with calculus, but I forgave him his wrong advice. I liked him very much.

During my education, private teachers helped me along the way. One of them was my piano teacher, Jadwiga (Jadzia) Rosenfeld, who was my mother's second cousin. Although Jadzia had attended the conservatory in Krakow and was encouraged by all her teachers to become a concert pianist, she decided to teach and returned to her family in Jaslo. Jadzia was twenty-three years old and had red hair and green eyes. She was very attractive and had a lot of success with men. For me she was more than an excellent teacher, and she was more than a cousin. I looked up to her, and I was influenced by her in many aspects of my life. I remember the day she confided in me that a young German from Berlin had asked her to marry him, and it was difficult for her to decline his proposal. They were in love, but knowing about Hitler's laws, she decided to be realistic, and told him, "This is not the time for a Jew to marry a German."

Just before the outbreak of war in May 1939, Jadzia married a man named Walter. Walter adored her, and I knew that she loved him too. She always called him "my giant." Walter was Jewish, over six feet tall and very handsome. He seemed to always protect her. Sadly, Jadzia was killed during the war. Walter was imprisoned in a concentration camp, but he survived.

Another tutor of mine often shared her wisdom of life with me. After my first French teacher, Pola, married and left Jaslo, I was taught French by a wonderful woman from Paris, Maria Malicka. She was not only my teacher, she also became a very dear friend. In fact she became one of the greatest friends I have ever had. Mrs. Malicka was a widow. After the First World War she had married Mr. Malicka, a Polish engineer. They lived in Jaslo. The couple did not have any children, and after Mr. Malicka died, Maria decided to remain in her husband's country and earn her living by teaching French and occasionally English. We spent a lot of time in conversation, walking in the park. Maria told me a lot about her childhood and youth, and she always inserted some lessons of life. She considered me almost a grown-up, and sometimes she discussed her relationship with her husband. She taught me a lot about love and interdependence in relationships. One day she told me how important it is for a woman to retain her self-respect in any situation. She also added that jealousy is dangerous and that we should never be afraid to speak up for our own values, even when they are unpopular. I remember her words: "Verbal manifestation of your jealousy will never have an effect. Rather, with your behaviour show your dignity and self-confidence. If you don't succeed, act according to your convictions concerning the relationship." I was maybe thirteen or fourteen years old, listening to this older woman who was giving me a very important lesson on love, friendship, and self-worth.

One day after I came home from school my mother told me that the time had come to learn another language: English. She assured me that I would have a very good teacher, who had just come from England after finishing her studies there.

After my first English lesson I wanted to quit. I found the English language very difficult, and I kept saying that the spelling and pronunciation were simply not coordinated. I was resigned that I would never be able to learn this most "difficult language." A year later, when my parents insisted that I learn, I agreed on the condition that Maria Malicka would teach me. And she did, although our classes were interrupted by the outbreak of the war.

Even after the war, when I studied political science in Paris and had the opportunity to learn English once again, I opted for basic German, which I already knew. After deciding to move from France to Canada, I was happy that we settled in Quebec. In Montreal I could speak French all the time. However, there in Montreal I decided once again to try and learn this "difficult language" with its very complicated pronunciation. My God! When I think about that I can only laugh, especially since I learned not only to enjoy English, I also managed to lecture on art, philosophy, and history in English for more than twenty years! I often thank God that I can write my poems, essays, short stories, and songs in this "difficult language."

In my school in Jaslo I often met three priests. Two of them were teachers at the school, and the third was a friend of the teachers. We had friendly conversations about our school events, about books that I was reading. Everybody knew I read a lot and I was familiar not only with Polish literature but with books that had recently been translated into Polish. For these three priests, I was a curious, smiling student. Each priest was very different in character. Father Jozef Gayda was a short man, quite heavy, and very jovial. He did not teach in my school but was always around. He was cheerful and had a keen sense of humour, and we often laughed together. When he died I went with all my classmates to his funeral in the neighbouring village of Warzyce. We were all very sad. This priest was everybody's friend.

In contrast, Father Ewaryst Debicki was very serious. Often before entering the classroom where he taught Catholic religion, he would speak to me in the corridor, asking me if I had written something new and what I was reading.

Father Jan Pasek was a tall, distinguished looking man, devoted to students and education. He often walked with Father Gayda in the park I would cut through on my way home, and would ask me questions about my plans and my future.

My conversations with these three priests reinforced what I had learned at home from my parents: that all people are equal, no matter what their religion, origin, or race. These discussions with priests took place during the time when Hitler was proclaiming "Aryan superiority" while emphasizing the inferiority of others. Once, Father Debicki, before entering the class where he taught Catholic religion, spoke to me about my special interest in different people in the world. We talked about different cultures and religions, and I remember our conversation vividly.

After we parted I went to the class where the Jewish girls were taught Jewish history and religion. The atmosphere in the school was friendly, and apart from religion classes, we were always together. We were a group of twenty-two girls who stayed together during the eight years of high school. Fourteen were Catholic, one was Protestant, and seven of us were Jewish. Of the seven, Bella Braun was killed with her mother, father, and sister; Renata Cukier was shot with her sister, Jasia, after being taken on a sleigh during a winter night (her mother and father had been shot beforehand); Lunka Safier is one of the group about whom I have no details; Hala Welfeld survived the war, but was deported by the Russians (her mother died in exile); Pola Grabschrift survived, though she was deported by the Russians, and her father died in exile; and me. I, too, survived. As I write this book, their smiling faces, our jokes, our dreams for the future, our curiosity about life, our expectations come flooding back.

It was not important that the Catholic and Jewish girls did not attend the same religious lessons. We were united in our dreams and expectations despite a world that was already shaken by the propaganda of hatred, which had also reached Poland. After so many years, I can say that in our school we had a sense of belonging to each other. However, there were moments when thunder resounded around us, especially in the years before the outbreak of the war.

Our religious class was taught by two very different teachers. Professor Chaim Diller was a deep-thinking scholar. Tall, serious, well dressed, he was respected by everyone in Jaslo. After Professor Diller died, a young man arrived. He was good-looking and modern and was interested in our questions. He was always ready to interrupt his lecture to appease our curiosity. His name was Chaim Schild. Since he was young, we were not intimidated by him, and he often based his lectures on beautiful legends. He also tutored Adam and me in the Hebrew language once or twice a week.

I remember one of the legends, a story about the Jews who, after leaving Egypt, received the Ten Commandments on Mount Sinai. According to this legend, God revealed Himself to His chosen people in the desert, not only to the people who had come out of Egypt but also to the souls of the Jews who would be born in the years to come. This legend comes back to me very often in my memories.

Chaim Schild perished with his young wife and his parents during the war.

* * *

When I was in Israel in 1972, I went to Sinai. With a small group, I flew in a small plane from Tel Aviv, and we landed near St. Catherine's Monastery. A young priest from the monastery guided us. It was difficult to comprehend that this monastery had been built in the desert so many years ago. After we visited the monastery, he showed us the "burning bush" where the Angel of the Lord appeared to Moses in fire, flaming out of the bush. As Moses watched, he saw that although the bush was on fire, it was not consumed by the flames. Moses decided to look more closely to see why the bush was not burned. (Rabbi Plaut in his commentary explains that the bush is in fact the soul.)

I looked at Mount Sinai (we did not have enough time to climb to the top), and I tried to imagine the time in history when the giving of the Ten Commandments took place.

An hour later we went by bus to Sharm al-Sheikh, and there I experienced one of the greatest moments of my life. Here I saw the white sand on the shore, the blue sea, and the magnificent blue sky illuminated by the strong sun. Serenity reigned. There was only one tent with a few Israeli soldiers and a little child, maybe two or three years old, playing alone in the sand. Someone who worked in the camp must have brought his wife and child there.

I was alone, although there were a few couples around me. I was sorry that I could hear them speaking as their voices broke the silence. Suddenly, I felt as if I had made a great and mysterious discovery. I thought that only in this place in the desert could God and humankind meet. The calm sea, the sky, and the white sand of the desert. I could not utter a word. Yes, here I was present when God gave the Ten Commandments. I did not pray with words, but my thankfulness for having the opportunity to feel this way was in my silence. Was this the grace of God bestowed on me in the split-second of a moment? This was not the Western Wall, the remnant of Solomon's Temple, but the experience was as if I had entered a figurative temple where everyone could enter, everyone who feels the Ten Commandments in their soul and tries to praise God with their thoughts and deeds.

In 1972, I wrote a book in which I collected prayers from different religions and tried to find their similarities.[24] I did not dwell on differences. Yes, all peoples are different, but if we emphasize their similarities and not differences, we are able to discover the unity of the human family. As I write these words I think about those three Catholic priests, the young Jewish teacher, and the Jewish girls in my high school who did not survive.

The thoughts about God and humanity never leave me. This is my sense of belonging to humankind.

In 1965, I wrote a book of poems in French, *Le Pain de la Paix* (The Bread of Peace). In one poem, "Le chercheur de Dieu" (The Seeker of God), I describe a solitary man, who as a youngster, sold newspapers on the street in New York during the day and at night studied various subjects in different disciplines. He learned a lot, entered university, and finished his studies. He was very successful, and in a few years he became a millionaire, living on Park Avenue in an apartment filled with magnificent works of art. One day, he saw himself reflected in a big rococo mirror. Here he was, a 50-year-old man who had achieved wealth but nothing else. He decided to travel throughout the world. He wanted to search for God. A week later he went to Barcelona, where he listened to children singing in an old church. He decided to continue his journey. He went to Jerusalem. On Friday night he went to a synagogue and listened to the prayers. He continued his journey once again, to Egypt, where he listened to the muezzin calling the worshippers to prayer. Then on to Mecca and Bangkok. He finished his journey around the world and came back to New York. He had studied all the prayers in the world, yet he still could not find God. One day he went to Central Park, not far from his apartment, and there he saw a little white girl trying to describe the sky to a little blind black boy. She said to him, "Through my eyes I will show you the world." There my millionaire found God.

A few years ago I was walking in New York on Fifth Avenue near St. Patrick's Cathedral, and there at the corner I saw my poem come to life. I noticed a young white girl describing to her companion the blue sky in a most poetic way. Her companion was a tall young black man. He was blind. He carried a white cane. I hesitated, but after a while I approached the couple. I told them that many years earlier I had described them in my poem. They laughed at first, but after they realized I was serious, they were very moved. My imagined vision had become real.

It was back in my high school in Jaslo in Poland where these hopes and the visions of a better, more just future were born.

Students often remember their teachers, but sometimes the teachers remember their students. I was in contact with Professor Jan Lisowski after I left Poland. Before he died, he asked his wife to write me a letter and asked me to write, to write ... always.

One day in Philadelphia I told my cousin Albin that I often think about Marcus Aurelius. A few days later, Albin brought me an English translation of *Meditations*. In it were printed the words I had learned in my youth: "Men exist for the sake of one another. Teach them or bear with them."

A Flicker, a Spark, and a Flame

T he young student Karol Wojtyla offered the voice of his feeling to poetry at a recitation contest in Wadowice. He recited fragments of Cyprian Kamil Norwid's poem *Promethidion*, and the words of poetry vibrated in the air. Without any doubt these words left their trace in the memory of this young man who recited Norwid's poem, and in the memory of listeners who were present where these words were pronounced.

Poetry ignites flickers of thought, but can this thought over the course of years ever transform itself into a flame?

In Greek mythology, Prometheus stole fire from the Olympic gods and offered his fire to humans, as a flicker, a spark, a flame. This was his gift of to humankind.

In a fragment of his *Promethidion*, entitled "I Will Ask This Eternal Man," Norwid wrote:

I will ask this eternal man
I will ask the history about the confession of beauty.
I will ask the eternal man because he is not jealous,
I will ask the eternal man who is waiting without lust,
I will ask this one without passion:
What do you know about beauty?

It Is a Form of Love

It goes through India, Persia, Egypt, Greece
in hundreds of languages and centuries of centuries,
in the granites russet – red and with gold

in marble – ivory – waiting afterwards.
This said to me Prometheus with a hammer.

The Shape of Love – Is Beauty – And Nothing Else.[25]

Norwid continues:

How much of this beauty
man saw in the world – in the great God
and in himself – in the dust.

As Prometheus offered the treasure of fire to all humanity, so Norwid offered Karol Wojtyla, the future pope, this thought: The Shape of Love – Is Beauty – And Nothing Else.

How much spirit we can discover in one sentence! In all corners of the world people search for consolation in the awareness that love exists, that there is someone upon whose feelings we can depend. This fragment, "I Will Ask This Eternal Man," touches all those who were born before us, those who live in our time, and those who will come after us.

We search for beauty in God, and at the same time through our behaviour we can allow ourselves to be shaped by that beauty or remain a "colourless" dust. Our dialogue is first with God and afterward with humankind. It is possible to become a "colourless" dust or to create in our being a "beautiful" dust. This dust will vibrate in the air one day, like the words of the poets, and the world in turn will become more beautiful.

In *Crossing the Threshold of Hope*, John Paul II writes:

For contemporary thought the philosophy of religion is very important – for example, the work of Mircea Eliade and, for us in Poland, that of Archbishop Marian Jaworski and the school of Lublin. We are witnesses of a symptomatic return to metaphysics (the philosophy of being) through an integral anthropology. One cannot think adequately about man without reference, which for man is constitutive, to God. Saint Thomas defined this as *actus essendi* (essential act), in the language of the philosophy of existence. The philosophy of religion expresses this with the categories of anthropological experience.

The philosophers of dialogue, such as Martin Buber and the aforementioned Lévinas, have contributed greatly to this experience. And we find ourselves by now very close to Saint Thomas, but the path passes not so much through being and existence as through people and their meeting each other, through the "I" and "thou." This is a fundamental dimension of man's existence, which is always a coexistence.

Where did the philosophers of dialogue learn this? Foremost, they learned it from their experience of the Bible. In the sphere of the everyday man's entire life is one of "coexistence" – "thou" and "I" – and also in the sphere of the absolute and definitive: "I" and "thou." The Biblical tradition revolves around this "thou," who is first the God of Abraham, Isaac, and Jacob, the God of the Fathers, and then the God of Jesus Christ and the apostles, the God of our faith.

Our faith is profoundly anthropological, rooted constitutively in coexistence, in the community of God's people, and in communion with this eternal "thou." Such coexistence is essential to our Judeo-Christian tradition and comes from God's initiative. This initiative is connected with and leads to creation, and is at the same time – as Saint Paul teaches – "the eternal election of man in the Word who is the Son." (cf. Eph. 1:4)[26]

Reading those words I am reminded of the African mother begging God for milk – the nourishment of her breasts and the nourishment of her inter-human love. The beautiful dust forms by itself. Norwid's *Promethidion* contains another fragment that illustrates Pope John Paul's vision of "how I see the Polish art in the future." Norwid wants the chapel where the Polish spirit would reign to

give symbol of blossoming signs,
where through stonecutter, woodcarver,
carpenter, woodcarver,
poet – and finally the martyr and knight
would rest in deed and in prayer.[27]

In another fragment Norwid writes:

And as the humblest prayer, an angel's call,
And between these, work into its right place will fall.[28]

For Norwid, it is not thought or knowledge that counts most. He considers the craft of the apostle and "the humblest prayer of the angel" the highest craft. He believes that "between these, work into its right place will fall." In his dreams, Norwid sees Polish art "as a flag on the tower of human works." Is this art in the life of the Pope John Paul II, who tries in love to find beauty without any blemish, a witness that the flicker of love implanted in the country of cornflowers and poppies was never extinguished?

Karol Wojtyla grew up with poetry. The love of his mother, the moral strength of his father, and the poetry of his homeland contributed to his understanding of the meaning of love. Pope John Paul II tries to build bridges between many different people. Maybe this pope is like a carpenter or a stonemason who builds a firm foundation for the future on a terrain of swamps and dirt. Maybe he is a sculptor who tries to sculpt souls, a stonecutter who breaks the stones of human indifference to suffering which is harder than the stones he broke while working in a quarry during the war. He is certainly a poet who knows how to dream, who can imagine a rainbow of people with different thoughts, cultures, and even religions living together in harmony. And finally, this pope is a martyr who, after celebrating Holy Mass, was wounded by a fanatic whom he later forgave. He forgave as a man; the rest depends on God. And this pope is also a knight – a Polish knight from the olden days, a Slavic and Romantic knight who in the name of his convictions is ready to give his all, his life. In work and prayer, this modern Prometheus brings a flicker of love.

Does Norwid help the pope in his task? Along with his prayers, the poetry that Karol Wojtyla recited with feeling and strength is present in his striving as he guides one billion Catholics and tries to influence the history of the centuries. Perhaps even now the shadow of the beloved poet Cyprian Kamil Norwid accompanies the pope during his walks in the Vatican gardens.

After the Second World War, Karol Wojtyla, already a priest, wrote the drama *Our God's Brother*. In the introduction we read that it presents a "study, the attempt to penetrate man." He dedicated his drama to the memory of Adam Chmielowski, whose name was well known in Krakow.

Adam Chmielowski had many talents and studied a great deal during his youth, first in Petersburg and later in the *gymnasium* in Warsaw. He also studied engineering, and he was a student in the Agriculture and

Forest Institute in Pulawy as well as in the Design Class in Warsaw. He studied painting in Paris and Munich. One of his friends was Henryk Sienkiewicz.

At that time, the Poles in the part of Poland occupied by Russia were fighting for their independence. There was an uprising in November 1830 and again in January 1863. Chmielowski took part in the second uprising and lost his leg in the battle near Melchow. The Tsarist authorities forbade him to live in the occupied part of Poland, and he later moved to Krakow. His paintings *The Sunset, Cemetery*, and *Insurgent* still hang in the National Museum there. He lived on Basztowa Street in Krakow and devoted all his time to painting. In 1880 he entered the Society of Jesus, taking his vows eight years later as a Jesuit brother in the presence of Cardinal Dunajewski, taking the name Brother Albert. He organized the Gathering of Brothers, serving the poor under the name The Albertans. In 1891, he founded the Order of Albertan Sisters. *Ecce Homo*, which he painted in 1879, is now in the Church of the Albertan Sisters.

The choice of this hero by Karol Wojtyla is significant. Brother Albert was a painter who, although he loved art, decided to dedicate his life to those whom he wanted to help recover their dignity. In 1983, Pope John Paul II beatified Albert. On December 13, 1988, the world premiere of *Our God's Brother* took place in the Slowacki Theatre in Krakow, and the next year, Brother Albert was canonized in Rome. Now there is a street named Adam Chmielowski in Krakow.

Adam Chmielowski, a talented painter who certainly knew how to express his feelings on canvas, decided to give his feelings to a new canvas of life. On this canvas passed the silhouettes of people who were often forgotten as they waited for someone to shake their hand, or for a bowl of soup, or to be acknowledged for their dignity.

In *Our God's Brother* Karol Wojtyla writes:

> Adam, left alone, sits for a long while, motionless in his chair. Then he wipes his forehead, pushes back his hair. Suddenly he rises. Very slowly he walks to his easels. He passes many of them indifferently before approaching *Ecce Homo*. Is not that painting more surely his than the others? He stops in front of it and, in spite of himself, bends down as if stooping under the weight of this subject. He lifts his eyes to the painting. Then he speaks very slowly.

Still You are terribly unlike Him, whom You are.
You have toiled in every one of them.
You are deadly tired.
They have exhausted You.
This is called Charity.
But with all this You have remained beautiful.
The most beautiful of the sons of men.
Such beauty was never repeated again.
Oh what a difficult beauty, how hard.
Such beauty is called Charity.[29]

After this confrontation with his own being, Adam decides to leave his present life and become Brother Albert.

One part of *Our God's Brother* is called "The Atelier of Destinies." The description of this "atelier of destinies" is significant:

The location and dimensions of this place will become clear in the course of the action. The people who will pass through it are, after all, a group remembered from history. But what matters most here is their destinies – the development of their destinies.

The two men who are now talking remain in the nearer and better-lit part of the studio.

Max: The newspapers are writing about your exhibition already.

Stanislaw: Yes, I saw them this morning.

Max: In my opinion they will cut you to pieces.

Stanislaw: That's what I expect . . .

Max: You antagonize everyone. That's not the way.

Stanislaw: Have you ever considered, Max, that we can transform little – ridiculously little – apart from ourselves? As artists we merely try to understand, or rather heed – you know what I mean – and reflect in our work an unexpected insight into our self, which, slowly transformed, has suddenly realized its own transformation. Then people come along, take an interest in the work of art, and through that work of art engage the artist who can so change his skin like a chameleon. They need this kind of encouragement. It means they can transcend themselves. And for that matter, it does not cost them much.

Max: I envy you such a viewpoint. You have quite a high opinion of your public. I must admit I would find it quite difficult to cope with something like that.

Stanislaw: Well then, why . . .

Max: You want to ask me, I suppose, why I paint at all. Well, certainly not for the public.

Stanislaw: I wouldn't dare pose the question like that. And yet, in spite of everything, a relation remains, a reference, a social mission.

Max: Then dissolve it on the palette, give it a coat of oil, and seal it with plaster! And now maybe you will add a word about responsibility . . .

Stanislaw: Ah yes, I think so.

Max: Excuse me – how big a responsibility?

Stanislaw: How big? . . . I won't reply to that, Max. I think the question is too personal. Besides, we know each other too well, and I have no desire to posture before you.

Max: Well then – how wide?

Stanislaw: To that I will reply. Yes. I am convinced about the mission of art.

Max: What mission? From the eyes to the brush? In saying that I do not wish to compare art with craft. Oh no, not at all. But one mustn't exaggerate. I value art to the extent that it stimulates me, gives me the impetus to which my true self inclines. And thanks to that, it tests how much can still be drawn from myself. After all, how a man's self works, how it grows and declines, is extremely interesting. But that is all. All. What more do you want? That is sufficient meaning. Around me, in others . . . ?[30]

When we read the words of Norwid and Karol Wojtyla about the mission of art, we perceive authors or painters who put their art on the pedestal of conscience. They provoke in the viewer and listener not only a sense of the mystery of their being but also the horizon of their vision of the world and of their understanding of humanity.

Is the "atelier of destinies" not a place where everyone sojourns and consciously or subconsciously "forges" and "sculpts" their own being?

If the word "conscience" occurs in every chapter of this book about Pope John Paul II as a builder of bridges, it is because conscience determines how we act in our lives. For some, conscience is the ever-present motor that drives their actions. For others it is just a useless screw. For some it is a source of never-exhausted strength, while for others it is like a stream of water where they can wash away their deeds. Then they consider their conscience superficially washed, as cleaned.

In the Metropolitan Museum of Art in New York there is a magnificent painting by Rembrandt, *Pilate Washes His Hands*. This painting becomes a challenge for history. Rembrandt, a Protestant, who had read the Bible every day since his childhood and who lived in a time and country where religious themes were not popular subjects for painters, must have believed in the mission of his art. At this time in the Dutch Republic, portraits were more popular than religious paintings. Luther did not believe in the power of painting. The Protestant world considered music to be the only appropriate accompaniment to religion.

Rembrandt searched in the Bible for an answer to one question: Who is this "man" created in God's likeness? Maybe this is why Rembrandt left 90 self-portraits in paintings and sketches. Perhaps Rembrandt searched in his own being for a way to understand the Bible. Maybe this is how he got to know God and Christ. Many of his paintings show conflict on the face of a man, conflict with conscience in this chiaroscuro of light and shadow. From this shadow appears the painter, who in his own conscience contemplated silhouettes from the Old and New Testament.

Rembrandt, the son of a miller from Leyden, may have watched the Rhine River and searched the water for the colours of humanity – water that was clear in spring, cloudy in autumn. I stand before the painting of Pilate in the Metropolitan Museum and think of Christ.

Rembrandt painted not only Pilate but also Judas Iscariot, who on the steps of the Temple gave back the silver coins of betrayal in humility and in suffering. Judas asked for forgiveness and then hanged himself. This painting of Judas created in the image of Rembrandt throws light on the conflict of humanity, painted with all its strength in the face of Judas. Judas tried to repent. In the painting (now part of a private collection in England), we see his face, distorted, deformed in all his pain and despair. Rembrandt often painted the faces of his subjects, showing their inner conflict as if their sense of justice was reminding them to obey laws.

The painting of Judas attracted the attention of Konstantijn Huygens, who was the advisor to the Duke of Orange. The Count commissioned a whole cycle of paintings on the Crucifixion of Christ, one of the greatest masterpieces of art. *The Crucifixion, The Descent of Christ from the Cross*, and *The Assumption* are the expressions of the greatest love of man for the man the Christian world calls the Chosen One and Son of God. Rembrandt, in his humanity, his eagerness to understand suffering, left for the world the image of Christ in the light and shadow of chiaroscuro, the drama of light and shadows he knew how to use to solve serious problems. Rembrandt also painted *The Circumcision of Christ*. The Blessed Mother holds her son, the Jewish child who should be circumcised on the eighth day of his life, according to Jewish law. This beginning of the covenant that was established between God and Abraham was respected in the family of Christ.

Beside these events in the life of Christ, Rembrandt also painted a few portraits showing only a face and silhouette of Christ. When we look at these portraits, we admire the spirituality, serenity, and beauty. We see in the face and in the silhouettes of Christ a man created in the image of God and who belongs to the whole human race.

The models for these portraits were always Jews. Rembrandt believed that since Christ was a Jew, then in his portraits he should return to that source for the features of the Saviour and founder of Christianity. Amsterdam provided him his models. Many Jews found their home there after being exiled from Spain and Portugal. The Dutch Republic offered Jews freedom of religion and protection, as they did to other different religious sects at this time.

One of Rembrandt's last paintings is *The Return of the Prodigal Son*. Why, almost at the end of his life, did he decide to eternalize on canvas the parable about the Prodigal Son? Love shines from the face of the father who puts his arms around his son. Perhaps Rembrandt is presenting himself, pleading to God to take him into his arms. Although Rembrandt had a very difficult life and often suffered, we see his love and faith in God in this painting. Maybe we see in it the prayer of all those who suffer. The father forgives his son, and in the painting, the son has lost a shoe, while rushing to his father. Does this almost insignificant detail have meaning? How many sinners run with a plea for forgiveness, and while running, are seized with their own fear? Their repentance is sincere.

Rembrandt knew that God is compassionate. Throughout the Bible we find descriptions of God's mercy and forgiveness. Besides the parable of the Prodigal Son, there is the story of Jonah. Jews read this story every year on the Day of Atonement, the most solemn holy day. On this day, Jews fast from one sunset to the next, and pray for the absolution of their sins. They pray to God for forgiveness. Both of these stories stress God's compassion if we repent sincerely. God does not want to punish us but rather tries to put us back on the road to repentance.

In the Book of Jonah we follow a man who did not obey God. Jonah was to deliver a message to the city of Nineveh. He thought that it was possible for him to escape from this mission given to him by the Almighty. However, God pursued the sinner, wanting to show him the road to repentance. Jonah tried to reason with God, but at one point he asked for death. It is interesting to see Jonah asking for punishment. However, God, still patient with a disobedient Jonah, sent a large fish, which swallowed the sinner. There in the belly of the fish, Jonah said a prayer, and in his prayer he remembered the loving kindness of the Creator. God listened to his prayer and commanded the fish to spew Jonah up onto the shore. The words of the Lord came to Jonah for the second time to deliver the message to the city of Nineveh. This time Jonah went to the city with God's message that within forty days the city would be destroyed. To Jonah's surprise the wicked people listened to his message of destruction and repented immediately. Maybe the most important part of accomplishing the mission was Jonah's dissatisfaction with God listening to the repenting people of Nineveh. It was true that its inhabitants were enemies of Israel, but God wanted to show Jonah that all people deserved his care.

This book which contains the words of God is significant, not only because of the loving kindness of God, but because it emphasizes that every individual deserves God's care, and that God has compassion not only for the righteous but also for those who disobey God's word. God is slow to anger and with all His might tries to teach people how to repent.

Jesus' parable about the return of the Prodigal Son brings in a very simple form the teaching of wisdom. The teachings of Christ certainly reached all people, educated as well as uneducated. What would be easier than to show the greatness of God as that of a father whose behaviour gives an example of sincere forgiveness, the outcome of love for each other? The caring father embraces his son, the sinner, with joy, and this brings hope to those who have committed errors and suddenly realize that they would like to find a path through repentance to the grace of God. In the Gospel according to Luke we read:

> And they began to celebrate. Now his elder son was in the field; and when he came and approached the house, he heard music and dancing. He called one of the slaves and asked what was going on. He replied, "Your brother has come, and your father has killed the fatted calf, because he has got him back safe and sound." Then he became angry and refused to go in. His father came out and began to plead with him. But he answered his father, "Listen! For all these years I have been working like a slave for you, and I have never disobeyed your command; yet you have never given me even a young goat so that I might celebrate with my friends. But when this son of yours came back, who has devoured your property with prostitutes, you killed the fatted calf for him!" Then the father said to him, "Son, you are always with me, and all that is mine is yours. But we had to celebrate and rejoice, because this brother of yours was dead and has come to life; he was lost and has been found."
>
> (Luke 15:24-32)

There is one God, but there are many jealous people like the brother of the Prodigal Son. He is immersed in his own concept of justice. He is cruel and angry and preoccupied with his own "noble" behaviour. He considers himself the more important son. Christ knew very well that weakness exists in every individual, and that this weakness can be temporary. What is more significant than to admit our own weakness and to try to overcome it? If someone considers themselves above others, that person is already showing their weakness, their own vanity, and in losing humility, they are even defying God. The awareness that God is the sole judge brings us to understanding – or maybe not understanding – the ways of God, and to accepting these ways as binding upon us. How many times do we reflect on our life? Often, it is only when we look for hope and want to overcome our despair that we search for the guidance of the Almighty, and through our own pleading do we feel the presence of God.

The last words of the parable show that at the moment of true repentance we should celebrate our victory over weakness. The fact of admitting our sin is an act of courage, and maybe it is a sin not to acknowledge the one who chooses to return and wants to start a different life in accordance with the laws of God.

I expressed my feelings in a poem I wrote about Rembrandt, entitled *Moses with the Tablets of the Law*:

God entrusted man
with the greatest treasure,
the ten commandments,
the key to man's conscience.
The tablets of the law
remain in man's hands.
It is up to man
to hold them high, very high,
or to break them into pieces
and throw them
into the abyss
of ignorance, apathy
and forgetfulness
of God's divine existence.[31]

Are we allowed to forget God's commandments? Or the story of Jonah, who found God's forgiveness? Are we allowed to forget the story of the Prodigal Son? Does God not teach us compassion and the art of forgiveness in these stories?

Are we responsible for the sins committed even centuries ago? Can we beg for forgiveness when we see injustice causing the suffering of innocents? Is it a sin that people come to God by different roads?

On December 7, 1991, on the occasion of the closing of the European synod, Pope John Paul II gave approval for the following prayer:

O Lord, our Reconciler, in the Christian communities of Europe our divisions, our egoism and the scandals of those who say they belong to Christ but lack the power and authority to work for peace, justice, and liberty, have weakened in the conscience of the people their faith in the new life which you have brought. Pardon us and have pity on us.[32]

On August 19, 1985, in Casablanca, Morocco, he greeted young Muslims with these words:

Christians and Muslims, in general we have badly understood each other, and sometimes, in the past, we have opposed and even exhausted each other in polemics and in wars.

I believe that, today, God invites us to change our old practices. We must respect each other, and also we must stimulate each other in good works on the path of God. . .

Dear young people, I wish that you may be able to help in thus building a world where God may have first place in order to aid and to save mankind. On this path you are assured of the esteem and the collaboration of your Catholic brothers and sisters whom I represent among you this evening . . . Then, I am convinced, a world can be born where men and women of living and effective faith will sing to the glory of God and will seek to build a human society in accordance with God's will.[33]

After returning from Santo Domingo in October 1992, the pope spoke about "The Act of Atonement" during the general audience in the Basilica of St. Peter:

Through my pilgrimage to the place where evangelization began, a pilgrimage characterized by thanksgiving, we wanted at the same time to make an act of atonement before the infinite holiness of God for everything which during that advance toward the American continent was marred by sin, injustice and violence. Some of the missionaries have left us an impressive witness. One need only recall the names of Montesinos, Las Casas, Cârdoba, Juan del Valle, and many others.

After five hundred years we stand before Christ, who is the Lord of all human history, to address those words to the Father that Christ himself taught us: "Forgive us our trespasses as we forgive." . . . The Redeemer's prayer is addressed to the Father and at the same time to all who suffered various injustices.

We do not cease asking these people for "forgiveness." This request for pardon is primarily addressed to the first inhabitants of the new land, the Indians, and then to those who were brought from Africa as slaves to do heavy labour.

"Forgive us our trespasses." This prayer is also part of evangelization.[34]

In August 1987, in a letter to the president of the United States Conference of Catholic Bishops, Pope John Paul II addressed the issue of Jewish–Christian relations:

There is no doubt that the sufferings inflicted upon the Jews are also for the Catholic Church a reason of deep sorrow, especially if we think of the indifference and sometimes the resentment that in particular historical situations have divided the Jews and Christians. Certainly this calls for yet stronger resolutions to cooperate for justice and true peace.[35]

John Paul II's guiding thought grows out of his profound belief in the goodwill of all people. He wants to pave a new road of collaboration with all people in the world. This road should be built in the name of love of each other and respect for each other. It is an outcome of the reflections of the representative of the Catholic Church after the Second World War and at the same time of a deep philosopher and a great poet.

In Wadowice where Karol Wojtyla recited the poem *Promethidion*, the words of the poet Cyprian Kamil Norwid ignited a flicker that glowed in the heart of this teenager from Wadowice. Norwid gave life to the flicker of Prometheus, who offered people fire. Fire gives warmth, and fire can harm. Fire can be useful and fire can destroy. It all depends on how it is used. This flicker became even stronger during the war, when Karol Wojtyla witnessed cruelty and hate. This flicker allowed Karol the poet to dream that after victory over hate we would be able to build a better world. Even during the war, wherever Karol lived or worked he strove through his prayers and his behaviour to create an atmosphere of warmth. This flicker gave him courage as a priest to write a drama about Adam Chmielowski, an artist who decided to leave the vocation of art to become a shepherd of souls. In "The Atelier of Destinies," the flicker became a spark.

This spark helps the pope to beg for forgiveness in the name of love for all humanity and in the name of spreading understanding. Love and understanding create warmth. During the prayer for absolution of the sins of the past we hear the strong voice of the pope, the same voice of the man who years before recited the *Promethidion* in Wadowice. This voice we hear in Canada, in Australia, in South America, and on the sands of the Sahara Desert.

The world is not deserted.

The journey started in Wadowice; it continued to Krakow and from there to the Vatican.

In the modest room of the Holy Father's quarters hangs a painting of the Virgin Mary of Czestochowa. Here, in his own "atelier of destinies," a good man works, dreaming of kindling a flicker of love in the hearts of all people. Can this flicker melt the ice of indifference to suffering and injustice?

In St. Peter's Square in the Vatican everything is quiet. A few lamps shine on St. Peter's Basilica, and there, high in a room on the upper floor, in another "atelier of destinies," in this room, a light flickers, late at night.

The pope is not sleeping.

The Long Journey of a Diary

A diary is a friend, a revelation of our own thoughts. It expresses our way of seeing, observing, judging, and feeling. It is an escape for some people, a sounding board without voice for others, a way of communication with our selves in a certain stage of life when we feel that we can trust an inanimate object and turn this object into a kind of witness of our experience. Years later when we read or reread the content, we can laugh at ourselves or admire our naïvety, and wonder about the time when these ideas emerged.

One day in 1939, my parents decided to send Adam and me by taxi to a city about 70 kilometres away from Jaslo. I packed a few outfits and my diary. The next day, September 1, the war started. Our parents joined us in Debica when the bombs were already falling from the sky. Poland was shaking.

My diary started a long journey in space and time. During all my wanderings, the diary which I kept from 1938 to September 1, 1939 – that terrible day which saw the start of a war that would scar the world – accompanied me wherever I went, even when we lived with forged papers. All I did as a precaution was to erase from the text the word "Hitler" and a few lines concerning Hitler's speeches, which echoed strongly through the radio stations of Europe. After the war, the four small notebooks of the diary travelled with me from Poland to Berlin, from Berlin to Paris, from Paris to Montreal, and from Montreal to Philadelphia. Other different papers I cherish may have been in a disordered mess, but I always knew where these four notebooks were. This was my treasured past, never to be forgotten, always to be kept close to me. These four little notebooks were a reminder of my youth and happiness. Although I did not read them for many, many years.

I recently decided to open some of the pages of my diary of my early years without studying and judging them. In writing this book I decided to share them with my readers, since these diaries contain the thoughts that I had during the shaping of my future outlook and my attitude to life. The world was trembling but I was a teenager. I loved life. I was curious. I was creative: I started to write poems at the age of eleven, and at thirteen I started to compose songs, music, and lyrics. I loved life and sang the beauty of life in my poems and my songs, in my laughter and in my jokes. My classmates loved my poems and popular songs.

When I returned to Poland for a visit after an absence of more than 40 years, my dear friend Dziuta Schoenborn handed me a copy of my "Navy Ballad" (navy because for eight years we wore navy uniforms – a navy pleated skirt and a navy or white blouse). I wrote this ballad about my eight years in high school. In it I described all my professors with a lot of humour. The ballad was funny but not offensive in any way. I looked at Dziuta and my past came back once again; the apartment where Dziuta lived before the war; the books that her parents had kept in a large library and were always ready to lend to all their daughters' friends. Dziuta had a younger sister, Zosia, who was Adam's age. They were all very dear to us. I looked at Dziuta, and I thought of her mother and her father, who were killed during the war, and Zosia, who was killed immediately after the war. Dziuta lost her family, and she lost all her parents' possessions. But why did she save my ballad? Maybe this was a reminder of our youth, with all its joy and happiness.

There in my diary I found the words about my first love, not only of life but for a man. My love was Marek Lille, a medical doctor who was fifteen years older than me. The Russians deported him to Russia, where he disappeared during the war.

My diary tells me that I learned to love watching American and European films. I loved Jeannette MacDonald, Nelson Eddy, Charles Boyer, and Jean Gabin, whom I adored. I also loved the Polish actors Eugeniusz Bodo and Jadwiga Smosarska. I also loved German and Austrian movies, especially *Unfinished Symphony* with Hans Jaray, which I thought was one of the best movies I had seen. I was reading the magazine *Kino* (Cinema). I loved Polish singers, especially Mieczyslaw Fogg. He sang one of my songs after the war, "Usmiech Warszawy" (The Smile of Warsaw), which was about Warsaw, a vision of the city rebuilt from the ruins, after being destroyed during the war.

The entry for October 18, 1938, reads: "On Sunday Marek said that anticipation, striving, longing for something is more beautiful than a goal." He also said that often after reaching the goal we are disappointed. I think about these words, and I recall the teaching of John Dewey, who said that when we build a home, we should not only think about this home in its finished, built state, but we should enjoy the way of striving for this home, the process of building.

How often in my life I thought about Marek's words before I learned about John Dewey. I believe that in order to enjoy life we have to always strive for something and, after achieving it, go farther. The professors whom I met during my early studies come to mind. Marek was not my professor, but since he was older than me (I was always interested in older men), he taught me something about striving, always trying to go forward, overcoming adversity, jumping if necessary, inventing new steps into the unknown without fear.

In my diary late that same night, I wrote about a student from the boys' school who died in a bicycle accident. Igo Krzyzanowski was well liked by his classmates, was an excellent student. He was only seventeen. I was very sad, and I wrote these words:

Life, life, what is it? We pass beside the tragedies. We dedicate a few moments. We shed a few tears of compassion and we continue to walk on a busy street. We will continue to ride our bikes, often we will ride with or without light. We will listen to popular music and go to high school dances without Igo Krzyzanowski, who was in our dance classes. Everyone will follow his own path and maybe even the memory of Igo will fade. Igo was coming back from his rendezvous with Ewa Degenfeld from the neighbouring city of Jedlicze. Life, a meteor, a star which is shining, burning strongly, and disappearing somewhere – in the depth of the world – covered with a tear.

Life – a day of the changing weather – life – seducing man with its mystery. We walk on the street and we don't know who is walking beside us, what is going on in the soul of this man we don't know. Who is he? Is he smiling? Is he suffering? Does he have a home? Does he love someone? We look into the future – we do not know if life will offer us happiness, sunshine or tears – whom will we meet, what will we see?

I look at these words, translated from Polish to English, and I wonder. God, I did not change. These thoughts, committed to my diary on October 18, 1938, remain with me, decades later. There is another entry in my diary for September 5, 1938, written at 1 o'clock in the morning after my first day in school.

I was nicely dressed in my new uniform when I met Professor Lisowski [we called him "Jasiu" among ourselves]. He was surrounded by my classmates. He looked at me and I realized that this is my last year of high school and I also realized that maybe for this professor it was also difficult to think about eight years spent with our particular class. He knows that at the end of the 1938–1939 year we will pass our baccalaureate exams and we will go out into the world. [My year was the first one which took part in a new program of *gymnasium* and Lycee. Before, there were only eight years of *gymnasium*, without specialized programs. Our Lycee offered us a program in the humanities.]

We came as children into high school, knowing that we would leave as adults. Our young professor became older. We gave a lot to each other. I look at the schedule for the next day.

In my diary was the schedule for the next day: Latin, German, History, Polish Literature.

I loved school. I was looking forward to starting again. In the courtyard where we spent our recess the asters were blooming. They were purple, the colour of lilac, and all the shades of pink. Were they greeting my class for the last time? Yes. Yes, this was my class and these were my teachers and my friends. I looked at the flowers, and I thought of nature, of this magnificent world created by God.

My fascination with nature and my admiration for God's creation never disappeared. During the war I remember I could not cut flowers because they were living things, and too many living things were being killed. In the book which I wrote in French, *Ne me demandez pas qui je suis* (Don't Ask Me Who I Am),[36] I tried to reason with myself, but still I could not cut flowers in the garden.

Years later a gardener explained to me that flowers live longer if we cut them and put them in fresh water and remember to change the water every day. Flowers and people. If flowers have fresh water every day they live longer. If people know how to love they are happy.

As I write about these long-past happy days, other memories of pain and sorrow return. Events and encounters become confused. There is an avalanche of thoughts asking me not to forget that I am a survivor, that I belong to a part of the vanished world.

I remember the summer of 1969. I was with my younger son, Jacques, in Nice on the Côte d'Azur. It was one of the most trying times of my life. I had lost Sigmond, my first husband, the father of my children. I remember the day. It was sunny and hot with no clouds in the sky. The waves were quiet, almost without any sound. I had my little notebook that I carried in my purse, and for a moment I watched the sky. I looked at my son.

I started to write. Jacques asked what I was writing. I only said, "You will see later." I looked at him. I was so grateful to God for my two sons. His brown eyes were watching me. It was Jacques who in this moment gave me the courage to breathe, to go forward. He wanted me not only to survive after my loss. I knew that he also wanted me to love life. How often in my writings I have compared children to flowers. In one of my poems I wrote:

> May the flowers grow
> in the gardens of humanity
> the happy children
> who do not know fear.[37]

How I prayed to God that my children would live in a happy world. God, how I looked at the Mediterranean and prayed for the children who would not know fear.

It was there in Nice that I wrote this poem:

And God Prayed at Dawn

God looked at the universe.
He caressed
And graced with His presence
The oceans and the mountains
The plains and the deserts.
He transmitted
To every creature on earth
The mystery of creation,
The instinct of life.
In that single moment
The branches of the trees
Resented the strength,
Coming from their roots.
The strength grew
And helped the flowers
to bloom.

In that single moment
The inert waves
Of the oceans
Began to move
For the first time.

They touched the shores
And the earth
Brown, Black, or Red
And the sand
Gold or white.

The earth was changing the
colour,
Depending upon the secret of
the heavens
And the rays of sunshine,
Sent to remind the world
Of the Master's existence.

In that single moment
Through the revelation
Of the divine and paternal
warmth
The mountains were taught
About their task:
To protect with their power
The immense and small,
Grandiose and weak earth
Against violent winds
And storms.

In that single moment
The flowers began to dance
On their stems.

A kiss of God
Touched their velvet lips
And this kiss
Was a gift of sweetness
For the pure beauty
Of existence.

In that single moment
The heart of the first man
Started to beat.
God implanted love –
The seed of the most mysterious
And the most fragile,
The greatest divine power
The inexplicable love
Mightier than the oceans,
Warmer than the rays of
sunshine,
Brighter than the light of day
Purer than the first snow,

More flagrant
Than a spark,
The source of fire,
Stronger
Than the mountains
And softer
Than the velvet lips
Of flowers.

The eyes of man
Glanced with curiosity.
His chest moved rhythmically.
The heart of man
Was beating
And at that single moment
Tried to become
His master.

His eyes received
The blessing of God
To see
Far away.
Suddenly
God touched the head of man
And man started to think.
Did the heart still remain
The master of man?

God did not want to answer
And man could not answer.

God
After uniting in man
The two divine blessings –
Sentiment and thought –
Stopped.
The absolute Master,

The designer of destiny,
The source of light,
God asked Himself
Who will be the master
After Him.

Man, provided with
Heart and brain,
Will he be able to serve
As master after God?

The sky and the white clouds
Enveloped the universe.
Creation is not finished
Sang the doves
Near the oceans.
"Unfinished"
Whispered the mountains.
"Unfinished"
Repeated the echoes.
"Unfinished"
Chimed the bells of flowers.

Man looked at the sky and the
clouds
And in his inability to grasp the
infinite
And notwithstanding the
mystery of life
But enchanted with the pure
beauty,
Began to walk forward.
God saw man walking away
And was seized by a strange
revelation,
He asked Himself,
Had He allowed man

To leave
Too soon?

Man
In the meantime
Searched for God
With his eyes.

He was pursuing his path
Through the universe.
He was afraid
And he discovered
Time.

God left for Himself
Infinity.
Infinity remained
Beyond the capacity
Of the understanding
Of man.

Now
God asked Himself
For the second time
Who will be the master
After Him –
The universe
Or man?

The arms of man were strong,
His hands agile,
His head fascinating
And his curly hair
Was falling on his forehead.
His eyes were big,
But did not know
The temptation

Of searching for the impossible,
Of reaching for the skies.

Man touched the trees with his
hands,
And God looked at him
From far away,
This man was made
In His image.

Man stood straight
His hands moved
From the bark of the tree
And touched his own lips
Trying to caress them.
At that moment
Woman appeared.
She had the velvet skin of
flowers
Her lips were half-opened,
She approached man with her
body.

Man in his first physical ecstasy
Enchanted with the body of
woman
Whispered the first words
God had uttered to him,
"I love you."

The two beings,
Holding hands,
The two bodies,
One near the other,
Were giving birth
To humanity.

The multicoloured universe,
The scale of colours,
Blue, white, and pink
Smiled at two masters,
The powerful God
And fragile man.

For the first time
After the burst of joy
The universe
Trembled with fear.

No!
God should not have left
The universe
At the mercy
Of a fragile being.
Fear of the universe
Entered the existence of man.

Man felt strange
The beauty, the colours, the rhythm,
Inspired him
To dance.
He danced
Enchanted
And in his first dance
He wanted to put his head
On a very strong shoulder.

He touched the palm tree,
He touched the mountain,
He touched the wave of the ocean.
"I need your strong arm,"
The echo repeated in the universe.

"My arm is around you,"
Answered God
"The palm tree, the mountain, the flower
And the woman you love.
My arm is love,
My arm is the blue sky,
My arm is around you
When your thoughts touch Me
And when your heart beats."

The first dew
Fell on the grass
Of the universe.
The tear of the Creator
Fell on the earth.

God had doubts
About human strength:
Were the heart and the brain
Enough
To continue
His work of creation?

"The creation is unfinished"
Repeated the Guardian Angel of earth,
God listened
To the words of the Angel
And started to pray.

The dawn
Was transmitting
The prayer of God to man.
"In the future
You will start the family.

In the future
You will build the bridges.
In the future
You will build the cities.
In the future
You will glorify My name."
So prayed God.

He continued,
"When you start the family
Choose love to illuminate your
home.
When you build the cities
Do not forget to let in the rays
of sunshine.
When you build the bridges
Do not forget the line of the
horizon.
When you glorify My name
Be sincere."

Man
After you have built
Do not destroy the family,
Do not destroy the cities,
Do not destroy the horizons,
Do not destroy My name,
Do not destroy the universe,
My universe created for you.

At the dawn of each day
God repeats his prayer
And sometimes
In the dew
You will find a tear
A divine tear.
You feel it in your eyes
Each time
Someone kills
An innocent man.
You feel it in your heart
When listening
To the cry
Of an unhappy child.
And to the whisper
Of the universe
"Man,
Why do you want
To destroy
The creation of God?"[38]

Although many years have passed since I wrote this poem, the sun of Nice remains with me. The slow motion of the waves of the Mediterranean comes back in my memory, waves as slow today as they were then. I know that my approach to God is the same as it was in my diary from the time of my youth. I stop for a second. I recall Psalm 100, the psalm of thanksgiving. Yes, I am grateful to God for letting me admire His creation.

In the classroom where I teach the course "How to Find Meaning in Life," I ask my students, who are teachers from Philadelphia, to read the poem "And God Prayed at Dawn" and write a short paper on any part of the poem which they feel is important in searching for meaning in life. Many people choose different parts, and only after do we discuss my way of feeling "of God in every dawn" and in every sunset.

No – I did not change from the time when I was in school in Jaslo.

During the war it was not always possible to write in my diary but I often wrote letters to God. I prayed in my own words for the survival of my family and for the end of the war, and even during that time my admiration for God's creation was strong in me. I cannot write about my life chronologically because my thoughts contain yesterdays and todays, yesterdays and tomorrows, waiting to come.

This autobiography is more than an autobiography for me. There is a stability of hope, prevailing in all the stages of my life. And this stability is my faith, often expressed in my prayers. I know that faith is not part of the lives of all people. Maybe that is why I search for the common thread in all religions of the world. For me the world is small, and people all over the world are the same. It does not matter if they are black, white, yellow, or of mixed colour; if they are short or tall. I think about the mother in the Sahara. I see in her the mother who wants exactly what I want. She wants her children to live in a free, just, and honest world, and she wants her children not to live in fear.

Clouds over Wawel and Vistula

A fter finishing high school and receiving his diploma in August 1938, Karol Wojtyla moved with his father from Wadowice to Krakow. Krakow, the most historic city in Poland, had many national and religious treasures.

"Anyone who wants to get to know the soul of Poland should look for it in Krakow," said Wilhelm Feldman, the famous Polish critic, writer, and editor of the newspaper *Dziennik Krakowski* (Journal of Krakow), who lived from 1868 to 1919. Krakow became the capital of Poland in 1038, and the residence of choice of Polish kings and counts. When Warsaw became the capital of Poland in 1611, Krakow remained the spiritual centre where the Polish tradition and the Catholic faith were interwoven.

In the centre of Krakow, on a hill called the Hill of Wawel, are located the king's palace, the cathedral, the ramparts, and the old walls. According to archaeological records, the oldest human traces here go back 50,000 years. The Cathedral of St. Waclaw and St. Stanislaw, the first Roman sanctuary on Wawel, was built at the beginning of the eleventh century by the Polish King Boleslaw Chrobry. Often called the "Cathedral of Boleslaw Chrobry," it served as a place of worship for kings and counts. A famous story describes the tragic death of Bishop Stanislaw, who according to the records was killed by King Smialy in 1079. The bishop's martyrdom was acknowledged by his canonization in 1253. Later Stanislaw became a patron of the Polish kingdom. There are also graves of several other saints here.

At the end of the sixteenth century, Krakow was called "Little Rome." Besides Wawel there are 60 Catholic churches in Krakow. Polish patricians and the inhabitants of Krakow congregated for many centuries at Kosciol Mariacki (St. Mary's Church). Like the Cathedral, it was a place of worship for all who lived in Krakow. The original Mariacki church was built out of wood, but in the years 1221–1222 it was rebuilt in stone in the Gothic style. This church possesses a very famous altar built by Wit Stwosz, the architect, sculptor, and woodcarver who came to Krakow in 1477 from Nuremberg and who later gave up his German citizenship. Every day at noon, the sound of the bell from the Tower of Kosciol Mariacki is broadcast by all the radio stations in Poland. In 1962 Pope John XXIII gave the church the title "small basilica."

Through Krakow flows the Vistula River. Like the Seine flowing through the heart of Paris, the Tiber in Rome, the Danube in Vienna, the Vistula is the source of many legends. Dreams collect in the flowing waters. Rivers are a living part of countries and of nations – the Euphrates, Tigris, and Nile in the Middle East, the Ganges in India, the Mississippi in the United States, the St. Lawrence in Canada, the Volga in Russia.

* * *

At the age of eighteen, young Karol Wojtyla did not think of entering the priesthood, although he was very religious, remembering well the day when he was present as a child during the Holy Mass in the Wawel Cathedral and saw for the first time Count Adam Sapieha, the archbishop of Krakow. He decided to study philosophy and Polish philology. For him, Krakow, besides having a religious significance, was a city of culture, offering him the possibility to develop his artistic abilities.

One of his first steps in the new city was to join Studio 39, the drama school of the Krakow Theatre Brotherhood. He also became a member of the literary section of the circle of Polish philology, the Lovers of the Polish Language Association, and of the Fraternity Society of Jagiellonian University Students.

He had an unusual ability to communicate with people, and in a short time had established friendships and gained the respect of all who were in contact with him. These extracurricular activities did not get in the way of his academic curiosity. It is interesting that people around him noted that he was able to concentrate on his studies and to follow the lectures very thoroughly. One of his friends pinned a card on his desk that read "Karol Wojtyla – Apprentice Saint." Somehow, in spite of a very heavy load of activities, Karol Wojtyla still displayed his religiosity in a way that was accepted by his friends as part of his personality.

Life in Jagiellonian University followed its traditions and programs in spite of the many clouds that were gathering over Europe. Students continued to study literature, poetry, and history despite the fact that throughout Europe, danger was imminent and frightening events were happening every day. The Nazis and the Fascist regimes were dangerous. Civil war was raging in Spain. The pages of European newspapers were filled with images of cruelty as the civil populations became victims. The world was watching, but only a small minority intervened in the vicious attacks that took place in Europe and Africa. The Polish newspapers carried many reports about the fighting in Spain, but the politicians tried to minimize the danger. The majority of the world's population appeared indifferent. Hitler promoted hate, and the Nazi propagandists within Germany and outside its borders were very effective. Teutonic legends and the operas of Wagner provided a good foundation for their work.

Kristallnacht, the Night of Broken Glass, took place in Germany in November 1938. Synagogues were destroyed and thousands of Jews were arrested and beaten; some of them were killed. In Krakow you could see Jews who had been expelled from Germany in a most cruel way.

Many people in the world believed that all Jews were rich. It was a myth. Some of then were in fact very poor. The Jews who came to Poland after being expelled from Germany were penniless, their money and possessions expropriated. It was almost impossible to find a place in the world for these poor Jews. Nobody wanted them. Hitler said on many occasions that people had compassion for the Jews, but since "nobody wants them, let us support anti-Semitism." German propaganda easily overpowered the voices of compassion. In the university where Karol Wojtyla studied literature, the Jewish students were ordered to sit on separate benches in the classroom. The Polish nationalists wanted segregation. Many Jews fought with the nationalists on the university campuses. These Jews had been born in Poland. Poland was their country. They loved Poland. But for the nationalists, the most important thing was that these Jews had Jewish blood. Anti-Semitism had always existed in Poland, but now the animosity escalated. German propaganda crossed the border.

Hitler, in his thoughts and speeches, echoed Nietzsche's philosophy. In *Thus Spake Zarathustra* Nietzsche says:

> Dead are Gods; now we will that Superman live. . . . I teach you Superman. Man is a something that shall be surpassed. . . . What have ye done to surpass him? . . . What is great in man is that he is a bridge and not a goal: what can be loved in man is that he is a transition and a destruction.[39]

Nietzsche wrote *The Antichrist* at a time in his life when many people believed he was insane. Nevertheless, Hitler's expansion of power and the Nazi fight with the Christian Church can be seen as the fulfillment of Nietzsche's dreams. Nietzsche began the campaign against the priests when he said,

> If we have even the smallest claim to integrity, we must know today that a theologian, a priest, a pope not merely is wrong in every sentence he speaks, but lies – that he is no longer at liberty to lie from "innocence" or "ignorance." The priest too knows as well as anybody else that there is no longer any "God," any "sinners," any "Redeemer" – that "free will" and "moral world order" are lies: seriousness, the profound self overcoming of the spirit, no longer permits anybody not to know this.[40]

Nietzsche's ideas and his ideal of the Superman were easily planted in the fertile soil of the German mind. Many Europeans who were not Germans seemed not to realize that the popular slogan and song *Deutschland, Deutschland über Alles* meant superiority not only over Jews but over Europe and the world. Later, during the war, the governor of occupied Krakow said, "And one day there will be not enough poles to hang Poles."

Nietzsche proclaimed that "The kingdom is in you," and the Nazi era showed the world the possibilities of a Superman who found the kingdom of God in himself. But in the history of philosophy it is important to ask why Nietzsche's ideas superseded those of Kant. How could Kant's philosophy about the existence of God be forgotten during the Nazi era? Kant believed in God, and this affirmation of faith guided his moral principles. Kant wrote,

> I am certain that nothing can shake this faith (faith in God) for if it were shaken, my ethical principles themselves would be

shattered. Hence we must not say: "It is certain that there is a God," but "I am morally certain that He exists."[41]

Those who affirm God's existence and feel God's presence recognize the link between God and humankind. This spiritual link between humanity and the universe contains a certain sense of belonging. We do not feel detached in our thoughts and our feelings from the universe, wherever we live. Touching the ground makes us feel that we do not float in the unknown, that we have a place prepared for us before we are born. The link with the unknown and between us exists through spirit. It is as if a breath of the universe is integrated into our existence, making us a part of the universe.

Years after the war, when he was a professor at the Catholic University in Lublin, the future pope lectured on Kant, saying, "It is known that practical reason in the concept of Kant is a reason which designs the path of the will."

It is this "path of will" that has directed the deeds and activities of Karol Wojtyla throughout his life. In the year preceding the war, Karol Wojtyla, while listening to the words of Hitler over German radio stations which were powerful enough to jam other programs, realized what the voice of hate could bring. The young student watched history developing; he watched Catholic colleagues fighting with his Jewish colleagues. These Jewish students did not want to sit on "special benches." Many people knew that sometimes Karol accompanied a Jewish student home to spare her humiliation. Maybe he belonged to that small minority of people who, while watching politicians, trembled. At the time, many politicians tried to accommodate the policies of Hitler by talking about preserving peace. Then, in 1938 a significant sign came from Berlin. Father Lichtenberg spoke out after the flames were raging during Kristallnacht:

> In a number of Berlin homes, an anonymous inflammatory rag against the Jews is being distributed. It says that any German who, from allegedly false sentimentality, helps the Jews, commits treason against his own people. Do not let yourself be led astray by such un-Christian thoughts, but act according to the clear command of Christ: Thou Shalt love thy neighbour as thyself.[42]

Speaking in Munich, Cardinal Faulhaber added his voice:

History teaches us that God always punished tormenters of . . . the Jews. No Roman Catholic approves of the persecutions of Jews in Germany. . . . Racial hatred is a poisonous weed in our time.[43]

Did Karol Wojtyla subconsciously decide in the year before the war to look for a tool to spread the real message of Christ? Maybe this "path of will" that started during this pre-war time allows the pope today to come forward and express his love for all humanity. On July 8, 1980, in Marituba, Brazil, Pope John Paul II addressed a crowd that included people suffering from leprosy and other debilitating diseases.

And you, who are you? To me you are, first and foremost, human persons, rich with an immense dignity that bestows upon you the condition of person — rich, each of you, with a unique, matchless personal philosophy. This is how God made you . . . . You are children of God, known and loved by him.[44]

The address shows not only compassion, but also his eagerness to understand every human being in any circumstance and to restore dignity to those whose lives have become "a path of suffering."

Speaking to farm workers in Recife in 1980, John Paul II said:

The earth is man's because God has entrusted it to man. . . . The earth is a gift of God, a gift that he makes to all human beings, men and women, whom he wishes to see joined together in a single family, and relating to one another in a fraternal spirit.[45]

Proclaiming the idea of a single human family and human spirit is the leitmotif of this strong man of God.

The young Karol was in love with Wawel, the cathedral that was shown to him for the first time by his mother when he was a child. He lived with his father in the basement of an apartment house, but he did not look at the rubble on the street that he saw through his window. His eyes were high above in the sky of Krakow, maybe watching the clouds. He performed in the theatre. He was an excellent actor, but he never acted offstage. He certainly was not an actor when he served Mass in the small church in the Debnik or in the Cathedral of Wawel. Often on Friday night he would walk in the district called Kazimierz, looking at the flickering lights of the candles lit by Jewish mothers at the start of Shabbat. The origins of this Jewish quarter can be traced back to the reign of Kazimierz Wielki (Kazimierz the Great).

Karol Wojtyla realizes today that whenever we see the clouds over any part of the world, we should act. There were many warnings before 1939 that were ignored. Things were happening in Czechoslovakia, Austria, and Spain, and they were moving fast. In 1938, when the Jews were excluded from participation in the Berlin Olympics, nobody objected. They were only Jews.

We should not forget that often artists are able to express concern in their works, a concern that represents the voice of their conscience. Picasso's painting *Guernica*, showing the cruelty of war, was one of the warnings for Europe. Chagall's painting *The White Crucifixion*, on which Christ on the Cross wears a Jewish prayer shawl, was shown to remind the Christians of the world that Christ was a Jew. After the war the Swiss theologian Karl Barth wrote in *The Church and the World*:

> The existence of the Jew probably is the symbol of the objective metaphysical fact independent of all intellectual counter movements, that the Christian roots of Western culture is alive.

Later in the book Barth added:

> Wherever the Christian revelation whose actual witness is the Jew is recognized, the struggle against National Socialism ceases to be accidental and superficial and becomes fundamental and essential.[46]

The clouds and the sunshine. The sadness and the light. The despair and the hope. While serving Mass, the young Karol Wojtyla was praying to Christ for the light of his guidance.

Winter Night in Zakopane

I n Poland in winter, trees covered with snow will shine, twinkling like the night stars in all their splendour. Their delicate tiny ice stars compete with the stars in the sky. They last only for a few hours. When we touch them, they disappear as the warmth of human hands cuts short their existence. Even so, their splendour lives on in the memories of those who cherished their life, in those who touched them not only with their hands but also with their eyes, the wondering eyes admiring nature's magnificent spectacle displayed on the stage of winter.

I often remember the winter night of a New Year's Eve in Zakopane on the road to Jaszczurowka not too far away. I recall the speed of the sleigh ride, the crisp cold air, the shining stars reflecting on the trees covered with snow. Adam and I were spending two weeks in Zakopane. Since Adam caught cold very often, the doctor suggested that he breathe the mountain air. My parents had a friend who owned a small guesthouse, and we were to spend our Christmas vacation there. My parents' friend took care of us, two teenagers who enjoyed skiing in the morning and skating in the afternoon. Adam and I started on the small slope on Gubalowka Mountain, which was actually more of a hill, and each day we improved, eventually climbing higher up the mountains. We thought of going all the way to the top of Kasprowy Wierch, but for the time being we were happy to listen to our instructor and follow his advice.

There was something exhilarating about going fast on skis, feeling the air on your cheeks and forehead and at the same time retaining equilibrium like specks of dust in the universe. Only those who enjoy skiing can share this love for the snow that provides a unique path, each time more seductive with its beauty, and for the wood burning in a fireplace in the evening, where despite the heat you can still feel the kiss of the wind on your cheeks.

On this journey to Jaszczurowka, I was very excited. The son of the owner of the guesthouse, who was ten years older than I, had asked me to go dancing on New Year's Eve in a popular café. Only once before, when I was in junior high school, had I attended a New Year's Eve party, with my cousin Jerzy. He told all his friends that I was seventeen years old, though I was fourteen at this time. I was always so proud to go out with Jerzy. He was tall, very handsome, with blond hair and blue eyes. Several times I told my mother that my future husband had to have blue eyes. My wish was fulfilled years later.

There in the café I danced and danced. We saw young people kissing but we did not kiss. My schoolmates always laughed when I was with boys, especially dancing with boys during dancing lessons. I knew how to retain my distance in my own way. My friends were right. I was waiting for my real, true love. I dreamed about this tall, good-looking charming prince waiting for me. I was looking for love and, in time, God blessed me. I was loved, and I knew how to love.

My poems and songs have been a major part of my life since the age of thirteen or fourteen. There were words that asked to be written, there were melodies asking to be composed, there was a night in Zakopane that found its way into my song "The Winter Night."

But outside the windows of my sheltered world, Europe trembled. I listened to the radio and read the newspapers, but my only reactions were my thoughts and melodies. I wrote songs such as "The World" and "The Storm." My songs revealed my feelings, first of despair and then of hope. For me, hope always prevailed over despair, and I exulted over life, nature, and the mystery of the Creator.

When I read about the life of the Holy Father and the joy he found while skiing in the Tatra Mountains, I sense an exaltation similar to what I experienced at Zakopane. I did not know the Holy Father at that time, but in our youth we both shared a great love of life, the kind that come from retaining equilibrium on two skis as they glide on the path to wonder. I strongly believe that these feelings have never disappeared. Age has nothing to do with the youth engraved in our beings, this youth that never left us, although we now look different and may walk more slowly. I also remember how my children were proud of me when we skied together in Canada, at St. Donat or Ste. Agathe. I know that something of this eternal youth is present when we go forward every single day. I believe that there are people who retain their enthusiasm for life and that this enthusiasm allows them never to forget the exhilarating moments of their youth.

One day, while listening to the Holy Father deliver his weekly Sunday message to the people in St. Peter's Square, I could hear and I could almost feel the enthusiasm in his voice. There was something youthful there, even at the distance from where I was listening. I know that the Holy Father remembers Zakopane, even after all his travels around the world. I know he could not forget. I believe that we have very similar feelings because we, I dare to say, love life. Loving life with such intensity somehow inspires others.

One day, when my grandson Sigmond was six, he told his teacher that for "show and tell" he wanted to show his grandmother, his father's mother, and have her sing one of her songs. Michel's wife, Barbara, called me, and the following Thursday I took the day off and travelled from Philadelphia to Ottawa to present my grandson's favourite song. The principal invited two other classes to join us, and I sang "The World on Fire," accompanying myself on the piano.

> World on fire, fire in the world.
> We don't know where to go.
> World on fire, fire in the world.
> In fear our children grow.
>
> Fights and riots teach how to destroy.
> Men kill because they're scared.
> Atom bombs are in the hands of men.
> They play with life and death.
>
> And somewhere a bird is singing a song
> and somewhere lovers dream
> and somewhere a poet
> is drinking a sweet wine
> in the mountain from the stream.

World on fire, fire in the world.
We don't know where to go.
World on fire, fire in the world.
In fear our children grow.

We sent our men so far away in space
to look for sunshine there.
Our world became so very small and strange.
We don't see the sun on earth.

And somewhere a bird
is singing a song,
a song of summer night
and somewhere a painter
is searching in the sky
for the rainbow
of his life.

World on fire, fire in the world.
We don't know where to go.
World on fire, fire in the world.
In fear our children grow.
Where on earth is God and where is man?
Who answers me today?
My little son is searching for my hand.

God teach us how to love.

I never asked my grandson why he chose this particular song. I only knew that he and the other children enjoyed it, this song that contained thoughts from other songs I had composed in my teenage years. These songs were my reaction to despair as I looked for solutions, looked to find hope. I did not know why I wrote "The Storm" or "The World" years ago and "The World on Fire" holding my son's hand. I simply asked myself a question and I responded – to myself. How many times was the world on fire in my thoughts?

The months preceding the outbreak of the war were especially frightening. In my diary I noted that just listening to the powerful words of Hitler made me afraid. The German people listened and cheered this madman. Why didn't Europe see the coming danger? During the 1938 Olympics, foreign journalists were welcomed on condition that they did not interfere in German politics. Jewish athletes were excluded and nobody cared. After *Kristallnacht*, Jews were arrested and sent to the Dachau concentration camp. Many Jewish businesses were destroyed, and cemeteries were desecrated. The world was numb and deaf. After all, they were only Jews.

Before the war, the silence, the apathy, the indifference to acts of cruelty allowed Hitler to pursue his programs and proclaim the superiority of non-Jewish Germans. He developed many methods of propaganda, one of which was to export anti-Semitism. He worked to persuade people all over Europe that Jews were the calamity of Europe, and anti-Semitism grew. In Poland the outburst of anti-Semitism was imminent. In Polish universities, Catholic students did not want to sit on the same benches as Jews.

One day my father came from his office with some new neckties. My mother asked him why he had bought all the ties on the same day and he answered that he had received a visit from a lawyer from Berlin who had suddenly been expelled from Germany. He came to Poland, and to support his family he travelled from one city to another selling ties to lawyers. I remember my father saying, "It can happen to me in a few months, if the world does not react to the laws in Germany."

Yes, there were other winter nights which did not resemble the night in Zakopane before the war. There was Christmas night in 1941, when my parents, Adam, and I travelled from eastern Poland to western Poland, from Brzezany to Jaslo, and there was a night when I walked along the railroad track in Frysztak, tears freezing on my cheeks. Life, life, life, the struggle to remain alive.

The years passed. When I married Sigmond in March 1946, we went to Zakopane for a five-day honeymoon.

Every day, I imagine a scale for my thoughts and when I look at the balance I try to see on one side memories, the past, and on the other my longings and expectations for the future. Each day I realize that no matter my age, my longings and my expectations prevail over the past. The past and my experiences allow me to go forward and believe in my own contribution to the future without thinking of the fragility and time limits of my own life.

The Quarry and the Lullabies

There are days in the life of everyone, every nation, every part of the world that are not forgotten. Poland and every citizen within her borders will never forget September 1, 1939. This Friday marked the beginning of the Second World War.

People were going to work as usual, when suddenly planes of destruction appeared in the skies over a few cities in Poland. Karol Wojtyla was on his way to Wawel Cathedral. There, on the first Friday of the new month, he would go to confession and receive Holy Communion. Despite the danger, he did not want to change his usual First Friday visit to the cathedral. When he arrived, the church was empty except for Father Kazimierz Figlewicz, who lived in the church compound. Father Figlewicz celebrated Holy Mass and Karol Wojtyla served. When we think about it, we realize that strong will has always a part of the personality of Pope John Paul II, who in different times of his life has been ready to meet challenges and overcome adversities without fear.

On that terrible morning, the people of Krakow were in shock. Polish citizens had confidence in the Polish army, but the army did not react immediately. The war had begun. Combat was taking place not only on some distant battlefield, or in the sky above us. This war was to be a different kind of war, as suddenly, international laws were abolished. There was one aggressor, one oppressor, one Nazi ideology reigning, and this reign was visible even on the first day of the war.

On September 6, the German army entered Krakow. The only city in Poland to try to defend itself was Warsaw.

Early in November, the German authorities assured the Krakow professors that the university would remain open. On November 6, all the professors were invited to a lecture on knowledge by *Sturmbannführer* SS Bruno Muller. All the professors of the Jagiellonian University showed up, and when they arrived there they were arrested on the order of a so-called *Sonderaktion in Krakau* (special action in Krakow) and sent to Camp Sachsenhausen in Germany. This action followed the usual pattern of the German authorities – the intellectual elite was the first target.

That same month, Wawel Cathedral and Palace were closed to Poles. The palace became the residence of Hans Frank, the Governor General of the so-called General Government. One of his first orders was to proclaim the obligation of public work for the entire Polish population from 18 to 60 years of age. By December 12, 1939, it was compulsory for people to have an *Arbeitskarte*, a certificate stating the kind of work they were supposed to perform. People who did not have a certificate were in danger of being taken at any time from any place to Germany, where workers were needed.

It was difficult to find work in Krakow, but Karol, with the help of a French teacher, got a position as a labourer in a German chemical firm, the *Ostdeutsche Chemische* works in Solvay. During the first winter months of 1939, he worked outside in the quarry all the time. The work was hard. Every worker had to load stones on a freight car. A few students who were not used to physical work were assigned a less stressful task, bringing the earth that was later placed under the stones. The only heat was from a small iron stove, a short walk away in a barracks. There in the quarry, as he worked alongside the other labourers, Karol came to understand the mentality and the hardship of the oppressed

After a few months, he became an assistant to a shot-fixer. This new position allowed him to stay inside the barracks. The workers around Karol respected his approach to life. They even detected that he was very religious. They called him a "student" or a "little priest." In later years, Pope John Paul II remembered the warmth the workers showed him. They treated him with compassion and often encouraged him to read. At night they insisted that he sleep, assuring him that they would take care of everything. They shared their bread with him, always saying, "You should eat something, you have to endure."

Today when I observe Karol Wojtyla as the Holy Father, and listen to his sermons, I see how this time of camaraderie with working people has left a profound mark on his being.

In Milan in 1983, the Pope said,

I do not hesitate to say that the following four years, spent among labouring folk, were for me a gift of Providence. The experience I acquired during that period of my life was priceless. I have often stated that perhaps I have given to these years a higher value than to a doctorate; which, of course, does not mean that I undervalue university degrees.[47]

In April 5, 1987, at a gathering of workers, he said:

Thanks to my personal experience I can affirm that the gospel appears to me in a new light.[48]

The philosophy he studied at university, along with the day-to-day philosophy of the working people he met in the quarry, allowed Pope John Paul II to develop a sense of compassion combined with precise reasoning that provides him with a source of great strength. He does not differentiate between types or "classes" of people. Everything depends on his abiding values. In philosophy there is primarily an elaborated thought; in common people, common sense and feelings give them the ability to decide how to act in life according to their ethics.

In Poland, many collaborators were seduced by the better rations of white bread, or sugar instead of saccharin. But Karol was strong and remained a decent human being. He could not be corrupted by the enemy. How often when we listen to the words of Pope John Paul II in different parts of the world, when we see him in Cuba, or in the United States, we observe the man who knows the crowds, the common workers, the intellectuals, and the politicians. Life brought Karol Wojtyla to stand beside the people who worked like slaves yet who still retained their integrity.

In "Material," in his series of poems *The Quarry*, John Paul writes:

1
Listen: the even knocking of hammers,
so much their own,
I project onto the people
to test the strength of each blow.
Listen now: electric current
cuts through a river or rock.

And a thought grows in me day after day:
the greatness of work is inside man.

Hard and cracked
his hand is differently charged
by the hammer
and thought differently unravels in stone
as human energy splits from the strength of stone
cutting the bloodstream, an artery
in the right place.

Look, how love feeds
on this well-grounded anger
which flows into people's breath
as a river bent by the wind,
and which is never spoken, but just breaks high vocal cords.
. . .

2
Passersby scuttle off into doorways,
someone whispers: "Yet here is a great force."

Fear not. Man's daily deeds have a wide span,
a strait riverbed can't imprison them long.
Fear not. For centuries they all stand in Him,
and you look at Him now
through the even knocking of hammers.[49]

This poem stresses the independence of thought. Thought is independent only if individuals believe in their thought. Pope John Paul II travels, shakes hands with millions of people, blesses people, kisses children, and gives sermons. He challenges the minds and hearts of those who, for many reasons, are hard as stone. He knows that all these people he meets, who kiss his hand, who come to worship Christ with him, need their own guiding thought for tomorrow. And today, as in his previous years of ministry, he does not fear and asks people not to fear if they have faith, as the closing words of the poem show:

Fear not. For centuries they all stand in Him,
and you look at Him now
through the even knocking of hammers.

There in the quarry Karol listened to the knocking of the hammers and understood that everything is possible. Because everything is possible, Pope John Paul II believes that in this new millennium he will continue to promote understanding. He will continue to challenge history and show the people that they can be united while respecting their differences.

In the quarry Karol got to know the material of stones. During his years of working as a servant of the Church, as a priest, as a bishop, as a cardinal and as a guide to millions of Catholics, he also got to know "the material" of people who, in spite of increasing dependence on technology, still possess their own ways of thinking and their own souls.

Karol Wojtyla, the labourer in the quarry, could not know what lay ahead for him, but he was certain that faith would accompany him on whatever road he chose. In the Solvay quarry the philosopher spent many hours with hammers, the tools they used to break the heavy stones. But even there the poet Karol Wojtyla searched for inspiration. He believed that even while breaking stones, an individual has to be inspired. In his poem "Inspiration" he writes,

Work starts within, outside it takes such space
that it soon seizes hands, then the limits of breath.
Look – your will strikes a deep bell in stones,
thought strikes certainty, a peak
both for heart and for hand.

For this certainty of mind, this certainty of eye,
for this vertical line
you pay with a generous hand.
The stone yields you its strength,
and man matures through work
which inspires him to difficult good.

With work then it begins: the growing in the heart and the mind,
great events, a multitude of men are drawn in.
Listen to love that ripens in hammers, in even sounds.

Children will carry them into the future, singing:
"In our fathers' hearts
work knew no bounds."[50]

The poem contains three lines that today look like a blueprint for Pope John Paul's papacy:

The stone yields you its strength,
and man matures through work
which inspires him to difficult good.

Karol Wojtyla learned the hard way how to be inspired to perform "the difficult good." He also knew that to mature means not only to perceive the truth we create in ourselves, but also to face reality and, if necessary, take proper steps to challenge the status quo.

With work then it begins: the growing in the heart and the mind,
great events, a multitude of men are drawn in.
Listen to love that ripens in hammers, in even sounds.

Pope John Paul II was inspired by his parents; the seeds of love and faith they implanted in him mingled with the pain of loneliness that followed the deaths of his mother and of his brother. These memories gave him an experience of the depth and fragility of the human condition. As a child he missed the warmth of his mother; as a youngster he suffered after his brother died, but he remembered the prayers and the rosaries repeated in his home with his family.

Karol Wojtyla witnessed the terrible cruelty of the Germans during the war. He listened in the air of Krakow to the lullabies of mothers singing in the evening when the innocent children were crying. These mothers knew that the children were hungry and that some of them were destined to perish in the gas chambers. During this time he showed his concern for persecuted human beings through his lesser-known activities. George Blazynski, in his biography of Pope John Paul II, writes,

There was another grimmer, less well-known side to young Wojtyla's activities during the Nazi occupation. Conspirational university classes and clandestine theatrical performances boosting the national morale were dangerous enough for themselves. But Wojtyla also lived in daily danger of losing his life. He would move about the neighboring towns taking Jewish

families out of ghettos and providing them with new identities and hiding places. He saved the lives of many Jewish families threatened with execution.[51]

During the war, besides breaking the stones at the quarry, he also carried them. As pope, also carries different kinds of heavy stones in his heart. Many events in history chronicle the injustices and prejudices of the past. This awareness is even heavier than the stones in the quarry. But as the guide of millions of people, he cannot ignore it. This load weighs heavily on his conscience, and in spite of his physical frailty he never forgets its presence.

Luigi Accattoli writes in *When a Pope Asks Forgiveness*:

It is the Pope's desire to re-examine the facts of history in the light of the truth and to take full responsibility for both the good and the bad so that the Church can move forward into the next millennium free from the burden of protecting its "image."

Accattoli has assembled over ninety examples of Pope John Paul II admitting the past faults of the Church and asking pardon for them. He entitles this section of his book "An Examination of Conscience." In twenty-five cases, he says "I ask forgiveness" in one way or another. Accattoli describes these pronouncements as

the most interesting of his entire pontificate, and his words are open wide to the future. They are surely very personal, for no one can put in the mouth of the Pope any expression of repentance for the Crusades or the religious wars. And no one can pit one pope against another pope.[52]

How true are the words in Accattoli's preface, when he describes these texts as "very personal." When we read these words and follow the life of Karol Wojtyla from childhood, we observe his determination to be faithful to his conscience despite the obstacles he meets. The same preface continues:

For example, during his visit to the Czech Republic in May of 1995, the Pope referred to the religious wars and then said: "Today, in the name of all Catholics and as Pope of the Church of Rome, I ask forgiveness for the injustices inflicted on non-Catholics in the course of the troubled history of these peoples."

In his Encyclical *Ut Unum Sint* (May 1995), after acknowledging that most other Christians suffer painful memories, he said: "To the extent that we are responsible for these, I join my predecessor Paul VI in asking forgiveness."

Again, in the month of May 1995, in his message marking the fiftieth anniversary of the Second World War, the Pope stated that "the Christians of Europe need to ask forgiveness, even while recognizing that there were varying degrees of responsibility in the events which led to the war."

On yet another occasion, in his message to the indigenous peoples of the Americas (October 21, 1992), he said: "As Pastor of the Church, I ask you in the name of Jesus Christ to pardon those who have offended you; I ask you to pardon those who have caused pain to you and your ancestors during these 500 years."[53]

In a meeting with the Polish journalist Jas Gawronski, at the turn of the millennium, the pope spoke about importance of conscience.

At the end of this second millennium we must make an examination of conscience: where we are, where Christ has brought us, where we have deviated from the Gospel.[54]

Conscience, John Paul II tells us, is essential in understanding the teachings of Christ, especially at time when the divisions between people can destroy our planet in a matter of seconds. The pope inspires people to think because he knows that every individual matters, that every single thought counts. Accattoli summarizes John Paul's link between guilt and responsibility:

For the most part, he has acted by himself and with a great deal of personal involvement, as is evidenced by the fact that most of his references to guilt and responsibility have been made during his travels, including the visit to Berlin in June of 1996, where he spoke of the lack of Catholic opposition of the Nazis, and at Vendée, France, in 1996, where he stated: "During those terrible battles [of the Catholic resistance to the French Revolution], many actions were marked by sin, both on one side and on the other."

The historian Alberto Monticone once stated: "In this request for forgiveness we have the ultimate key to the travels of John Paul II." When the Pope speaks to a people, he recognizes the responsibility of those Catholics who had gone to that people before him. If he had not traveled, perhaps he would not have asked for forgiveness.

Pope John Paul II continues to travel and to ask forgiveness with a will that is stronger than his physical power, because he has taken upon himself a responsibility for the second millennium. He once confided that shortly before he was elected pope, Cardinal Wyszynski said to him: "You must lead the Church into the third millennium." But he wants to do that less burdened by the weight of history, better reconciled with the other Christian communities, and with a bond of friendship with every religion and with all men of good will. And if that should cause some degree of confrontation with history, it will not be the end of the world. After all, he is a prophetic – as well as a missionary – pope.[55]

After centuries of disputes, many of which ended up on the battlefields, Pope John Paul II widens the horizons of thinking and tries to stop the spread of hate and the killing of innocent people. There exists only one truly powerful weapon against injustice, and that is knowledge.

Can one individual make a difference in the world? Maybe yes – if, like Karol Wojtyla, this person knows how to look for inspiration in the quarries working with stones, and then in the evening, while walking home, listens to the lullabies of mothers who tremble for the lives of their children. The dust of the stones, and the lullabies, mingle in the air. Yes. One individual can make a difference.

The Flames of War

Every time I light a candle and watch the emerging flame, I think about this mysterious fire, first twinkling timidly and then remaining steady and moving only when there is motion in the room. Whenever I am in a room where a fire is burning in a fireplace I wonder how a few pieces of wood can provide such soft warmth. I admire the flames dancing gracefully and the wood slowly changing shape.

During the war I saw other flames – cruel ones, without mercy. Some were ignited by the enemy. Others were allowed to ignite by all those who did not care to prevent them until it was too late.

I remember the summer of 1939. The fields of wheat were green and then turned to gold, the cornflowers and the red poppies smiled, the sun shone. But far away the flames of war were being carefully prepared, waiting for the moment when they would turn cities and villages and people into ashes.

I remember when I first heard the word "homeless." The first "homeless" were the Jews of Germany and Austria, who were very poor. Nobody wanted them. Who would like to give a home to the homeless Jews? There were more and more boats loaded with people who had nowhere to go. One of these boats, the *St. Louis*, headed for Cuba but was refused entrance to the island. The boat then sailed to Miami, but the American authorities would not receive the passengers. They were sent back to Europe, where most of them lost their lives during the war.

Hitler started the war with the Jews, but later decided to spread his power, annihilating those whom he considered inferior. He wanted to rule Europe, and then the world. He systematically indoctrinated people in Germany with the idea that humanity should be divided, that equality of humankind was unrealistic, that all those who would follow him would acquire a very special status. He promised that one day his people would decide who would live and who would die.

Hitler was preparing for war, and the world did not react. Early on September 1, 1939, the sun was shining. There were no clouds in the sky when the German planes crowded the sky and started to drop their bombs. High above, German pilots were bringing death and flames, destruction and despair. Already on this, the first day of the Second World War, those of us living in Poland experienced the outcome of the cruel orders given by a madman whose followers were executing innocent people on the city streets. The battlefields were still empty and the civilian population became the first target of the mighty German army.

I watched the sky and trembled as the walls of the apartment in Debica where we were staying with Regina Herzig, my father's sister-in-law, shook with the force of the explosions. We had arrived there the day before from Jaslo because our parents, foreseeing the war, believed that Jaslo was in greater danger than Debica. In the vicinity of Jaslo were the oil fields. Our parents were supposed to follow the next day. The apartment walls shook, and in one day our world collapsed. Until September 1, Adam and I were teenagers loving every moment of "our life." We looked forward with hope and faith in the future unfolding before our eyes. Observing the shaking walls was terrifying. Now we realized that everyone was in danger. We wanted to stay alive, and this determination to survive became our leitmotif. We knew that "our world" was a part of a "greater world" affecting our destiny and the destiny of people around us.

In the afternoon of this first day of war our parents arrived, even as the air attacks continued. Every few hours we watched the bombs, never knowing if our house would be hit next. We did not have shelters. Each bomb attack lasted five to ten minutes, and afterwards there were tears and we heard people screaming. Many people died, or were left to die.

The Polish army was not prepared. The city where we were was defenseless. By the third day of the war nobody could get gas for their cars. During that day, my father walked with me through the streets of Debica. The air attacks were fierce, and we were forced to lie flat on the ground almost every hour, watching the bombs fall. Each time the planes approached, the birds would congregate together, flying in groups, as if to warn us that the planes were coming.

On the fourth day, we left Debica for Majdanek Sieniawski. A few days later, on the first day of Rosh Hashanah (Jewish New Year), we met German soldiers for the first time. They entered the village without any fight. I remember we were praying in the home of a Jewish shopkeeper behind his little store.

The German army was well-equipped and advanced rapidly. The only city that fought back was the Polish capital, Warsaw. People there tried to defend their beloved city. In other parts of Poland countless homes were destroyed and many people were killed.

The nightmare had begun. My father decided to go back to Jaslo, and we were forced to travel there by horse and buggy. When we arrived at the outskirts of Jaslo, a peasant from Majdanek Sieniawski offered to bring us to our home town. My parents contacted our best friends, Helena and Jan Kosiba. They informed us that persecution of the Jewish community had already started and that my father was in greater danger than the others because he was known as an enemy of Nazism and of Hitler. He had often denounced National Socialism in the courtroom, and he had also written a movie script dealing with Hitler's policies, which was supposed to be filmed that autumn.

My father and Adam did not enter the city. A friend of my father's, a judge, offered his home in the forest outside Jaslo as a place to hide. My mother and I returned to our apartment.

A few days later, according to the pact between Hitler and Stalin, the Russians occupied half of Poland. At the end of September 1939, Poland was divided into two parts. Western Poland remained under German occupation, and the eastern part became a part of Russia. Jaslo was situated in southwestern Poland.

My parents decided to cross the border between the Germans and Russians near the San River illegally. According to my parents' plan, my father, Adam, and Adam's friend, Marian Meller, were supposed to go a few days before my mother and me. But after they crossed the river, they were arrested at the border and taken to prison for crossing the border illegally. In prison, Adam became ill with a high fever. The prison authorities were afraid it might be a contagious disease, so they released my father and brother, who then made their way to Lwow. A few days later a very strong *Aktion* against Jews started in Jaslo. The immediate response of the Germans was to burn the synagogue.

Marian was supposed to be freed a few days later but ended up being sent to the Soviet Union, where he stayed until the Polish army was organized. He enlisted and came back to Poland at the end of the war as an officer. He was the only one of his family who survived the Holocaust. After the war he studied engineering and emigrated to Palestine, where he took part in the creation and defence of Israel. He lives with his family in Haifa.

My mother and I prepared to follow my father and Adam. We looked around our apartment, at every picture, every carpet, every piece of furniture, every book, that was a part of our beloved home. Through the window, I could see the park. I watched the birds as they flew or perched on the roof of the courthouse where my father had defended so many people and earned a reputation as an honest, good man who fought for justice. He had helped many clients, including many people who remembered that they could turn to him even if they could not afford to pay.

A few days before our departure, Mrs. Kosiba came to collect our most precious paintings and carpets. She wanted to keep them for us until we came back after the war.

One afternoon before we were supposed to leave, a German officer appeared at our apartment door and announced that our apartment would be occupied that same evening by a group of his men. He would allow us to stay in two rooms. When he left, my mother luckily remembered that in my father's office were hundreds of issues of the magazine *Gerechtigkeit* (Justice). This magazine was published in Vienna by Irene Harand, an enemy of Hitler's. My father had supported her from the beginning of her courageous fight against Nazism. We knew that if they found any copies of *Gerechtigkeit*, we would pay with our lives. We did not have much time, so we decided to burn all the papers in the oven. We rushed and succeeded in burning all the magazines in a few hours. Later, when the Germans came, they asked why our apartment was so hot.

Two days later, when we left, we took with us two suitcases and a pillow in a blanket, our only reminder of home. I looked back one last time into the dining room, where our piano stood alone. And our days of wandering began, days and nights that will be forever engraved in my memory.

We crossed the border in Sanok, on the San River. Crossing the border meant walking across the bridge dividing western Poland, occupied by Germans, and eastern Poland, occupied by Russians.

A man we did not know approached us on the bridge and said that he had heard our name, and since he had great respect for my father, he offered to help us. He carried my mother's suitcase and told us that although arrangements had been made, and the Russians had even been paid to let a group of a hundred people cross the bridge, he did not trust them. He told my mother that as soon as we crossed the bridge he would take us to a Polish family of his acquaintance who lived nearby. There, he said, we could spend a quiet night, and in the morning we could take the train to Lwow. My mother agreed. After crossing the bridge we went there, then an hour later we heard shots. The group we had broken away from had been forced to go back because the Russians would not accept them. Among this group were my uncle Mulo's sister-in-law with her two children. We had asked her to go with us to the peasant's home, but she refused. A lawyer from Rymanow was shot. I remember his name, Wimmer. He had argued that he did not belong to the group and was only waiting for the arrival of his wife and little son. I do not remember the name of the man who saved us. The next morning we discovered that, of the entire group, we were the only three people who remained in the Russian part of Poland.

The peasant who gave us shelter during the night took us to the railway station. Before we left, a young Ukrainian woman said to me, "It is possible that you will meet Russian soldiers on the road. Don't trust anybody. They should not find out that you came from the other side." Looking at me she added, "Just smile and say *Zdrastwuyty* (good morning)." She was right. We were in a wagon drawn by two horses. A soldier approached us, carrying a long rifle that was different from the rifles used in Poland. I remembered the woman's advice and with a broad smile said, "*Zdrastwuyty*." It was like magic. He did not ask for any papers, he did not ask questions, he let us pass. We arrived safely at the station, and after a few hours we reached Lwow.

I had been in Lwow before the war. It had been a beautiful city with a distinct culture reflecting the population of Poles, Ukrainians, and Jews living together while preserving their own traditions and cultures. This time the glamour of the city was gone. In a few weeks the city had changed. Everywhere you could see posters with the faces of Engels, Marx, Lenin, and Stalin. Here and there you could read slogans with powerful words promoting the Communist Party. Loud radio stations "taught" people how to embrace the new "faith" of communism, and Russian Soviet songs reminded everyone about their new rulers.

Right after our arrival my parents rented a small apartment of two furnished rooms on a very quiet street, Krasinski Street. The apartment was in a small two-storey house surrounded by many trees. We did not have any money, as my father's cash had been taken by a German police officer during the trip from Majdanek Sieniawski to Jaslo. The officer stopped us and asked my father for our documents. He took my father's wallet but gave back only the documents, saying that he really liked the wallet.

We were never rich. We had left our beautiful apartment, and my parents had looked after our excellent education. We had many pictures, because art was a very prominent feature of our home, but my mother did not even have any jewellery except one gold watch and a string of pearls from her mother. My father looked for work in Lwow. Naturally he could not go back to his profession as a lawyer. Under the Russian occupation he knew that he could only work in an office provided that the office needed someone who knew Ukrainian. My father knew it well because he had been born in Stryj, in eastern Poland. He hoped to get a position as an administrative employee or a bookkeeper. After days of searching, he eventually found work in the office of a vermin extermination company.

Adam immediately went to high school, and I decided to study music at the Lwow Academy. I wanted to study composition, and I dreamed about becoming the conductor of an orchestra. I also wanted to enroll in drama courses. The conservatory and drama courses were free. I tried to look forward to learning despite the political climate. Every day, Adam came home from school disgusted. Students were taught Marxism and Communism. They also had to attend public meetings glorifying the power of the workers and the proletariat. The ideology was to promote Communist power and to strive for the unity of workers throughout the world. I especially remember one evening when Adam came home very shaken. His beloved teacher of Polish literature had been badly beaten by the hooligans who came to a public meeting and wanted to teach the "Polish patriot" how to behave.

Shortly after, I went to the drama school, only to find that starting the next day all lectures and plays would be taught in Ukrainian instead of Polish. I decided to drop drama. I went to the director, a famous Ukrainian poet, Havryluk, and said that since I didn't speak Ukrainian I could not continue my studies. He tried to persuade me that the Ukrainian language was not difficult, but I stayed firm in my decision.

One day my father came home and told us that he had lost his job. The company where he worked had not been doing well. Again my father started to search, and finally after many weeks he found work with a wholesaler, overseeing invoices. Many workers had been sent there from Russia. After a few months my father discovered that people were stealing the merchandise, and he reported this to the man in charge of his department. In this company, honest people were dangerous, so next day my father lost his job. This was the last place my father would work.

At this time, I realized that my studies were less important than the well-being of my family. In February 1940 I went to the conservatory and explained to the director, Jan Soltys, that I could no longer attend classes in the morning. He did not want me to leave my studies and told me that in his opinion I was too talented to quit my studies in music. He said he would try to find me something that would not require attendance at classes so often. Then he asked me to sing. He liked my voice and said that if I were to study voice, he would find me a professor-tutor, one of their best teachers, and suggested that I should study with her when I could. Because I played the piano, my second subject would be piano, and he promised to make a similar arrangement with the piano teacher. I accepted this offer with great joy.

The next day I found work as a cashier in a small restaurant. I had to work from eight o'clock in the morning to four in the afternoon. I received a salary and lunch. This lunch was very important because for us to eat well was not easy, and we were too proud to ask our relatives who lived in this part of Poland for help. My father was a very proud man. Around this same time I remember taking my favourite blue dress to the flea market and selling it. I got the dress for my birthday in 1938, and I loved it, but I was happy to bring money home.

From my job in the small restaurant I was promoted to a very big restaurant near the famous Lwow Theatre. It was hard work and I had to work until late in the evening, after the restaurant closed. I had to take the money home before depositing it in the bank the next morning. Late in the evening after the tramways stopped, I would walk almost an hour to our apartment. Today I wonder that I was never scared to walk alone in the dark night. Besides my pay, I always brought home half my lunch because the sandwich I was given to eat was huge, with lots of cheese or meat, and I would cut it in half and bring home the uneaten half in the evening.

A few weeks later, I was called to the manager of the restaurant where I worked. The manager said that he felt I was too intelligent to work as a cashier and recommended me to the head office. Starting the next day I would go to work in the bookkeeping section. I was happy that at least I did not have to work in the evening. I did not know the Russian alphabet, and since Adam was studying Russian at school, I asked him to teach me. That evening my brother introduced me to Russian writing and reading. It was certainly not easy, but I was confident that I could overcome the obstacles provided I did not become discouraged. At the same time, being aware that I did not have any idea about statistics, I decided to enroll in the Economics Institute, where I could study without attending too many evening lectures. I was required to pass exams which were supposed to prove that I knew the material. This was something completely new to me.

In the head office I met my superior. His name was Mr. Sharapow, a short, stocky man, very jovial but at times serious. His assistant was a handsome young man, Lusia Kremer from Kiev. I don't recall Sharapow's first name, but I remember that these two men became very helpful later in our hour of need. I learned during this difficult time that in every regime, in every nationality, were different people with different attitudes and behaviours. I worked and I learned a lot. I was always interested in numbers and I could use my ability to count in my head. When I started to study economics I never left the conservatory. I continued to study voice with a wonderful teacher, and I studied piano, although I did not have a piano to practice on.

One night in May 1940, the police came looking for my mother's brother, Dr. Samuel Goldman, a medical doctor who was temporarily living with us. He was from western Poland and had also crossed the

San River, running from the Germans. His wife, Lunia, and his little daughter, Dzidzia, were supposed to follow him but had had some problems and decided to stay in their home town. My uncle was not home when the police arrived. The next day we found out that the Russian authorities had decided to arrest all the men who had arrived from western Poland and send them to work in Russia. That same afternoon I was stopped by a Russian neighbour. I did not know him but I knew his two children, who often played on the street near us. This Russian was a policeman. He told me very abruptly that the following night, together with all the other people who came to Lwow from western Poland, we would be taken far away into Russia where the Russians needed a workforce. He added that the soldiers who were to carry out these orders were not supposed to use force. He looked at me and said that we were on the list to be deported.

The next night, the Russians hammered on our door no fewer than eleven different times. Each time when they came to take us away I showed them that I had a job and was a very valuable student at the Lwow Conservatory. The most important item I had was a letter from the Director of the Conservatory stating that I was especially gifted. To this day I do not understand how we avoided deportation.

The next morning, Mr. Sharapow greeted me, saying, "You are lucky that you were not deported." And he added, "Lusia went to the railway station. He wanted to help you and your family." An hour later Lusia came. He was completely drunk and asked me to come to his office. He told me that he was a member of the Communist Party but that he could not see his brothers and sisters be taken away against their will. All the people that he saw at the railway station were his brothers and sisters and he did not approve of what had seen.

A few months later his mother came from Kiev. I met her and she asked me if she could meet my parents. During the visit I arranged, she told my parents the story of her life. During the revolution her parents and her husband, Lusia's father, had been shot in front of her. They were wealthy people and very well educated. She was taken with her little son to the Urals. The child went to school and first became a member of the children's "pioneer" organization. These children were indoctrinated from early childhood with the principles of communism. Her son eventually became a member of *Komsomol*, the youth party, and as a young man became a member of the Communist Party. His mother told my parents that she had never told her son how her parents and his father had died. She spoke Ukrainian and therefore she could converse with my parents. We believed that she wanted to share the story of her life with somebody.

In the Economics Institute I met a very interesting director. His name was Boris Fiterman. He was from Charkhow. There are Russians who prove the point that I stress very often in my teaching, that we should never, never put people in categories. If we do we are taking away a part of their humanity.

One evening after classes I stayed longer at the Institute and told Boris Fiterman how happy I was that we had not been deported to Russia. At one point I told him how afraid I was of Germans. He asked me if I had a special reason to be so afraid, and I answered that I was Jewish. He looked at me and took out a map of the Soviet Union. Pointing his finger in the vicinity of Stalingrad he told me that since I was Jewish, it would be better to go to Russia than to stay in Poland. Keeping his finger on the map, he said that he knew that the Germans would attack sooner or later, and that they would even reach deep into Russia before they would be stopped.

Years later when we got the news about Stalingrad, in my mind I saw Boris Fiterman from Charkow, his map, and his way of teaching me Russian politics.

Searching at Night
for a Path of Light

On February 18, 1941, Karol's father was alone in their apartment when he suffered a fatal heart attack. On this particular day, after work Karol had gone to his friends, the Juliusz Kydrynski family, to pick up the supper prepared for his father by Mrs. Kydrynski. When he arrived home he found his father dead. It was a terrible blow. Karol was stricken by death once more, and he suffered greatly. The death of his mother and his brother had already left a mark on him. However, growing up he was always aware of the presence of his father, who had taken care of him and taught him how to cope with life. His father attended to all the daily responsibilities without complaint. Besides the love and warmth that accompanied Karol during his growing years, his father had given him lessons of endurance. Now he was completely alone. His father had not even had a chance to say goodbye.

In the basement of the small apartment on Tyniecka Street, Karol knelt beside the inert body of his father the entire night. With his prayers, the sensitive son was paving the road of his father's last journey. During that lonely night guarding the beloved body, Karol searched through prayer for courage to endure the pain. He did not ask why it had happened to him. He knew that he had to accept the verdict of destiny. And his memories mingled with the words of prayer, the memories of a close and happy family. He recalled the conversations with his father during their long walks together. Always fresh in his memory were the hours when his whole family had said the rosary together in their apartment in Wadowice. His family struggled together, prayed together, and dreamed together. A secure feeling of serenity emanated from his parents. He had always admired his father, a military man, who attended to the daily household chores when his mother was sad, weak or ill. This everyday love provided him with a positive outlook on life in spite of the difficulties. How often during his work in the quarry his father's words came back to him, how often he listened to his mother's voice saying to the neighbour, "Karol will be a great man, or maybe a priest." Yes, in this family they struggled together, they prayed together, and they dreamed together. His brother Edmund had become a medical doctor, but even this fulfilled dream was cut short.

Karol's few true friends in Krakow showed their concern for him during his grief. In his greatest pain, however, Karol was strengthened by the belief that the Virgin Mary, Christ, and God were watching over him. He remembered the words written on the sundial in the church in Wadowice: *"tempus fugit — aeternitas manet."*

Krakow was silent, the frost decorated the windows of the small apartment, the wind carried the dust from the quarry, and sweet melodies were sung by mothers whose children did not want to sleep.

Do grown people who are in pain and cannot sleep listen to the wind? Do the sweet melodies of mothers singing to their children stop for a moment and let the frost melt on the windows? What are these melodies entering the rooms where grownups cannot sleep? Do they sound like the blessing of someone who, with a tune of serenity, allows us to close our eyes and believe that the night will bring happy dreams? Do we need tales and stories perhaps even more than logical arguments, which so often appeal only to our mind with techniques on how to resolve problems, while excluding dreams and songs and poetry as nonreality? Maybe this "nonreality" offers us the atmosphere of a poet or a writer or a mystic who insists on the emotional ingredient in our posture in life.

The streets of Krakow were sometimes silent and sometimes bursting with the screams of those who were taken, arrested, persecuted. This was the reality of war. This was the cruel presence of hate that excluded all pity. It was well-orchestrated cruelty conducted by those who knew how to use the instruments of death in different forms and disguises. This was the cold philosophy promoting the superiority of one category of human and trying to prove that anyone designated as "subhuman" should be annihilated. Was it the night of the war where God's commandment would be abolished as trains carried people to the abyss? Was it possible that evil might persist, and that along with victims there would emerge indifferent bystanders acting as if they were immune to the tragedy of those who were the target of killing? Yes, Karol Wojtyla would see the streets of Krakow as they were. He walked those streets and asked himself if it was possible to awaken humanity in humankind. He did not believe for one second that cruelty and hate would win.

While walking through the streets of Krakow, Karol would wonder why a certain percentage of the population in many countries occupied by the enemy collaborated and sold themselves for money. How could these people be corrupted by the propaganda of hate and not see the ugly side of the politics of having one goal only: to take away, step by step, the dignity even of those who were collaborating?

In these moments of struggle with reality Karol looked for non-reality for something that could appease reality and logic for a moment. Was this an escape or simply a way of searching for the courage to believe that all was not lost and that faith in God and God's protection would serve as reconfirmation of humanity's worth? Karol knew the world's literature, and perhaps Dante's description of hell reminded him of the existence of the power of goodness and the power of evil.

In Canto 1 of the *Inferno*, Dante says,

Midway upon the journey of our life
I found that I was in a dusky wood;
For the right path, whence I had strayed, was lost.
Ah me! How hard a thing it is to tell
The wilderness of that rough and savage place,
The very thought of which brings back my fear![56]

At the beginning of Dante's work, the pilgrim establishes the leitmotif of his journey to God. He is lost, and he asks for help. The first person Dante meets is Virgil. In the dark wood, the Roman poet offers to guide him. Virgil asks Dante "to climb upward to that happy mountain, the origin and cause of every joy":

While I was stumbling down to lower ground,
Before my startled eyes appeared a man
Whose voice seemed weak from long-continued silence;
And when I saw him in that desert place,

"Help me, pity me," I cried, "Whate'er you are,
A living man, or specter from the shades!"
He answered me: "No man am I, though once
A man I was – from Lombard parents sprung
Who both were citizens of Mantua.
Late in the time of Julius I was born,
And lived in Rome while great Augustus reigned,
When false and lying gods still held their sway.
I was a poet, and sang the worthy son
Born to Anchises, who escaped from Troy
After proud Ilion was burned to ashes.
But why do you return to so much woe?
Why not climb upward to that happy mountain,
The origin and cause of every joy?"
"Are you then Virgil – that great fountainhead
Whence such a flood of eloquence has flowed?"
I answered him abashed, with forehead bowed.[57]

Recently, during a private audience, the pope told me that he had always enjoyed poetry and still does to this day.

If someone considers poetry as a source of ideas, transcending the past and treating the present only as a temporary state leading to a better future, then poetry can become a very powerful weapon and a source of hope.

Karol Wojtyla also loved the theatre. In 1940, as George Blazynski explains, he was very active in the underground Rhapsodical Theatre, under the guidance of Mieczyslaw Kotlarski.

This small group performed many plays and epics by famous Polish poets. Despite dangers, the group presented different plays. The actors and the audience tried to find strength and escape for even a short time from the daily routine. For an hour or two, in a room with a small stage, the reality of the street was not present. One afternoon a witness experienced Karol's excellent rendition of a very moving part of Adam Mickiewicz's *Master Thaddeus*, the scene of the dying priest Robak. Robak says that he fought for Poland but he does not remember his deeds, he remembers only the suffering. The Polish patriot, a quiet hero, revealed his true nature; Poland was worth suffering for if it was needed. The same witness recalled that the loudspeakers outside were delivering a public address to the Polish population proclaiming the victories of the German army. Karol did not stop reciting the poem and the audience listened in silence.[58]

During the war, people created many defence mechanisms in order to remain lucid and not sink into depression. A Jewish theatre was organized in the ghetto of Warsaw, where poets were able to present their works, especially songs. A well-known actress, Diana Blumenfeld, who survived the war, said to a friend in 1946 that there were people in the ghetto who asked the performers how they could "sing and dance on the graves." Her answer was, "We just wanted to reaffirm that we were still alive."

In the same Warsaw ghetto there was an orphanage for poor Jewish children that had existed in Warsaw long before the war started. The man who dedicated his life to running this orphanage was the doctor and famous writer Janusz Korczak. Dr. Korczak was highly respected in Poland. He wrote many books for children and others, both fictional and theoretical works, such as *How to Love a Child* and *The Child's Right to Respect*. His works were based on his expression of love for children.

During the war, Dr. Korczak tried to keep the children busy. He played with them and created a cheerful atmosphere. When the children were hungry, he asked them to use their imagination and think that instead of dry bread they were eating sandwiches with sausage. In the evening, he tried to organize entertainment.

In *Warsaw Diary, 1939–1945*, published in London after the war, Michael Zylberberg described an evening in the ghetto when the children recited poems by Isaac Leib Peretz. In one of the poems, called "Brothers," the author says that white, brown, black, and yellow mingle together. All human beings are brothers and sisters. They were created by one Father and one Mother. God created them all. The whole world is their Fatherland.

Dr. Korczak tried to spread spiritual strength and the spirit of oneness among the children he cared for. He never betrayed his love for children. At one point, the Nazi authorities decided to destroy the orphanage and send the children to a concentration camp. The Gestapo approached Dr. Korczak and informed him of the plan to take the children away. They said that he could remain in Warsaw but he pleaded with them, asking if he could stay with the youngsters until the end. He asked the Gestapo to allow him to speak to the children and tell them that they would have to leave the orphanage. The Gestapo agreed. So Dr. Korczak went to see "his children," as he always called them, and in a joyful voice told them that they would have to pack, that they were going on an excursion to look at trees and fields and to breathe the fresh air. The children got ready and went with Dr. Korczak to their final destination. In the train Dr. Korczak sang songs with them. He later perished with "his children."

Verdi's *Requiem* was performed in the ghetto of Terezin. Rehearsals took two years. Every few days some members of the choir disappeared. They were replaced immediately. It was due to the strong will of a few people who finally performed the *Requiem*. A survivor who attended the performance recalled that when the last words *"libera me"* (free me) resounded in the air, the audience was proud. The human spirit had won.

In seeking the beauty of creation, in having reverence for life, in striving for confidence in faith and God, people find the bridge to hope. The theatre in Krakow, and the artistic performances in Warsaw, Terezin, and many other places are the best example of resisting apathy and fear.

Besides the theatre, Karol found a source of strength in a sincere and deep-thinking friend, a humble tailor, Jan Tyranowski. Pope John Paul II remembers how this quiet man, who often deplored that he could not express his thoughts clearly, was able to talk about God and tried to explain who God was. John Paul II remembers especially one conversation at twilight in which Tyranowski uttered words as though speaking to himself about the depth of evangelical possibilities. So often it happens that the thoughts of different people meet across the ages and across space, the famous and those people not known to the public express the same ideas.

Reading about Jan Tyranowski and his thoughts about God reminds me of the poems of Michelangelo, who said that if thoughts do not ascend to Heaven they are in vain. The tailor from Krakow and the famous poet, sculptor, and painter glorified the name of God in a similar way. Jan Tyranowski entrusted his thoughts to Karol. He influenced the future pope, helping him to shape his character. He became a sculptor of Karol's being in a way that only great poets and sculptors can. This simple tailor, contemplating God and the world, interpreted in his way the works of St. John of the Cross and the thoughts of St. Teresa of Avila. These two saints became very important to the young Karol Wojtyla. St. John of the Cross offers the source of this thinking. Through his works he allows anyone to discover the roads that lead the soul to the union with God.

The life of St. John of the Cross was very difficult. Everything he achieved was the result of his own hard work. This small, frail man, lived in poverty as a young child, understood the poor and the sick and was able to bring people to a longing for the mystery of God. One day St. Teresa said these words about him:

> One cannot speak of God to Padre John of the Cross because he at once goes into an ecstasy and causes others to do the same.[59]

This ecstasy transcended the ages and crossed national borders to capture the spiritual imagination of many people around the world. This mystic, born in the sixteenth century, touched the thoughts of the mystic Jan Tyranowski in twentieth-century Poland. The tailor from Krakow offered Karol Wojtyla, a future pope, a very special path to follow.

To study the works of St. John of the Cross requires the willingness of keen analysis of every line and sometimes of every word. This precision and clarity of expressing every nuance of feeling and thought is perceived by those who search for the depth of the human soul on different levels. In the poem *The Living Flame of Love*, we read in Stanza 3:

> O lamps of fire!
> in whose splendours
> the deep caverns of feeling,
> once obscure and blind,
> now give forth, so rarely, so exquisitely,
> both warmth and light to their Beloved.[60]

St. John of the Cross wrote his "commentary on the stanzas that treat a very intimate and elevated union and transformation of the soul in God" at the request of Dona Ana de Penalosa. The commentary on Stanza 1 offers us a glimpse of the depth of the theologian and philosopher, a humble man and a poet:

This flame of love is the Spirit of its Bridegroom, who is the Holy Spirit. The soul feels him within itself not only as a fire which has consumed and transformed it, but as a fire that burns and flares within it, as I mentioned. And that flame, every time it flares up, bathes the soul in glory and refreshes it with the quality of divine life.

Such is the activity of the Holy Spirit in the soul transformed in love: the interior acts he produces shoot up flames, for they are acts of inflamed love, in which the will of the soul united with that flame, made one with it, loves most sublimely. Thus these acts of love are most precious; one of them is more meritorious and valuable than all the deeds a person may have performed in the whole of life without this transformation, however great they may have been. The same difference that lies between a habit and an act lies between the transformation in love and the flame of love; it is like the difference between the wood that is on fire and the flame that leaps up from it, for the flame is the effect of the fire present there.[61]

In the commentary on Stanza 3, St. John of the Cross writes:

O lamps of fire!

First of all it should be known that lamps possess two properties: They transmit light and give off warmth.

To understand the nature of these lamps and how they shine and burn within the soul, it ought to be known that God in his unique and simple being is all the powers and grandeurs of his attributes. He is almighty, wise and good; and he is merciful, just, powerful, loving, and so on; and He is the other infinite attributes and powers of which we have no knowledge. He is all of this in His simple being, the soul views distinctly in Him, when He is united with it and deigns to disclose this knowledge, all these powers and grandeurs; that is: omnipotence, wisdom, goodness, and mercy, etc. Since each of these attributes is the very being of God in His one and only suppositum, which is the Father, the Son, and the Holy Spirit, and since each one is God Himself, Who is infinite light or divine fire, we deduce that the soul, like God, gives forth light and warmth through each of these innumerable attributes. Each of these attributes is a lamp which enlightens it and transmits the warmth of love.[62]

And suddenly the image of "lamps of fire" brings a vision and a feeling: the vision is the guiding light and the feeling is of warmth.

The commentaries of St. John of the Cross reveal his humility combined with his eagerness to transmit his thoughts in an accessible way. Not only was he a poet who wrote for the sake and beauty of art, he was also a theologian and philosopher who tried to communicate the most noble ideas in a form that could be understood by educated and less-educated people. Together with his friend, St. Teresa of Avila, he knew how to pave the road to love God and to teach the love of God.

At twilight in the apartment of the tailor, Jan Tyranowski, young Karol Wojtyla crossed the borders of the war, and somewhere far away God lit "the lamps of fire."

The Apostle of Hope

The autumn in Poland was sad
in 1942.
Planty Park in Krakow
searched for the sun
in vain.

Huge, black clouds
floated in the sky
and the rain was falling.

Sometimes the rain brings relief
to the thirsty trees
or to people
thirsty for the pure air.
This rain was different;
this rain cried war.

The drops of rain
were bringing gloss
to the golden leaves,
transparent drops of rain
transparent
like the drops of tears.

Krakow was crying.
The tears were flowing
along the trees
and the tears were flowing
down the faces of people,
people during the war.
And in the air
wandered
the lullabies,
the lullabies of the mothers
who did not have food
for their children
and the lullabies
of the Jewish mothers
who knew
that for their children
beside the threat of hunger
was the threat of death.
The lullabies
vibrated together
with Chopin's carol
"Hushabye baby Jesus –
hushabye."
It was a strange war.
The enemy was fighting
not only on the battlefields.
The enemy fought with children,
with women,

with men
without uniforms
and without arms.

The rain was falling
and the tears were flowing.

Along the street in Krakow
walked a young man;
he walked bent.
He passed the park;
he walked slowly.
Each step
was bringing him
to a new destiny.

The young man stopped
before the front door
at No. 3 Franciszkanska Street.
Before the door
he straightened his back.
He looked at Krakow;
he looked at the sky
and there, far away
between the clouds
he saw a tiny ray of sun.
This tiny ray of sun
brightened the face
of Karol Wojtyla
and the front door
of the bishop's palace.
Karol Wojtyla
entered the priesthood.
Was this front door
an arch of triumph
for the young man?
The bishop

Count Adam Stefan Sapieha
greeted the young man
with a smile.

The years passed by.

On November 2, 1946,
the young priest Karol Wojtyla
celebrated the Holy Mass
in the crypt of St. Leonard
in Wawel Cathedral.
It was a quiet mass
for the souls
of the mother, father,
sister and brother
of the young priest.

The young priest
wanted to honour
the memory of the family
through his love
and his affection
which are able to reach
beyond the physical existence
of the loved ones.
The souls listened
to the Holy Mass
and maybe
from far away
the mother caressed
her son's hair
and whispered "Lolus (Karol),
my heart,
the heart of a mother,
knew
that you would become
a priest."

On July 28, 1948,
the young priest walked
on foot
to his parish.
At the corner of the fields
was a small chapel
of St. John Nepomucene.
The chapel
at the corner of the fields
remembers
the sun was burning,
July was hot.
The young priest
knelt,
prayed for a while
ardently, sincerely
his prayer burning
like the sun in the sky.

The chapel did not forget
Karol Wojtyla.
Does the chapel have a soul?

In December 1963
Jerusalem
greeted Karol Wojtyla
with the sun.
There in Jerusalem
the sun
is golden and powerful.
It penetrates the soil
and gives an aura
to life,
to the city of God
and the prophets.

The man walks
on the stones

and feels
the holiness of those
who sanctified this soil:
Isaiah, Jeremiah,
Jesus
and maybe even Mohammed
in his vision.
The sun is golden and strong
and penetrates the soil.
The prayers are sincere.
The man, who prays there,
closes his eyelids
but the sun
stays
in his pupils.
The warmth of heaven
leaves an imprint
with a kiss,
a delicate kiss
of Jerusalem.

Does Jerusalem have a soul?

Karol Wojtyla
walked slowly
along the Road of the Cross
and maybe thought
of Pope John XXIII
who died
on June 21 of the same year.
Maybe Karol Wojtyla
thought of healing
the wounds of humanity.

Pope John XXIII
gave to the church
a vision of the future
based on respect

of man for man
– on brotherhood.
Pope John XXIII
did not forget Bulgaria
during the war
and maybe there
in Bulgaria
the lullabies of the mothers
were wandering
in the air
and with their sweet melody
were asking someone
to listen to them.

Karol Wojtyla
walked slowly
along the Road of the Cross.
Karol Wojtyla
prayed there
in Jerusalem
and maybe thought
that
the light of Jerusalem
radiates
through the whole world,
and the small chapel
of St. John Nepomucene
in Niegowici,
before which
he knelt
on the road
to the parish
radiated
with the strong golden sun
of Jerusalem.

On January 13, 1964,
the snow was falling

in Krakow.
The Notre Dame Church was
white,
snow-white.
The snowflakes
of pure whiteness
greeted
the new archbishop
Karol Wojtyla.
The snowflakes were as
unblemished
as the thoughts
of a poet-priest,
who loved
God and man.
Christ was blessing
from far away
the new shepherd
of the souls
in Poland.

The jasmine bloomed
in Krakow
in May 1967.
Pope Paul VI
nominated
the new cardinals.
Karol Wojtyla
became a cardinal.

The trees in Krakow
transmitted the news
to the trees in Wadowice.
The jasmine in Wadowice
remembered
that 47 years before,
the mother of Karol Wojtyla,
in the room

where she gave birth
to her son,
asked
that the window be opened.

In 1969 Cardinal Wojtyla
visited
the Remuh Synagogue
on Szeroka Street in Krakow.
He was wearing a black soutane.

The white smoke
appeared
above the Sistine Chapel
on October 16, 1978.
Cardinal Jan Wojtyla
a Pole
became the shepherd
of 700 million Catholics.

And there
high above Michelangelo's
cupola
on St. Peter's Basilica
the old lullabies
wandered
in the air,
the old lullabies
from years, years ago.

After a while
the lullabies flew
far away.
Silence reigned
in Rome.

But at midnight
the Polonaise in A-major
called to fight
against hate.
It seemed that Chopin
wanted
to awaken the world
and the hearts of people
on the earth.

The apostle of hope
started his journey.

God was blessing the world.

The Dawn of a New Era

On October 22, 1978,
the soft wind caressed
St. Peter's Square
and the foreheads
of 3,000 people
who came
to see and to hear
the new Pope, John Paul II.

And
he came.
He came together
with his parents.

He came together
with Poland,
with the Vistula River
flowing slowly
in Krakow.

He came,
with the Polish poplars
and the weeping willows.

He came,
with the Polish poets,

Adam Mickiewicz,
Juliusz Slowacki
and Cyprian Norwid.

He came,
with the Polish fields
singing the glory of Christ
during the harvest
in summer.

He came,
with the Virgin Mary
from Czestochowa
and with the reminiscence
of the clock,
from Wadowice.
He remembered the inscription
*"tempus fugit —
aeternitas manet."*

He came,
to celebrate as a pope
his first Holy Mass
in St. Peter's Square.

In his heart

were all those
whom He brought with him
and one thought:
Tempus fugit,
aeternitas manet
(time flies,
eternity remains).

He was starting now
his journey in time.
He wanted to contribute
something
to eternity.

Time and eternity,
watching the skies and men.

And now he, Karol Wojtyla,
became the shepherd
of millions of people –
Catholics and
others.
Karol Wojtyla
cared for humanity.

The skies were watching
all people on the earth

The streams flowing
throughout the world
were docile
and transparent.

The feelings
in the heart of the new Pope
were docile, pure
and transparent –
and in these feelings was joy –

of a servant of God
who wanted also
to become a servant
of humanity.

The philosopher,
the poet,
and the priest
became one.

The hills of Rome
were listening
to the man
with the foreign accent.

At the end
of his sermon
he said:
"Pray for me.
Help me to be able
to serve you.
Amen."

With these words
came a promise
to eternity.
He wanted
all men
to help him.

Maybe at this moment
St. John of the Cross
sent from high above
"the lamps of fire"
with light and warmth
to every man on earth.

The Cupola of Michelangelo

retained
the caress of the wind
and the words
of the new Pope.

This was the beginning
of a new era

The Pope, John Paul II,
loves life.
He knows how to transmit
the zest for life
to all those who know him.
He carries with him
the flag of love.
This flag he carried
before he came to Rome
while teaching the young
students
philosophy,
while swimming, skiing,
playing ball
with young people
in Poland
allowing these young friends
to call him
wujek – "uncle."

Pope John Paul II
is courageous.
His courage
and his dreams
do not have
any foreign accent.
They are the dreams
of men
in different
corners of the world.

The Pope
wants to build
bridges.
The difference
between the pope
and men
is
that the pope
believes
in building
bridges,
and men
across the world
are frightened;
they do not know
how to accept people
who are different from them;
they are afraid
of those
whose skin
is darker or lighter
than theirs.
They are afraid of those
who pray
in different places
of worship.
They are afraid
of melodies
which sound strange.

Is God in Heaven
God of all men?

The crowd was still there
in St. Peter's Square.
After the Pope finished the Mass
and went to his quarters,
the wind caressed

as before
the foreheads of people
who were congregating
a while longer.
Maybe,
they were repeating:
Pax vobiscum —
Peace be with you

The rainbow
appeared in the sky,
the rainbow
of millions of colors.

Grosvenor Avenue in Montreal

Nobody cherishes a home more than someone who has been homeless. My family home was an integral part of the lives of four people who created an atmosphere of love. We did not have fireplaces in our apartment, but our home was warm. When I use the word "warm," I remember that in my parents' room there was a wood stove covered with pink tiles. Inside the stove were pieces of burning wood, and they provided the room with the right temperature. In this room and in the room that I shared with Adam where there was stove was made of white tiles, I often turned out the lights and opened the door to watch the flame sparkling and shining.

Throughout the war years we were homeless. We wandered from one place to another, always with two or three suitcases, but we did not lack warmth. Most of the time we were together. Being homeless is comparable to being hungry. We were homeless for five years. We were also often hungry, but we could always appease hunger with a few potatoes or a piece of hard bread. I remember that I often dreamed of good food. I also never forgot that after the Germans came to Lwow and we received a very small ration of bread, my father divided the bread into four pieces and then, knowing that I did not feel strong when I was hungry, divided his piece into two. My mother and Adam were less sensitive to hunger than I was. When people are homeless they dream of building a home, a small home somewhere in the world, somewhere quiet and peaceful.

During the war I would say repeatedly, "If I survive I would like to have my own typewriter and a piano," and then I would add, "I would like to have a real home."

I remember that after we were liberated, with the first money he earned, Adam bought me a typewriter and a small upright piano. This old typewriter is still with me in Philadelphia. At the time, Adam could not buy me a home. When I left Poland I was sorry that I could not take the piano with me. During the war I did not stop composing songs. In one of my songs, "Spring in January," I asked if spring would ever come for us. In the last part of the song I wrote that maybe there are many people who even though they didn't compose songs, they still dreamt of a home as I did. My song also spoke of all those homeless men, women, and children, who were longing for a day without being afraid of bombs falling from the sky or the noise of approaching tanks. How many of those people during sleepless nights listened for the approaching steps of policemen in heavy boots in fear and trembling, scared that those violent men in heavy boots would stop at their door?

There was another song that my mother loved, "The Song of the Soldier," in which the soldier says he is going into the unknown, to the front, and writes a letter in which he asks his mother to pray for him. He says that he knows he is leaving his home behind. He knows that God is with him, but he also knows that no one is waiting for him in this distant place where he must fight. In his letter the soldier asks his mother to pray for his safe return. From far away the wind brings the melody of the old trees, and in his imagination the soldier sees quiet waters. He asks his mother to touch his hand even in a dream, because he wants to be nearer to her.

I also wrote "The Little House in the Forest," a song about a tiny house without radio or newspapers, the house of my dreams, where the dawn would greet me with a smile every morning, and in the evening night would greet me with shining stars. I did not forget in this song that soldiers were still somewhere far away, near the Vistula River or near the Tiber. Maybe the soldiers were also dreaming about a tiny home where peace reigned. How many of them had composed letters to their loved ones? How many of them did not have time to write? How many of them wrote the letters and did not have the opportunity to send them? How many words of love remained in their thoughts?

* * *

When the war was over and we eventually arrived in Paris, my husband Sigmond decided that I had to have a piano. We were living in a hotel near Porte St. Cloud, and when the piano arrived, the hotel owner said that in the history of the hotel he had seen many things, but no one living there had ever bought a piano. I can still remember that small upright piano with its excellent sound.

Often in Paris, during our long walks together, I shared with my husband my dream of one day having our own home. Sigmond and I loved to walk in the evenings and on weekends. From Porte St. Cloud we moved to another hotel near la Place de la Madeleine. This hotel had two beautiful sunny rooms and I found room for the piano near the window. Finally we moved to an apartment at 7 rue Raynourd, where from our kitchen window I could see the Eiffel Tower in the sun or at twilight.

One day, Sigmond brought me a beautiful antique mother-of-pearl button. It had an exquisite design of a little house. He gave me this button, saying, "For the time being I cannot offer you a home but I can give you this button." The next day Sigmond went to the jeweller and had him make me a brooch. The button was set in a frame of gold and I loved it. I always wonder how it is that people in love often follow dreams together and try to incorporate their dreams, each into the life of the other.

Sigmond was the only member of his family to survive the war. He fought as a partisan in the forests and was a specialist in mining bridges. He suffered for a long time after being seriously injured and although he could never forget the past, only in Paris did he regain his love for life. He had been a Polish diplomat in Paris, although he had not belonged to the Communist Party. The Communist regime believed him to be well qualified for the position, because before the war he had worked for a while in the Polish consulate in Vienna. A textile engineer and economist, he was very well educated. He had studied in Austria, Belgium, and France. At Christmas in 1948, under the pretext of signing a commercial agreement between Poland and France, he was asked to go to Warsaw for three days. Since he did not belong to the Communist Party and was well known for his political views, the Polish authorities decided to keep him in Poland and would not allow him to return to Paris.

In a short telephone conversation he told me that I would be asked to come back to Warsaw with our son, Michel. He strongly advised me not to come. When a member of the Polish embassy asked me to go back to Poland, I refused. As a result, I was asked to surrender my diplomatic passport. I remember the day when that passport was taken away. After that, letters from Sigmond stopped. He had been arrested and for three months I did not know if he was alive or dead. He was released after three months, but he lost his position in the Ministry of Commerce and Industry and was not allowed to come to France. Finally he left Poland after 12 months with the help of an organization. I was alone in Paris with my young son for 18 long months. Luckily, my parents and Adam were also in Paris and they helped me through this difficult time. After Sigmond came back in July 1950, he said he could not live in Europe anymore. In 1951, Canada became our next home.

We had lived in an apartment in Montreal for a year when one of Sigmond's friends came and told us about a small house on Grosvenor Avenue in Westmount, a very beautiful location with many trees and not too far from the centre of Montreal. Sigmond did not have time to visit the house, so he asked me to go and see it. I fell in love with the semi-detached brick cottage. I was so excited I ran to use the public phone in Macy's Pharmacy. I remember every detail. At the corner of Grosvenor Avenue and Sherbrooke West, I realized that I had found the home of our dreams. A week later, while I was with Michel vacationing in a small *pension* in the Laurentian Mountains, Sigmond arrived for the weekend and said, "I bought the house for us." My dream had come true. We moved to our new home in September 1952. Everybody on the street spoke English. Within a month Michel, who spoke only Polish and French, had learned how to speak English with his friends. I'll never forget how on the first day he played with a little girl and little boy on the street, he came and asked me what "shut up" meant. At the time I did not know.

Our neighbours were wonderful. My nearest neighbour, Angeline Murray, was French Canadian, and through her I became acquainted with the neighbourhood. Michel started to ask me to cook Canadian meals – he wanted steak, pea soup, and apple pie *à la mode*, which I learned meant with ice cream. He was immediately adopted by the neighbours and their children.

Our life was not easy, but we started to love Canada. We felt free.

Sigmond eventually established a small import company in the basement of our home, importing sunglasses from France and Italy. I helped him with the business and at the same time I started to write poems and books in French. Our home was our castle. I remember the day that my neighbour Angeline painted her kitchen ceiling. I decided to do the same. I painted the whole kitchen, but I could not succeed in painting the ceiling white. Finally I opted for blue clouds on the white ceiling. Sigmond laughed, saying that I had created a sky for our kitchen.

Our piano, which we had brought from Paris, did not like the Canadian climate. We had to have it tuned every six weeks, and finally the tuner offered us an old Canadian-made pianola. I painted it gold to match the antique furniture of our salon. Today this piano is in Adam's small country house in St. Donat in the Laurentians, west of Montreal.

My parents and my brother, Adam, joined us in Canada in 1952. It was my father's decision. "If we survived the Holocaust together," he said, "we should not be separated by the ocean." It was not easy for Adam to leave Paris, where he had studied mechanical engineering and had a very responsible position in French industry, but he came anyway. There was another reason that especially prompted my father to come to Canada: he adored Michel.

By now, it was time for Michel to start school. We tried to enrol him in a French language school, but not knowing that these were Catholic schools, we discovered that Jewish children were not allowed to attend them. We received a letter informing us that since Jews paid taxes for English schools, Jewish children had to be educated in English. (This policy is no longer in place.)

In April 1956, my father died. This loss was tremendously difficult for my family and me. My father was the best friend and best mentor I had ever had. His influence on Michel had been immense. It was my father who taught him the laws of morality and goodness.

The happiest event of our life in Montreal was the birth in September of that year of our second son, Jacques, named after my father.

There on Grosvenor Avenue we created the home of our dreams. Everything we cherished was there: the culture, the music, the art. We created Paris and Rome anew in our Canadian home. Books about paintings and poetry started to fill our bookcases. Music resounded as my mother, Jacques, and I played the piano.

After finishing English high school, Michel decided to get his B.A. in French. He applied to Collège Notre Dame in Montreal and was the first Jew to be accepted. Ten years later, at a students' reunion, one of the priests told Michel that Cardinal Léger had given permission for him, a Jew, to enrol there. Michel's best friend, a French Canadian, told Michel after a few months at the college that at the beginning he had been unhappy that one of his classmates was Jewish. "I did not know any Jews personally," he said. "I only knew that they were different. Now I realize what it means to get to know people and to understand them."

Michel enjoyed his studies at Collège Notre Dame which gave him the incentive to study philosophy. After obtaining his B.A., he entered l'Université de Montréal, where he earned a degree in law. He continued his studies in philosophy at McGill University, and after getting his master's degree, he entered the Ph.D. program in philosophy at Dropsie University in Phildelphia. Today, Michel lives in Montreal, where he is a judge and a writer. A few years ago he became a member of the Board of the Collège Notre Dame.

A few years passed, and during 24 hours in September 1967 our world collapsed. Michel recounts this critical time in Montreal in his book of short stories *Jerusalem Breezes*.[63] I will let him set up and describe the scene because he has a profound insight into what I was experiencing at this most difficult time in my life.

I woke up to the Piaf-like voice rising to my bedroom from the living room downstairs. Although it resounded more melodious and less full, the accent in English was a mixture of Paris and Jaslo, heavier on the Paris, yet charmingly soft. The piano vibrations held a resonance of treble, and I did not feel the deep lull of a bass. The lateness of the hour and the seemingly acute awareness which appears after tranquil sleep and tends, suddenly, to make of the child in us a philosopher combined with the richness of the melody to nudge an overflow of emotions into an all-encompassing imagery. Suddenly all the pieces of the life of the person I had been thinking of came together, as if I had been intoxicated by an embracing intuitive comprehension. I sat at the top of the stairs and envisioned the scene.

My mother sat on a small, square, gold, four-legged Louis XVI stool. The upholstered seat was flatly pillowed, sky blue, the same colour as the rest of the living room, including the curtains, except for the gold rim on the moldings just below the ceilings. Being a child, it took me a while to realize that this living room was actually a salon, and that all the other living rooms I had seen in Montreal were not large dens without books. The furniture, paintings, sculpture, in the salon, like the inhabitants of the home, except for my one and only Canadian-born brother, had immigrated *in toto* from our 7 rue Raynouard, 16eme arrondissement, Paris apartment, across the street from the park from which the Trocadéro and the Champs de Mars appeared. The large ornate, gold-framed rococo mirror, at the end of the wide, double-sized room, reflected the large chandelier and a white sculpture of the head of a smiling little girl adorned in her braids. One of two Persian, blue-motif carpets which covered the floor was visible in the middle of the room, from its far side. A small yet tall, circular beige marble table, also gold legged with a golden ledge, was centred so as to allow room for a large Louis XVI chair, now noticeably empty, where my father often sat listening to my mother singing her songs, and frequently accompanying her by his harmonious whistling. In the mirror, a barely visible sofa stood in a corner-nook. All the material on the seats and on the backs of the chairs, as on the rest of the furniture, depicted colourful pastoral scenes inhabited by angels or young, regal, handsome men with their hair in buns and by dainty, pretty maidens. On the immediate top left of the mirror hung a portrait of a fair lass embracing and being embraced by two cherubic children. The top right corner of the mirror exhibited a painting of guests in a similar salon, although larger, which one would expect to find in a French palace; and a little further, the finest painting of all, from a museum, also in a gilded frame, like all the others, of a dark haired, voluptuous gypsy, wearing a red bonnet and a black dress adorned with crimson, holding in her hands handiwork of flax. The profusion of red in the painting combined with the brown dancing eyes to give life, echoing a carefree gypsy melody in the girl's expression.

The room streamed with light, which burst with dazzling radiance in the mirror, beaming from the wall lamps on either side of a large fireplace which was never used, but was preceded by a regal break-front of material similar to the furniture, standing on four curved, gold legs. On the mantle of the fireplace stood an antique gold clock with a white face. The timepiece was centred between two rather plump reclining angels; ever since I could remember, I had heard its chime only a few times. To the right of the mantle, another large Aubusson armchair, and in the corner-nook of the front portion of the double-roomed salon, a brown wood–inlaid, finely polished vitrine with curved bay windows displayed tiny porcelain, silver, gold and semi-precious stonewares on brown silk–lined shelves. On the left of the mirror, which could be seen upon entering the room, from either the regal, windowed double-doors of the front of the living room or the single wooden door at the end of the room, where previously there had hung a reproduction of the *Mona Lisa*, was a portrait of my gentle but strong, handsome, expressive, sad, blue-eyed father, who had passed away two years ago. Below the portrait, a rectangular, light-grey marble table edged to the wall with a few small prayer books with metal covers, of the type which were brought back as gifts from Israel. It was here that my mother would pray before she ate breakfast in the morning and before retiring at night. Each family member was blessed and prayed for, along with the world, around a central prayer for peace in Israel. It was beside this table that my mother sat on the stool, playing the piano, immediately to the left of a round blue-cushioned hassock, where I often sat listening to her sing.

The small hands at the gold-painted piano were smooth, only slightly lined, with red fingernails cut short. A loose gold braid-stranded bracelet and an occasional ring were put aside on the music-sheet ledge to avoid clanking the keys. The short, but not tiny, figure of the brown-haired, round-faced woman with the small, finely sculpted nose seemed to be one with the piano. Playing it was her way of relaxing, of entering another world, a world of yesterday, bringing it into her present and, subconsciously, perhaps, trying to figure out the next step in the future of her two sons.

She was left with them on the passing of my father, her husband, when the present void in the house suddenly set in on the night of the 29th of September, 1967. Within a matter of hours, on the 30th of September, my grandmother – my mother's kindly, also round-faced, smiling, tiny mother – passed away. It was my grandmother who brought from her large estate-home of Kalne eight children, with governesses, language tutors and piano specialists, from a tiny village of the Poland before the Holocaust, classical music and the accompaniment of the piano to my grandfather's deep, melodious voice. That autumn night had somehow linked itself tragically with the Second World War in Poland and, perhaps even more so, with the fact that during the war, my mother had been able to save her immediate family (father, mother, and younger brother), and here, without a war, that had not been possible.

I remember the stillness of the house during the year of mourning when that piano was never touched. Yet my mother was determined to give us as pleasant and happy a life as possible, while providing all she could materially by frequently taking the arduous business trips which my father had so often gone on. She was determined to maintain her healthy, positive outlook on life and to heed the order given to her by my eleven-year-old brother, who had been closest to my father, upon our return to the lower Westmount house from the hospital where my father had died: "I forbid you to look like a poor widow who needs pity."

I realize, only now, that from that moment on, resolve was in my mother, the same resolve which carried her and her family through the war. Looking back and now, I see the easy smile, the bursts of laughter, the more youthful attitude to life than mine, to which I have grown accustomed, the optimism, the innocence bordering on naivete, the fresh, spring-like creativity of character, and the selflessness. The calamity left much sadness but not a trace of bitterness. Her creative spontaneity has flowered in published books of poetry, over one hundred songs, music and lyrics in Polish, French, and English, an M.A. in comparative education, a Ph.D. in philosophy, a meaningful philosophy of purpose which she teaches in a course entitled "Ten Steps in the Land of Life" while being attached to an Ivy League university.

The radiant expression of awe, the illumination on her face, the sudden short silence which you know to be a prayer or a psalm of thankfulness to God for something, have remained. The youthful enthusiasm has not become the least bit tainted by her graduate education. She never dissects that without which there would be no poetry in life. A sunset has remained the same marvel for her that it was when her father, my grandfather, a writer, lawyer, poet of life, first pointed one out to her when she was a little girl travelling on a train to a vacation on the Baltic Sea. To this day, she points out sunsets, flowers, oceans, and trees to us with, I am sure, the same child-like expression she showed her father on that train ride prior to the war, years ago. The child has remained in her; and it is this that she brings out in us and others. Whatever is unblemished, fresh, spontaneous, disarming, continually surprising, touching the noble emotions, allowing the sentiments to be released, appealing to the finest of instincts her being evokes.

I recall a lecture in philosophy which we both attended as fellow students in a Ph.D. program, given by Dr. Israel Efros, a philosopher-poet professor from Israel, a scholar well over eighty, a giant of a kind, gracious man. He spoke of Sadya Gaon's commentary on Genesis, the creation. While everyone was taking notes, my mother had tears in her eyes, thanking God for being able to participate in such a lecture, appreciating the miracle of creation. Education kindles her poetic nature as it quenches that of others. In her travels to distant cities with my daughter, her grandchild, she steps into the historical, regal images of the furniture of the salon. She enters palaces, gardens, sprinkled with fountains, recounting tales of those who had once lived in these surroundings, sharing with my daughter the classical background music of that era, and even occasionally springing up for a quick dance. She holds my daughter in those hands which I so often recall on the piano, and particularly playing that song which accompanies me on my continuous journey to Jerusalem: "I walked, I walked, through life on my road to Jerusalem."

This song, so meaningful for Michel, later became the main song of the cantata *The Little Shoes*.

The Voice

The voice
resounded in the world
the voice was strong and kind
at the same time.
The man who came from
Krakow,
who knew history,
who learned in his youth
about misery and oppression
about cruelty and injustice,
spoke to millions of people.

He spoke to the millions
but his voice
was reaching every man.
For him each man represented a
unique world,
a unique entity.
Each man was different
in his uniqueness of feeling
of understanding
in his capacity of thinking
in accepting his mission
to contribute a spark
of God's will
in building a better future

or to choose another path
and instead of building –
to take part
in preparing
a future of darkness.

There are also other men
passive, indifferent
dangerous in their apathy
to history
unfolding itself
during their lifetime.

The voice of a man
can vibrate in the air
and remain
in the bark of the trees
for centuries.

One man can touch
with his emotions
the fields of wheat
and the waves of the rivers.
The gentle wind
will retain
the sound of the voice.

One voice can provoke an echo
to carry its message
to the remote lands.

The air and the wind
will obey
the plea of the voice.

A voice can bring a storm
and a caress.

One voice can stop the war –
one voice can inspire.
On December 11, 1978,
the world listened
to the strong voice.
The voice belonged
to Pope John Paul II.

The spiritual guide of Catholics
spoke on the day
of the thirtieth anniversary
of the Universal Declaration
of Human Rights –
about respect
and religious freedom.

What are these human rights?
Who was the first
who gave every man freedom?

Thousands of years before,
God proclaimed human rights
in the Ten Commandments.
How many people forgot
the laws of God?
How was it
that December 11, 1978,

was only
the thirtieth anniversary
of the official Declaration of
Human Rights?
Where were the other years,
centuries, millennia
when human rights
were forgotten?

The tablets of the Law
were broken
more than once,
during long, long years.

How many billions of tears
sank into the soil
in all parts of the world,
when human rights
were taken away?

Maybe John Paul II
thought of St. Francis of Assisi,
one of Italy's patron saints
who preached to the poor,
to those who were hungry not
only for bread
but for dignity?

On February 25, 1979,
John Paul's voice
was blessing
the tenderness of love.

The street cleaner's daughter
was married.
The Pope celebrated the
ceremony.

Can one woman from the crowd
be blessed
on the day of her wedding
by the highest authority
of the Catholic Church?
Yes.
She can –
if on the throne of St. Peter
there is someone
who knows
how to descend to the street
and make people feel
that he really cares.

Was the wedding
of one of the daughters in Rome
not the best example
to respect the wish
or a dream
of one individual
from the crowd of strangers
or maybe –
for John Paul II
no one in the world
is a stranger?

On June 2, 1979,
Poland was smiling.
Poland was breathing
a breeze of hope
that came from Rome.

For one day or a few days
a country – a satellite
of the Soviet Union –
experienced a glimpse of
freedom.

The trees were carrying
the strong voice
of a man, a pilgrim
who came to address his
countrymen.
They were his brothers
united in the faith
of their ancestors
since 966
when Poles converted
to Christianity.

On Victory Square
appeared a huge cross.
Beneath the cross
was a replica
of the Black Madonna
of Czestochowa.

John Paul II
addressed one million people.
They were listening
to each word.
They were taking
into their inner beings
strength and determination
to survive.

The communist regime
could not silence
the voice of the crowd
rhythmically repeating,
"We want God, we want God."

Pope John Paul visited
Czestochowa, the Nation's
Shrine,
and prayed.

The Black Madonna
watched the Pope-Slav
who so often
was transmitting
the power of love
and understanding of suffering.

Pope John Paul II
visited also
the Kalwaria Zebrzydowska
shrine –
Where as a child
he came with his father
and his brother
after his mother died.
Later on as a priest or as a bishop
he often prayed here for the
strength
and illumination
of thoughts.

In Wadowice
the Pope
became Karol
Lolek – for a short time
Wadowice was smiling
assuring their son
that the streets
remembered his first steps
as a child.

The peaks of the mountains
watched the native of Wadowice
and wished him
to be strong – as strong
as the mountains.
Do the memories
stored forever

encourage us
never to forget the past?

Our past offers us a lesson,
the joys and sorrows
help us
to form our own judgment
of the events of history
in which we play a part
not only as spectators
but also
as co-creators.

Who are we?

Are we the yesterdays and
todays
mingled together,
shaping our way
of perceiving history –
the history of countries
and the history of our own life?

We accept our inability
to penetrate the universe
of the Creator
but at the same time
we strive
to understand more
to fulfill
our unexhausted willingness
to touch the unknown
or to catch a glimpse
of the mystery of destiny
even
without understanding.

Do our feelings,

the most delicate vessels,
allow us to act
sometimes
in spite
of our powerlessness?

When we think
about the first pilgrimage
of John Paul II as Pope
to Poland
we observe his participation
in history
and his choice
to play an active role
in abolishing the rules
threatening the freedom of men.

In his choice
his feelings were present
his good will
to leave an imprint of hope
not only for his countrymen
not only for Poland
but for the world.

It was during his first visit to
Poland
that John Paul II
visited Auschwitz.

The Pope
celebrated the Holy Mass
for the living
who suffered in the camp
and after he prayed
for those who lived in his heart
he wanted to meet
beyond life –

The sky listened to the whisper –
"I kneel before
all the inscriptions
that come one after another
bearing the memory
of the victims
of Oswiecim in (their) languages
Polish, English, Bulgarian,
Romany, Czech, Danish,
French, Greek, Hebrew,
Yiddish, Spanish,
Flemish, Serbo-Croat,
German, Norwegian,
Russian, Romanian,
Hungarian, and Italian."

After –
as it was recalled
by John Cardinal Krol, of
Philadelphia,
the strong voice of the Pope
stopped for a while
and then
the soft voice continued:
"In particular, I pause . . .
before the inscription in
Hebrew.
The inscription awakens
the memory of the people
whose sons and daughters
were intended
for total extermination.
This people
draws its origin
from Abraham in faith
(cf. Romans 4:12)
as was expressed
by Paul of Tarsus.

The very people
that received from God
the commandment
'You should not kill'
itself experienced
in a special measure
what meant by killing
is not permissible
for anyone
to pass by this inscription
with indifference . . . . "

Pope John Paul II
stood in this place
where human rights
were abolished.

The human rights
went into the smoke
from the chimneys.

Does the air retain
the smoke from the chimneys?
Do we observe the human rights
only for one day
when they are commemorated?

On October 2, 1979,
New York waited.

The streets of New York
and the skyscrapers
were whispering.

Pope John Paul II
came from Rome
and will address
the United Nations.

What will he say,
this guide
of millions of Catholics?
How will he approach
the assembly
of voices of the world?
Is this voice of a man
from Krakow and Rome
strong?

Will this voice
leave
an echo
in far away Peru
or in Madagascar?

Will this be only a voice
or a dialogue
of one conscience
with another,
one conscience
of a priest-
poet-philosopher
with the conscience
of the messenger
of a small, tiny country
or with a messenger
of a country of power?

Will this voice of conscience be
the greatest judge
of future decisions
of the Assembly of the United
Nations?

Will this voice
repeat the commitment
of John XXIII's encyclical

Pacem in Terris
of the year 1963?
and the Second Vatican
Declaration
on Religious Freedom?

Will the Guide of the Church
defend the rights of man?

John Paul II
praised peace
and the General Assembly
listened
to a man
who did not forget
the lullabies of the mothers
during the Second World War
and the prayers
of the mothers
whose sons fought as soldiers
on the fronts
or in the forests as partisans.

For what did these soldiers
and participants fight?

Were they fighting
with weapons of death
for peace?

Here in the United Nations
the Pope was bringing
the most powerful weapons
which are often left
on the shelves
covered with dust.
The Pope was bringing
the weapons

of love and understanding ,
for one's fellow man
in the deserts
and in the overpopulated cities.
The delegates listened.

The strong man
reminded them
of their mission:
to be guardians
of peace.

The words about peace
flew over the roofs
of the building
of the United Nations
and maybe the trees
and the skyscrapers
of New York
repeated the words
of peace.

Late at night
the stars watched
the city of millions of people
and millions of souls.
On November 26, 1979,
the voice
stopped
for a while.

Mehmet Ali Agca
tried to assassinate
John Paul II.

A killer
wanted to silence
a strong voice.

The Holy Father was saved.
He suffered.
After days of suffering
the voice
resounded in the world
once again.

It was destiny
that wanted
the voice
to continue
its journey.

On December 27, 1983,
John Paul II
celebrated Holy Mass
at Rebibbia prison
and visited the man
who wanted to kill him.

On December 1, 1989,
John Paul II
had a private conversation
with Mihail Gorbachev
in the Vatican.

There were two Slavs
in one room,
a Pole and a Russian.
Each of them
representing
a different world,
one the world of faith
the other the world
of the totalitarian regime
built on discipline
and terror.

In the world of faith
man has the right
to converse with God
any time
according to his beliefs,
in the world of discipline
and terror
man becomes
a screw in a huge machine
obedient
to the rules of a country
in which the conscience
is buried
in cemeteries
with unmarked graves.

The keys to the cemeteries
belong to the watchdogs
of injustice.
But in the steppes
of the Soviet Union
late at night
the wind carries
the cries
of those
who did not want to be
pawns on the checkerboard
of life and death,
pushed left and right
against their will.

The world was shaking.

With its sound,
the strong voice
was breaking
many barriers
and touched

the forbidden grounds.

Without battles and fights
on the fronts
and streets
history was changing.
People started to breathe –
there was more freedom in the air,
more and more.

In 1989
the Berlin Wall was destroyed.

The voice wandered,
wandered, wandered . . . .

Walking Through Jerusalem

Light and stones. The strong light from above gives power to the stones below. The stones seem to be united with the light from heaven. Are the stones sacred? No! It is the light from far away, from the kingdom of the Almighty, that blesses the memory of those who have walked on these stones. You walk and you wonder. There is a very special feeling of reverence for these stones. Why for stones? Because these stones carry in their depths the steps of people who tried to bring light from above. The prophets had only one message: "Love your God with all thy heart, with all thy soul and with all thy might."

Why do people across thousands of centuries need this message to be repeated again and again? Why have so many children still in their mothers' wombs lost the divine light before they were born? Why were they too weak to retain this light? Amidst the confusion of generations, the prophets appeared, to preach, to teach, to prepare a path on which all humankind would walk in peace. You walk on the stones in Jerusalem and you wonder why you, a fragile soul of the 20th or 21st century, have these thoughts of reverence for the light above.

This is more than reverence. Perhaps it is the awareness of being linked with history and the moment in which we live. After witnessing the genocides of the past, after seeing the machinery of the Second World War using sophisticated gas chambers, many people today long for the grace of God to descend and allow them to meet spirituality suspended in the air through the light on the stones. Why is this your reaction in spite of your weakness? If we want to acquire our equilibrium after contemplating our feelings, we try to remind ourselves of the prophets. They created this atmosphere of mystery. There in the air you hear the mysterious sounds, the melody of silence. And you, you alone provide the melody to your thoughts with a leitmotif, "Love your God with all your heart, with all your soul, and with all your might." These words became a credo. Isaiah, Jeremiah, Christ, and Mohammed repeated them. The words of love become more than words. Suddenly they mean hope, hope against all atrocities and calamities. In these words is the eternal hope for the light of God, which will never be extinguished. If this hope were to vanish, humanity could not survive: we are too weak to believe only in ourselves. When I touch the dew early in the morning, no matter where I am, I will look for one drop in which the light from Jerusalem lives and lets me breathe. Why that drop of dew? Because dew disperses quickly. We have to know how to admire its short existence. And we prolong it by remembering it. In a poem called "And God Prayed at Dawn," I once wrote that God cries when innocent people die. Beside the light from heaven in the morning dew is maybe the tear of God.

When we walk barefoot on the dew we feel the sacredness of the soil to which one day we will add our own dust.

I remember when I came to Jerusalem that first time in December 1970. Even the way I was dressed revealed my feelings. Whenever I enter any sanctuary I try to be dressed "for God." How strange it must sound, but this is the way I feel. I remember the words of Gandhi, who said, "All roads lead to the same God."

I asked my friend, who had driven me from Tel Aviv, to leave me alone at the Western Wall. I stepped out and walked slowly to the Wall, the remnant of Solomon's temple. I touched the first stone and suddenly my eyes filled with tears and I wept out loud. I was not ashamed even though there were people around me. I cried, cried for a long while, speaking to these stones, asking them how it was that millions and millions of Jews across the world repeat the word "Jerusalem," those wandering Jews down the centuries who were not blessed with being able to touch the stones, which at this moment were endowed with strong light. I looked for God in my soul and I asked again and again – why was this blessing bestowed on me? Why did I deserve to stand there, feeling the stones that were warm not only because of the warmth of my hand? Here I was in 1970, after I had lost my husband, the father of my two sons. I felt lost so often. The only way to survive was to pray in my own words. Some of the prayers composed by others did not really belong to me. I wanted to pray – as me – although many years later I realized that I was merely this grain of dust. Here near the Western Wall I prayed, I prayed for my sons, Adam, for my family, my friends, and … "I prayed in Jerusalem at the Wall" for the peace of the world.

There, I wrote the beginning of the song which was later to become the main theme of my cantata, *The Little Shoes*. I would never forget my encounter with Jerusalem.

After I came back from the trip to Jerusalem, I composed "The Road to Jerusalem" one night at three o'clock in the morning, in our home on Grosvenor Avenue in Westmount in Montreal. I thought that only the walls of our salon were listening – I did not know that Michel was listening to my song from the top of the stairs.

A few months later, this song became the main theme of my cantata, *The Little Shoes*. I had seen pairs of little shoes in the concentration camp at Majdanek one day after the liberation in October 1944. The camp had already been converted into a museum by the Polish authorities. I was a young journalist, and had been sent there to write about the museum. I had never been in a concentration camp and this museum gave me the experience of cruel history where witnesses were screaming – with their silence. All that remained were their shoes – little shoes, big shoes, the shoes of men, women, children. They were shabby, for the better shoes had been sent to Germany. You could almost hear their footsteps. The names of the manufacturers were inscribed – there were shoes from Warsaw, from Amsterdam, from Saloniki in Greece. The guide showed us a letter to Berlin in which the director of the camp was asking for more poisonous gas. Then he showed us a huge barrack with a mountain of tins on which was written "Zyklon B." Each tin of crystals would form enough gas to poison 150 people, but still the camp authorities thought they needed more. With me were journalists from different countries. One journalist could not believe what he was seeing. "No, this is impossible. No! No!" he kept saying in French.

When I returned from Majdanek, I wrote an article entitled "How to Awaken Man in Man." It was published the next day in the Polish paper. It later became the preface to my collection of ten short stories, *Ten Silhouettes Under the Sign of the Swastika*.

When several months after I composed my song "My Road to Jerusalem" I thought of my visit to Jerusalem, I decided to write the cantata *The Little Shoes*. While composing it, the light on the stones in Jerusalem lingered in my memory. I dedicated the cantata to the memory of Wlodek, Sigmond's son from his first marriage who died along with his mother, Hela, during the war. Whenever the cantata is performed I believe that through the silhouette of one child, people come closer to history and understanding the tragedy of the Holocaust. The little shoes become a symbol for suffering.

In my cantata I describe a little boy, Zev (his Hebrew name; in Polish he was called Wlodek). Zev tries to provide bread for his mother and his younger brother. He takes risks; he goes to the streets of Warsaw where he is caught by a policeman.

To have sad, dark eyes in Warsaw
was a crime.

Zev is sent to Auschwitz.

At the dawn of a beautiful day
on Sunday
he died.

Zev goes to heaven, and the angels tell him he is a righteous man, one of the 36. According to the old Jewish legend, the very world reposes on 36 righteous men. Zev is unhappy, and he asks only for his shoes, the shoes that he left in Auschwitz. He wants to run in the world, the world of misery and fear, the world of hunger and war. He wants to see all people free tomorrow. The angels tell him that instead of his shoes he will get wings. The giant angel says,

You will fly into tomorrow
Forty years from now.

Zev and the giant angel fly to Jerusalem and there they hear the song:

I walked, I walked through life
On my road to Jerusalem.
I walked, I walked through life
On my road to Jerusalem
through Paris, Moscow, and Rome
through New York and thousands of towns
through the mountains, forests and streets
right and left, up and down.

From far away I came
Jerusalem, Jerusalem
I came here to pray
Jerusalem, Jerusalem.

They walked, they walked through life
on their road to Jerusalem.
They walked, they walked through life
on their road to Jerusalem,
through Auschwitz, Gross Rosen and camps
Warsaw ghettos, Treblinka and war
when they whispered, *"Shema Israel"*
on their road to Jerusalem.
They will never be forgotten

Those who whispered your name
who were dreaming about you
but who never came.
They live always in my prayer
at the sunset when I pray
and at dawn
they touch my hands
with millions of hands.
From far away I came
Jerusalem, Jerusalem

I came here to pray
Jerusalem blessed be your name.
I prayed in Jerusalem at the wall
I prayed in Jerusalem at the wall
I prayed for the peace of the world
I prayed for the peace of the world
I repeated my old Hebrew prayer
which my mother taught me one day
and I wondered
if the choir of angels
prayed with me
for every man on earth.

I prayed in Jerusalem at the wall
I prayed in Jerusalem at the wall
I prayed for the peace of the world
I prayed for the peace of the world
I was praying for Jews and for Moslems,
for all Christians, all Buddhists, all men
I was praying for those who were forbidden to pray

And my voice went up to Heaven
at the wall of Jerusalem
my old prayer so eternal for all my fellow men
at the sunset the sun was smiling
waving to me through the clouds
for a while I closed my eyes
waiting for the stars.

I was dreaming about people
joining hands across the seas
building bridges through the mountains
over hate and enemies.

And the flowers whispered softly
peace had come into the world
God was happy, God was singing
in Jerusalem at the wall.

I prayed in Jerusalem at the wall
I prayed in Jerusalem at the wall
I prayed for the peace in the world
I prayed for the peace in the world.

And one day when my dream will come true
men will never kill other men.
All the children will live without fear
and enjoy the daily bread of peace.
All the rivers in the West in the East
All the mountains in the South in the North

they will listen to God who will sing
In Jerusalem at the wall.

And suddenly an explosion
interrupted a song –
a bomb exploded at noon
on a beautiful day
on a street
of Jerusalem.

Zev approached the giant angel
in the sky all blue and white
and whispered:
"Why? Why? Why?
Why?"

Zev goes back to heaven, and there he sees the earth, where violence prevails. Again he asks for his shoes. He wants to return to earth to go to the streets where people are hungry for love. He sees the flowers breathe. He wants the children to smell the flowers. And God says,

"You are a just man
and your wish will be granted.
Where do you wish to go?"

Zev says that he wants to fight misery and hunger, injustice and suffering. He asks God to let people open their fists and join hands. And God says

"I cannot open
the fists of men.
Men have to open them
by themselves.
I gave men
the power of thinking,
I gave men the power
of love,
I gave men a free choice
of using their hands
and their minds,

I gave them the universe
of enchanting beauty.
I watch men
and I cry,
Zev do you hear me,
my little boy,
God cries with you."

Zev asks again:

"Can You help me, God?
Can You help me, God?"

And the cantata ends as it began:

In the museum of yesterday,
I saw the little shoes,
they were standing in the corner,
the little shoes.

Despite all the years that have passed since 1944, I still try in all my lectures, and in all my courses, to awaken humanity in humankind. I wrote *Building Bridges* because Pope John Paul II understands my feelings. In his letters he encourages me to be myself. I feel a great ally in this Catholic Pope, John Paul II, who wanders around the world and tries to awaken humanity in humankind. Pope John Paul II travels as a guide for millions of Catholics and I wander throughout the world alone. In my small, humble way I try to do the same.

When my stories were published in Paris, I looked around. Paris was beautiful, people were smiling, and there so often I asked myself how to rehumanize people after the war. How many of us became immune to suffering, seeing on the big screens movies depicting the atrocities of war, the naked corpses, people digging graves for themselves? After a while the public refuses to see it again – "We saw it already." Why is violence and cruelty displayed rather than decency or justice? Was Socrates right when he said that he was more interested in humankind than in the cosmos? When we see a faceless and nameless crowd we do not feel any connection but if we know one person from the crowd and we try to remember the shape of their face and their name, we become more involved in history.

When I got my fellowship at the University of Pennsylvania in 1980 after I finished my Ph.D., I undertook the project of rehumanizing our society by searching for meaning in life. After interviewing many psychiatrists, psychologists, and social workers who were asked to answer my seventy-two questions approved by the university, I was invited to give a lecture on the meaning of life to social workers who had finished their studies at the university. I remember one social worker, a man thirty or thirty-one years old. After I delivered the lecture he asked me if I would say something about my life. Later on my book *Ten Steps in the Land of Life* was published in the United States and in French under the title *Dix Pas dans le Pays de la Vie*. He understood that my eagerness to awaken man in man stems from experience in life which shaped me more than any university education.

I will continue this work of "rehumanization" until I die.

The Longest Journey

The longest journey
of Pope John Paul II
took only twenty minutes
or maybe less.

From the Vatican
to the Jewish synagogue in Rome
is not far.

The sky watched the Pontiff
entering the limousine.

The Old and the New Testament
were about to encounter
each other
in the place of worship
of Roman Jews
after 1900 years.

On this day of spring,
April 13, 1986,
the waters of the Tiber
were flowing slowly
as they had
for millennia
before.

They wondered
why the successor of St. Peter
undertook
this difficult journey.
Pope John Paul II,
almost at the end
of the twentieth century,
decided to remind the Christian
world
of its spiritual link
with the past.

Was it because
he cared to build bridges
after centuries
with all those
who were suffering,
persecuted?

Was it because
he was a just man
who learned
about massacres and killings,
who learned
about shameful deeds
committed in the name of faith

recorded
in the history of mankind?

Was it because
he did not want to perpetuate
crimes of humanity
and remain indifferent
to the future
unfolding itself
day by day?

Was it because,
as a child,
young Karol Wojtyla
was taught
in the city
where he was born
about Jesus Christ
who descended
from the House of David?

There in the city
of his childhood and youth
he read in the New Testament
the words of Christ:

"Love the Lord your God
with all your heart
and all your soul
and with all your mind –
this is the greatest
and the most important
commandment."
(Matt. 22: 32, quoting Dt. 6:5)

Pope John Paul II
also knew
that the Roman Jews

like Jews
throughout the world
recite the morning prayer,
the affirmation of faith:

"Hear, O Israel,
the Lord is our God,
the Lord is One.
Blessed be the name
of his glorious majesty
for ever and ever.

You should love the Lord,
your God
with all your heart
and with all your soul
and with all your mind."

Christ recited this prayer
every day in Judea.

Jews recite this prayer,
Shema Israel,
in their homes,
in their synagogues.

Even in Auschwitz
many of the Jewish prisoners
recited this prayer
while walking hungry
in the mud –
wearing tattered shoes
or barefoot.

Who were these Jews,
the descendants of slaves
who left Egypt
and whom God protected?

Who were these Jews
in the desert,
who were taught freedom
and who promised
to be guardians
of the Laws of God?
600,000 people
experienced the revelation
on their way
to the Holy Land.
Moses became the recipient
of God's wisdom.

Besides 600,000 people
and Moses
there were other witnesses:
the desert
and the mountain,
the tiny grains of sand
and the mighty Sinai.
The grains of sand
reminded man
that he comes
from the dust
like the grains of sand,
and the mountain
majestic and indestructible
reminded man
of the power of God –
and
maybe
this mountain
reminded man
that he is more
than the grain of sand –
maybe this mountain
reminded man
that God gave him a soul –

a soul in which
there is a spark
of God's mystery
which remains with him
during his life
and beyond life.

There is a Jewish legend
that besides people
who were present
in their physical existence
in the deserts,
the souls
of the future generations
of Jews
witnessed the revelation
before being born.

These souls waited
to come on the earth
in the centuries
and millennia to follow.

Was the soul of Christ
on Sinai?

Were the souls of the disciples
of Christ
and the souls
of the apostles
of Christ
present there?

Who were these people
to whom Christ preached
the laws of God?

His disciples

and his apostles –
they were all Jews.

Christ also said:
"Love your neighbour
as you love yourself."

In the Old Testament,
in Leviticus 19:18,
we read:
"Thou shall not take vengeance
nor bear any grudge
against the children
of thy people,
but thou should love thy
neighbour
as thyself."

Christ knew the scriptures
and tried
to repeat them
while teaching people
how to love.

Pope John Paul II
never forgot the words
about loving the neighbour.

There in Wadowice
were the neighbours,
schoolmates –
he did not make a distinction
between Catholic neighbours
and Jewish neighbours –
they were all his friends.

Karol Wojtyla
got the greatest lesson

from his father
who loved Christ
and the little boy
started to love Christ
as his father did.

Karol Wojtyla
interpreted the words of Christ
in his own way.
He understood
that if you hate anyone
you commit a sin
against God.

The letter of the Bible
and the teachings of his father
were engraved
in Karol's feelings –
they were his inspiration,
they guided his steps
on the road
to Christ's longings.

Is it important
to be taught humanity
at a young age?

In the home of his Jewish friend
Jerzy Kluger,
young Karol
listened to the quartets
performed
by his friend's father
and his father's friends,
Polish Catholics.

There was harmony
and beauty

in the rendition of music –
not one false note
was heard.

John Paul II
entered the synagogue.
The president
of the Jewish community
and the chief rabbi
greeted him warmly.

The Bishop of Rome
repeated the words of Isaiah:
"The Lord, who stretched on the
heavens
and laid the foundation
of the earth
and who chose Abraham
in order to make him
father of the multitudes
of children. . . ."

In these words
the link between the Old
Testament
and the New Testament
came back
after 1900 years.
After 1900 years
the head of the Church,
the Man
who followed the dreams
of Pope John XXIII,
the co-author
of the Second Vatican Council,
started
with this journey
another journey

based on "common heritage"
drawn from the law
and the prophets.

When John Paul II
recited Psalm 118
in Hebrew:
"O give thanks to the Lord
for He is good,
His steadfast love endures
forever.
Let Israel say:
'His steadfast love endures for
ever,'"
some souls in Heaven
were blessing the Man
who decided to build bridges
over hate.

The day of spring,
April 13, 1986,
wrote a glorious chapter
in the history of humanity.

The Roman sky was silent
but the sun touched the forehead
of Pope John Paul II
entering the limousine
taking him back to the Vatican.

"May the Flowers Grow" ... and Philadelphia

There are many treasures in life. It depends on family structure and family values whether these treasures remain forever cherished, or whether they disappear, or are hidden, never to be found. Some people come with certain treasures when they are born and some are blessed with treasures which are inherited. Some treasures can be kept in our being and others are outside, in the world around us. For some people a treasure is a small farm, for others a castle. When my father wrote that I should always love truth, he offered me choices, but at the same time he knew how to endow me with the moral ability to fight for this truth no matter when or where.

One day when Michel was four or five, I came into the room unexpectedly and overheard a conversation has was having with my father, his grandpa, whom he affectionately called *Dziadzius* in Polish (and whom he refers to the same way even today). "I promise to do it," said Michel. I remember my father gently saying to him, "Michel, if you are not sure that you will keep your promise, you should rather say 'I will try.' Only when you are absolutely certain that your promise will be kept should you say 'I promise.'" Michel never forgot this lesson. To this day he knows that if he makes a commitment he must be true to his word. A simple sentence awoke in Michel a sense of responsibility, and in conversation with him, my father had taught his grandson how to think.

I remember when my father wrote that I should always love truth, he offered me choices but at the same he gave me the moral strength to fight for this truth, no matter when or where.

When Michel was six or seven years old he spent a lot of time with my parents. He caught cold quite often and he used to say, "Bring me to *Dziadzius* and *Babunia* ("grandmother" in Polish). *Babunia* knows how to cure me very fast." On one of these occasions I overheard another conversation between Michel and my father. They were sitting in the living room, listening to the radio. The broadcaster was talking about Nobel Prize winners. Michel caught the name Nobel and asked my father who Nobel was. My father explained to him Nobel's role in history, that he had invented dynamite and, seeing the effects of his invention when it was used as a weapon, was very sorry. His invention made Nobel a wealthy man in a short time. He felt guilty and set up a fund to be used as an annual prize for people who promote peace and who work for the "good of humanity."

Another conversation took place a few months later, also in my parents' house. It showed me how Michel could formulate his opinions in front of my father.

Again they were listening to the radio. The broadcaster on the talk show asked the audience in the studio and the listeners to answer the question, "Who is more important in life, a man or a woman?" Before anyone else could answer, Michel said without hesitation, "A woman is because she gives birth to a child."

When I think about influences during the formative years of a child, I find that the shaping of character is as important as teaching the child how to read and write. When Michel was older he often talked to his father about justice. Sigmond suffered a lot in his life but he was a compassionate man and the war had not changed his approach to God, in spite of his suffering. He taught Michel to always be aware "before whom we stand." He taught Michel that we are responsible for our actions to God and our fellow human beings at the same time.

Michel dedicated his book *Jerusalem Breezes* to Sigmond, with these words: "Dedicated to the memory of my father, Sigmond Shore, a noble and fine man of word."

Sigmond loved his sons and tried to implant strength of character in them. It was interesting that he treated Michel and Jacques, who was eight years younger, according to their personalities. He tried to spend a lot of time with Jacques, as they both loved watching sports and certain television programs. Often, I listened to their conversations and I admired Sigmond for instilling confidence in his younger son at a very early age.

Jacques was eleven years old when he lost his father, but very shortly after Sigmond passed away, I could see Jacques trying to follow his father's attitudes to life. While observing Jacques, I often thought of Sigmond. Sigmond lost his mother at the age of ten, and her death left an indelible mark on him. But in spite of it, Sigmond found a way to enjoy life, and one day he even said to me that his mother had left a lot of happiness in him. His love for life was again on trial when he found out after the war (during the war he fought in the forest as a partisan) that his wife, his son, his father, his stepmother, a sister and stepsister had perished during the war.

After meeting and marrying me, he regained his zest for life and knew how to appreciate every day.

There was something remarkable in Sigmond's strength when he helped people in distress. When Elio, his part-time bookkeeper in Montreal, suffered a terrible tragedy (his wife and his 19-year-old son were killed in a fire), Sigmond decided to act. Elio, originally from Italy, had emigrated from Morocco with his wife, Adele, and two sons. They were very happy in their adopted country. Marco, his elder son, was an excellent student and just a few weeks earlier had received the highest award in Quebec. He studied engineering at McGill University. The day the fire broke out in the apartment house where they lived, Elio, with his younger son Aldo, jumped from the third-floor window, but Marco and Adele perished.

Aldo was not injured but Elio had broken his leg and became severely depressed. Sigmond offered Elio and Aldo our home, and they lived with us for several weeks. During this time Sigmond spent his free time with this man who had lost his equilibrium. Elio started to walk again and gradually regained his mental strength in our home. I realized later that Sigmond, by giving him the example of someone who overcame the tragedy of losing his wife and son, had helped him greatly.

Their conversations took place mainly in the dining room, and very often Jacques was there, since he liked to do his homework with someone in the same room. One day, after Sigmond passed away, Elio came and talked to me in that same dining room. Jacques was doing his homework as always. At one point Elio started to complain. We talked about his loss, and I told him how difficult it was for me to go forward as well. We did not know that Jacques was listening. Suddenly, my eleven-year-old son raised his head, stopped writing, and said, "C'est la vie." (We always spoke with Elio in French.) I will never forget this "c'est la vie." In my son's voice was a maturity beyond his years. I understood that his father had given him the strength to go forward in life. Elio and I did not continue our conversation. Jacques had the wisdom of acceptance, and he gave strength to grown people, to us.

From generation to generation we transmit our way of seeing, of feeling, and it is up to us to carry on while keeping in mind where we live and the people we meet. My brother Adam and I are the products of our upbringing and of the history that unfolded before our eyes. We retained the values of the past and later adapted them to our new surroundings. Through his work and his knowledge, Adam achieved very important positions in his profession, in France, in Canada, and now in the United States. He was the executive director and president of an industrial enterprise. He often quotes our parents. Not long ago told me that one of his friends asked him why he gave charity to a man who came to his office, one of many who came for donations. His friend said that many of the people that came to him did not deserve charity. Adam told him what his own father had said, many years before. "If ten people come to you for charity and nine of them do not deserve it, remember that maybe the tenth one really needs it. You do not know who this tenth one is, therefore you should support all of them." As I listened to my brother, the atmosphere of our home in Poland came back to me in Philadelphia where we both live now. Changing countries, getting to know new people, and adapting to new cultures had not diminished the lessons of yesterday.

As I write this book about Pope John Paul II and about my own life, I think that if this book aims to build bridges, I should show my attitude in every issue of life that I consider significant.

I respect myself and my values, but at the same time I have the same respect – absolutely the same – for the values of people from different cultures, religions, and upbringings. Not only do I respect them, but my feelings are also very often involved in experiences with people whose culture or religion is different from mine. I remember one day I was in il Duomo in Milan on the evening of All Souls Day. Thousands of candles had been lit by worshippers in memory of their loved ones. I did not know anyone in this cathedral, but seeing the flickering lights was a moving experience. Serenity and silence spread through all those long naves. I do not know why, but I am sure I will never forget that evening. I also know that whenever I am in the Vatican I go to the crypts of Pope Julius II and Pope John XXIII. I say a Hebrew prayer near the place where Julius II is buried. I am grateful to him for inspiring Michelangelo to paint the Sistine Chapel and leaving us the "Genesis" with the *Creation of Adam*. I also stand near Pope John XXIII's burial site and thank him for initiating the Second Vatican Council, after witnessing the atrocities committed against Jews in Bulgaria.

In Philadelphia on All Souls Day, I go to the Roman Catholic cathedral, although this is not my holiday. I ask one of the priests to open the door to the steps leading downstairs, where John Cardinal Krol is buried, and I say Kaddish, the Jewish prayer for the dead in Aramaic. This is my prayer.

When I read about Buddhism or the religion of Tao, I admire the concepts.

When I read the al-Fatihah prayer of Islam I find connections to Judaism and Christianity. When I interpret the parable Jesus told of the Prodigal Son, I reflect about the gift of forgiveness. I read "Canticle to the Sun" written by St. Francis of Assisi as a song about seeing nature as the creation of God and it means a lot to me. I am also grateful to St. Francis for having the strength to leave an affluent family, to work for the poor, and at the same time to teach people how to admire the sun, the moon, and to freely express their feelings. It was St. Francis who inspired poets and painters. Without him we might not have known Dante or Giotto. Without St. Francis, the Renaissance could not have taken place. When I read St. John of the Cross explain his poem "The Dark Night of the Soul" as the "spiritual illumination and the union of God through love," I enter the sphere of mystical wisdom. The concept of seeking union with God through love becomes a road to spiritual purity. I begin to understand this great saint, who is not my saint, as someone who searched God through the scriptures and through his own humility and strength. He is not only a man of Christianity, he is a man who brings us all closer to God and humanity. For me, he crosses the boundaries of religions.

When I write this book about building bridges with different cultures and beliefs, I am writing about widening the horizon of understanding. When we try to build bridges we have to know about people: who they are, and why they are as they are. I try to help build these bridges from a place of humility, as a pawn on the chessboard of the world. I must be sincere when I talk about my way of seeing life, or this book will not contain the truth as I perceive it.

Thomas Merton wrote in *No Man Is an Island,*

If I am to know the will of God, I must have the right attitude toward life. I must first of all know what life is, and to know the purpose of my existence.[64]

Through being acquainted with different forms of worship and beliefs, my way of thinking enables me to appreciate others. How easy it is to misjudge people about whom we know nothing.

An encounter with a landscape, with a painting or with people often changes our lives. Suddenly, the secret self-dynamics are awakened, and feelings dictate to us how to enter a new road, how to make decisions that would not be made without this encounter. The impact provides us with the hope of reaching for new horizons. Only years later, while judging our position in the light of our reasoning, do we become aware of our courage, which prevailed over unseen difficulties.

My life was changed when Father Joseph Papin of Villanova University saw my small book of poems, *May the Flowers Grow*, on the desk of my late and very dear cousin, Dr. Albin Schiff. Those poems on Jewish topics prompted Father Papin to write to me in Montreal, asking me if one short excerpt from my book could be included in a Villanova publication. I gave permission and a few months later I met Father Papin. At that time I was completing my master's degree in Comparative Education at McGill University and was hoping to advance to a Ph.D. in aesthetics. Father Papin told me that as a survivor of the Holocaust I should rather take my Ph.D. in Philosophy, with special emphasis on the Holocaust era.

He recommended Dropsie University to me, and I followed his advice. Dropsie University was interested in my topic for a Ph.D. thesis on the Holocaust and offered me a two-year scholarship. I decided to commute from Montreal to Philadelphia for two days every week. Jacques was already at the University of Ottawa, and I could focus on my own studies.

Immediately after I made my decision, Michel, who had finished his studies in law at the University of Montreal and had obtained his M.A. in philosophy at McGill, followed my example and pursued his studies in philosophy at Dropsie University. My Ph.D. program was very interesting. We were surrounded by renowned scholars such as Solomon Zeitlin, Jacob Agus, Ephraim Efros. During this time I recalled with gratitude those other professors who had been a part of my life: Guy Rocher from the University of Montreal; Roger Magnusson and Nicholas Coccalis (my M.A. thesis advisor) from McGill; and Dr. Moses Tannenzaft, who taught me English for four months after I first arrival in Montreal. While I was studying in Philadelphia, many memories surfaced from my previous schools and universities which had helped to shape my character and my way of thinking. During the war, the director of the Lwow Conservatory, Jan Soltys, believed in my musical abilities. He convinced me to stay and study, although I had to earn money for our livelihood since my father could not find any work as a lawyer. I listened to Jan Soltys and later on his letter would save my family and me from deportation to Russia. And it was while studying political science at the University of Paris that I learned how to debate with even the most ardent of adversaries.

Dropsie University offered Michel and me many different approaches to philosophy and history. In December 1972, one of my professors, Dr. Solomon Grayzel, invited me to deliver a lecture on the Holocaust at a colloquium sponsored by three universities: Villanova, Dropsie, and Lehigh. I accepted, and in order to prepare for it, I decided to visit Yad Vashem, the centre for documentation of the Holocaust in Jerusalem. I wanted to search for documents that would show the humaneness of the Holocaust victims even at the moment of death. I also wanted to find the testimonies of non-Jews who had helped Jews during the war.

After studying some of the documents, which had never been examined until then, I chose to quote some excerpts in my lecture, which I later published in my book entitled *Forty Years After Darkness*.

When six million Jews died, some letters remained – those which were not destroyed or which were not sent from Jewish homes by strangers. These strangers very often did not know to whom the letter belonged. They were only a few words on a piece of paper, which may once have represented a treasure; words of love addressed to dear ones; or perhaps a description of an unforgettable sunset, which in many places disappeared together with their authors. Some letters remained. [65]

Of the letters that remained, two had travelled a long way. These two express the thoughts of many, many people. As a remembrance of the victims of the Second World War, these two letters became symbolic and should never be forgotten.

The first letter was written in Polish at the Majdanek concentration camp. The letter was signed Jozef Kalisman. He wrote this letter on the eve of his death. It is addressed to his wife. No one knows if this letter even reached her. No one even knows if the wife of Jozef Kalisman survived. All that is known is that Jozef Kalisman was killed in Majdanek. One part of the letter reads:

Death is not terrible, if we do not know about her. It is only a fraction of a second.

This man, who knew he was going to die, tried to describe his death as nothing terrible. He wanted to console his wife with loving words in the time of her sadness. Only two sentences talk about death; the rest is a love letter. A man who knew that he would die asked his wife, a woman whom he loved very deeply, to go on without him and enjoy life. He encouraged her not to despair. He assured her that one day the war would end and life would once again be beautiful. He went on to say that she should find someone else with whom to share her life, that sharing was a natural way to continue life, and that she should not deny herself the joy of it. He concluded his letter by saying,

My dear, please forget everything; but when many years from now you look at my picture, think only that I was somebody who loved you sincerely.

This letter, which was found after the war and sent to Yad Vashem, contains the most human legacy of all: remember how to enjoy life. The words "somebody who loved you sincerely" speak for all those who loved life and who wanted to transcend the limits of their own lives by this love. These people never believed that Hitler would win; they always tried to foresee a bright future. It is important to remember the circumstances in which this letter was written, and the place where it was written, Majdanek concentration camp.

In those places of horror, the vision of tomorrow gave strength to those condemned to die. Why? Because these people, who were condemned to die, still loved life and were concerned with life even after death.

I also wrote about the letter that I saw in 1946 in Paris.

This second letter was written by a French Jew, a young poet. At the top of the letter, displayed at the exhibition in France immediately after the war, is typewritten information: "A letter from prison written by a young poet who took part in the resistance." This letter is addressed to the poet's mother.

The young poet wrote about the joy of living and the joy of participating in the fight for a better tomorrow. He asked his mother not to cry, because for him, it was worth the sacrifice of his life. In his imagination, the young man saw the world after the war. He was certain that this world would be beautiful and just. In the small room of an old house near the Champs Elysées in Paris, the letter shone in the sun. The ray of sun endowed the letter with a special light. Was the sun trying to attract the attention of those people visiting the exhibition, to the words of a fighter for whom the future was more important than his own death?

The two letters, of Jozef Kalisman and the French poet, cannot be forgotten. In them there is a plea and a wish; there is the thought of two men, an immortal thought, to remind survivors that no bullets can kill the spirit of man. The two men who wrote these letters left the legacy of the six million who died: Remember to enjoy life. If you enjoy life, if you appreciate life, you will try to build the world according to the vision of the victims and their deaths will be honoured.

Say Kaddish, but do not forget to sing a song afterward. Somewhere far away, the six million who perished will know that their dreams are part of our present, and of the future for the generations who come after us.[66]

During one session of the Colloquium in April 1973, I delivered the lecture and finished with my poem "The Cry from Warsaw." [67]

I remember a spring
like the others before.
I remember the rays of sunshine.

I remember the fields covered with grass,
the green forests,
the flowers and gardens.

I remember a bird,
an enchanted bird,
blessing its nest with a song.

I remember young girls,
who smiled every night
at their lovers
on the eve of death.

I remember one spring
and a stream of blood
in 1943.

I remember men,
handsome and strong,
long, long ago.

My friend,
do you understand?
No, you will never understand.
In my country of today,
in this blessed country,
it is hard to understand
the suffering of yesterday.
We have grown blind to suffering.

I remember many kinds of men,
some of them with the hearts of stone,

some of them with the heart of a child.
They did not want to die
at the age of twenty,
twenty-five years ago.

Millions were dying then
every day on the cross –
the cross of hate.

My brothers speak to me each night.
From far away I hear their cry,
the cry from Warsaw.

Across my memories,
their shadows appear.
Their eyes are watching me,
I see them in my beating heart.
They live there:
the children who never became men,
the women who never became mothers,
men, hounded beings,
who whispered:
"We do not want to die."

And I remember men
who did not whisper at all.
Heroes without words,
they carried their heads high,
their hands strong as hammers
Resolved to fight,
Only their hands.
For their minds knew
that they could never win
against the foe.
They fought for dignity
and for one page in history
to be written after their death.

The page is still unwritten,
for the conscience of the masters of history
is sound asleep.
I walk through the streets of Paris.
I enter the Opera.
I listen to *Faust*
by Gounod.

The devil on the stage is kind,
very kind.
Why did I see so many devils
in my life?
The devil is dancing.
How many dancing devils have passed by
on my journeys,
laughing, grinning, cruel,
but they could not take from me
the love of life.

My brothers in Warsaw
loved life as I do.
They died
because no one was listening
to their cry.
No one condemned their useless deaths.

I walk through the streets of New York.
I stroll down Fifth Avenue.
I look at the windows full of light.
They are too bright for me,
and in the middle of all the lights
I see the darkness of Mila Street
and I hear Chopin
from far away,
Chopin played by my friend.
The "Polonaise in A major" follows me.
It is mighty and great.
My friend is dead,

but his music is still in my ears.
Chopin accompanies
the cry from Warsaw.

In Carnegie Hall,
I close my eyes.
I want to forget my past.
I dream with the orchestra.
The conductor is my master
in the enchanted world of harmony.

An hour or two pass by,
And suddenly, the soloist,
with one note of despair,
reminds me of you,
you, who are gone,
and you,
and you.

I travel round the world.
At La Scala in Milan,
I search for the music of peace.
The *Oratorio* of Haydn
is merciful
for those who look for mercy,
powerful
for those who are powerful,
human and deep, for those who suffer,
weeping along with me.

In Vancouver near the ocean,
I watch the quiet waves
and listen to their song.
Time is passing,
fast as the wind.
Where are the children
who did not grow?

The cry from Warsaw follows me,
in Venice, in Calgary,
in Los Angeles, in Geneva.
On any street, any noise,
reminds me of other sounds
of other streets,
where noises mingled
with the staccato of machine guns,
They still rise up to heaven
night and day.

In San Francisco,
on the Golden Gate Bridge,
I ask myself:
Will I find my own bridge one day,
the bridge between my past
and my present?
Yes, I will.

When the ear of the world
will touch the soil
to kneel in repentance
for what it has done.

When the hands of the world
will join to build
a happier tomorrow.

When the eyes of the world
will see the truth,
when the heart of the world
will be strong enough to love,
then the cry from Warsaw
will pass away.

My lecture was very well received, and during the colloquium many scholars and clergy people presented their views on the Holocaust. One of the main speakers was Cardinal John Krol of Philadelphia, who was of Polish descent. I was introduced to him and our friendship began at that point. He invited me to a meeting in the archdiocese, where he listened very attentively to my ideas about spreading understanding among different religions, races, and ethnic groups. Our friendship lasted from then to the day of his death in 1996. It was a warm relationship between two people often speaking Polish.

In 1974, I finished my studies in Philadelphia. The Dropsie University authorities had decided that since I had delivered a lecture on the Holocaust and I used some material from the research for my thesis on the Holocaust, I had to change my dissertation topic. I chose to write about Julian Tuwim, a poet who was very well known between the wars in Poland. I passed my oral and written exams (together with Michel) in 1974, and I decided to write my thesis in Montreal.

That same year, I met my second husband, John Edward Greenberg. I married Eddie, as I called him, in December 1974. He was a good, warmhearted man, a widower with three grown-up daughters, Mona, Gail, and Ava, who was the same age as Jacques. Born in Canada, Eddie tried to understand me and my way of thinking. I had great respect for him. I knew that he had taken care of his paralyzed wife and his three daughters for several years.

Like many other students, I did not complete my thesis right away. I was back working in business for a few years, doing my academic work whenever I could find the time. During my trips overseas, as always, I would visit museums and art galleries and I would expand my knowledge through many different encounters. One day while travelling to Europe I encountered Dr. Victor Frankl, with whom I had corresponded many years before from Montreal. He had survived Auschwitz and believed that if we have discovered meaning in life we can overcome our obstacles and difficulties. During my studies at McGill I had thought to write on meaning in life after reading his classic book *Man's Search for Meaning*. Dr. Frankl created logotherapy (logos in Greek means "meaning") for psychiatric patients. I planned to offer a structure – ten steps leading to finding meaning in life for everyone. I visited Dr. Frankl in Vienna in 1976. Our conversation lasted for two hours. Among other topics we also discussed the contribution of Dr. Albert Schweitzer in the twentieth century. I had admired Dr. Schweitzer for many years and I mentioned how grateful I was that after reading my book of French poems, *Le Pain de la Paix* (Bread of Peace), he had sent me a handwritten letter. Incidentally, this letter written a few days before his death is considered to be his last handwritten letter. In the letter Dr. Schweitzer commented on my poems and appreciated my ideas on peace.

At the end of my visit, Dr. Frankl invited me to his lecture in the *Wien Poliklinik.* I noted the young doctors listening to the lecture. They were very receptive to Dr. Frankl's methods and showed their appreciation. After the lecture Dr. Frankl introduced me to his students. He not only approved of my way of structuring the search for meaning in life in ten steps, but he also suggested that I establish my own centre, concentrating on teaching about the meaning of life. This encounter gave me a lot of courage.

I visited Dr. Frankl once again a few years later with Michel. Michel's M.A. thesis was on "cultural dialogue." I was very proud of my son, who in 1966 was one of two Canadian students to attend the University of Peace in Belgium. This University of Peace was organized by the Dominican priest Père Dominique Pire, who had received the Nobel Peace Prize. It was as a result of this experience that Michel decided to write about cultural dialogue. It was interesting to listen to Dr. Frankl and Michel discuss this subject and the possibility of a road leading to understanding between different people from different cultures. Dr. Frankl once again left a great impression on me, and Michel found the visit very special.

Now both my sons were grown up. Michel was working; Jacques, had finished two degrees – one at l'Université de Montréal and the other at McGill. Both of them were married. I decided to get down to writing my Ph.D. thesis, and when, in 1979, Adam was transferred to Philadelphia, Eddie and I decided to move there, too. One reason for the move was the climate. Eddie had had tuberculosis many years before, and in his later years the Canadian winters were becoming difficult for him. Eddie was very supportive while I was writing my thesis. He had been an accountant in Montreal, and after much searching he found work in Philadelphia.

In our first year there, I taught two courses at Gratz College. The next year, in 1980, I received my Ph.D., and the University of Pennsylvania offered me a fellowship in the School of Social Work, accepting my proposal on "ten steps in the land of life" as very valuable for people working in the helping professions.

It was only after I finished my work at the University of Pennsylvania that I established my own centre, The Lena Allen-Shore Center. Gratz College sent me students – teachers doing their master's degree who wanted to pursue their education. For a short time I also worked for the University of the Arts.

During this time, my dear friend Father Papin played an important role in my decisions. He believed that my idea of creating interdisciplinary courses for teachers could be very beneficial, especially in our era of specialization in one discipline.

Eddie helped me with his practical mind and gave me a lot of his time during those first months. I started with two courses; today there are 20 different courses that combine history and art, philosophy and art, philosophy and love, philosophy and education, and philosophy and life. Although Father Papin was there when the seed took root, he did not live to see the Center bloom. He died in 1981.

Many posters are displayed on my classroom walls. I often give them captions in the spirit of Eugène Delacroix, the French painter who wrote that "painting is the bridge between souls." On one of the prints, the *Praying Hands* by Albrecht Dürer, I wrote, "May we join hands with all those with whom we never joined hands before." With these words I often start some of my courses dealing with history or prejudice.

Around a long table sit my students, who live in a country made up of many different races, religions, and ethnic groups. I supplement my lectures with my songs. In a corner of the room is an upright piano. I realize more and more how I feel about the world around me. In 1993, I wrote in one of my poems,

America is not only
the country
of skyscrapers
and highways,
America is also
A country of dreams.

1993
Where have the dreams gone?
Where?
The drugs, the child abuse,
the danger on the streets,
the subway,
where fear reigns –
And the dreams, the dreams,
the dreams.
The American dream did not die.

How should we bring
the dreams back?
How should we take care
of children,
and bring security
to the subway
and to the streets?
How should we build the
shelters
for the homeless?

How should we create
a rainbow of colours
where black, yellow,
and white men
will understand each other?

When we watch the sky
and see a rainbow appear
in all its splendour,

there is a harmony of colours
on the rainbow.

Did you ever watch
the harmony of colours
in the rainbow?

I know
that there is no country
in the world
where dreams are as strong
as in the United States.
It is because the United States
was created from dreams,
at the base of the United States
are the dreams of the pioneers
and of those who came
to Ellis Island.

Try to imagine
the Irish man from Dublin
when he saw
the Statue of Liberty
for the first time.
The Irish man brought with him
an Irish song.

Try to imagine
the Italian
who came from Treviso.
In his luggage
he had a bottle of wine
to toast America.
And this Jewish immigrant
from Vitebsk
whose only wish was
to bring his children
to American soil.

There were others –
these people who lived
in the country,
they were brought as slaves
from Africa.

On plantations in the South
the songs were born.
The songs were born
from nostalgia, pain,
and the dreams, dreams, dreams.

The dreams were like
bouquets of flowers
intermingled
with prayers
and the music rose
up to the sky.

In New Orleans,
people listened
to jazz –
the rhythm, the rhythm,
the rhythm
and the blues
of many dreams.

So often
the dreams are shuttered.
So often
the dreams lay on the ground –
they disappeared for a while –
but the dreams
were never killed.

Somewhere in the Indian song
there was a cry
and the nostalgia

of those who lived
on American soil
before the followers
of Christopher Columbus came.

The pioneers and the Indians,
the slaves and the immigrants
they all struggled.
The pioneers and the
immigrants,
they struggled
and they sang songs.

The song came
from the Southern plantation,
the marches of the French
and English soldiers
mingled together
with Indian chants
and the melodies
of the Russian, Irish, Mexican
or Puerto Rican lullabies.
In this music of time
there were American hearts
beating together
in the rhythm
of the dreams,
their dreams.

I do not consider
anyone
who lives on our planet
to be a stranger.

We breathe the same way,
we are born the same way
and in the same way, we die.

Our tears are transparent.
Yes, the tears of a black,
yellow, or white man
resemble each other.
They are all crystal clear.
They are transparent.

Yes, the tears of a black,
yellow, or white man
resemble each other.
They are crystal clear.
They are transparent.

And
what do we want?
We all want to be happy
and to be loved.

I am American,
I am Canadian,
although I was born in Europe.
I started to dream about America
long, long ago.
Do you know,
that people dream
about America
miles and miles away?

There in different parts
of the world,
somewhere in Europe,
in Asia or Africa
some people dream
about the distant land,
located between the Atlantic
and the Pacific Ocean,
called the United States.

I remember there in the darkness
of the Second World War
as a young girl
I dreamed about a distant land.

In our dreams
the frontiers do not exist.
We cross the borders
without any passport
and without any visa.

During the Second World War,
I was far away
from Ellis Island,
I was far away
from the Statue of Liberty
but in my dream
the Statue of Liberty
watched over me.
It was great to know
that somewhere far away
there exists the Statue of Liberty.

Sometimes I think
that our dreams allow us
to withstand
cruel reality.
I teach teachers.
In my classroom
around a long table
I teach people
through art and philosophy
how to dream.

Many of the teachers
talk about their students.

They worry about them,
they bring to my classroom
hundreds of classrooms –
many children of today
do not know
how to dream.
The children are sad.

I want their children
to dream again.

(Presently I have dual citizenship, Canadian and American.)
A few years later, I wrote in another poem:

If every parent
would instill in her child
a sense of respect
for human life,
maybe our streets would be safer.
If every parent would provide his child
with a home, a real home
where children are kissed every night
and "good night" brings warmth
and love strengthens a sense of belonging
to a family, to a community
maybe there would be
fewer drug addicts.
If every parent would instill
in his child
a sense of justice
and teach the child about the difference
between good and evil,
maybe there would be
less violence and less crime.
There is also another danger
growing in the country –
prejudice.
The barriers abolished
for several years
are coming back
like a devil,
appearing in the corners
of the cities,
and the parks,
and proclaiming the power
of his destruction.

We can create
rehabilitation centres
for the drug addicts
but we cannot create
rehabilitation centres

for the fanatics –
and any fanaticism
brings a disaster,
fosters terrorism
and provokes
more anger and hate.

I teach teachers.
Once in my classroom
a student, an excellent teacher,
brought a quilt,
a huge beautiful quilt
made forty-five years ago
by his family.
This student-teacher
grew up in Maryland.
He told us
that there were fourteen in his
family
and they earned their livelihood
by making quilts.
All the students around
admired
the beautiful, colourful quilt
and the quilt became
a symbol of unity.
Those families, similar
to the family of my student
built America.
They were creating the quilts
of strength
the strength of different colours.

I often mention my experiences.
I am including my thoughts
in the poem
about the country
where I live.
Why am I doing this?
Why do I feel that I should do
so?
I believe
that only
by expressing the personal
approach
to issues
which are dear to us,
we can create an atmosphere
of universal understanding –
yes – from personal to universal.
Every member
of the human family
is a link in history.

The years passed by fast – so fast. Eddie died in March 1990. For fifteen years I had experienced a relationship built on trust and respect. A good, great man was gone, and there were many difficult steps to climb again – steps to overcome loneliness and steps of sorrow for someone who loved life. I had to struggle again.

In one of my songs, I wrote,

You struggle and you fight
with the currents of your life.
You feel your tears and pain
in the snow and in the rain.

You close your eyes and dream
of yesterdays gone by.
You search in your own heart
for someone, for a guide.

The silence stops.
I hear the song
of childhood days,
and of my home,
from far away
in time and space
I see my father's smiling face.

He sings for me
from high above
of love, of never-ending love
and he repeats
an old refrain,
go out and face life again.

As the years passed, some of my close friends died. I lost my dear friend Father Papin in 1981. In 1996, I lost another dear friend, the Cardinal of Philadelphia, John Krol. I realized after his death how much I had cherished my conversations with him. Our conversations took place first in the archdiocese and later, after he retired, in his private residence.

I will always remember one visit in 1993, in the Thomas Jefferson Hospital, where Cardinal Krol had been admitted. I knew that he had to spend Christmas in the hospital. On the first day of Christmas in the afternoon, Donna, my daughter-in-law, took me to the hospital since I don't drive in the city.

At the information desk I asked for Cardinal Krol and I said that I had spoken to the archdiocese where the secretary had given me the number of his room. The receptionist asked me if I was a member of his family. I answered that I was only a friend but would appreciate it if the nurse on the floor would ask the Cardinal if he wished to see me.

The Cardinal was happy to see me. He was alone. He told me that forty people had come before noon to celebrate Mass with him, and now he was alone. At that moment I realized that he was more vulnerable than ever. We started to talk. The nurse came and wanted to take his blood pressure. However, the Cardinal asked her to come back later. The Cardinal told me that he felt weak and that he was not young anymore. When he told me this I approached his bed without thinking and put my hand on his shoulder. I held his hand for a moment and said, "Your Eminence will regain his strength – you have to be strong." Suddenly I realized that my hand was still on his shoulder. I went back to my chair and we continued our conversation. As I was about to leave, the Cardinal called me to his bed. He put his hand on my head and said, "I have to bless you." I knew that in the Cardinal's blessing was his prayer and his heart. When I came downstairs, the air outside was no longer cold – or maybe the blessing of the Cardinal had left its warmth with me.

We met several times afterwards, always in his residence. At this time the Cardinal was in a wheelchair, always attended by his secretary, Father Robert Powell. Besides being a priest, Fr. Powell also had a Ph.D. in musicology and was an accomplished pianist. The Cardinal had a piano in his salon and often asked me to play my songs. One morning around Christmas 1995, after I played, the Cardinal asked Father Powell to play and sing one of Irving Berlin's compositions, "Count Your Blessings." Father Powell sang and we all hummed the melody.

I also remember that after he saw a video of the performance of my cantata in Polish, he asked me to sing for him "My Road to Jerusalem." Another of my songs which the Cardinal liked very much went:

I hear the nightingale and
I wonder why his voice is so soft
and sweet.
On summer nights I hear the
thunder
and I see many trembling trees,
who is there high above
who is there, who is there
high above
and everywhere...

During what was to be my final visit with him, Cardinal Krol said that he had a gift for me. It was a book. With his trembling hand he wrote a dedication for me.

A few months later the poem "The Cry of Warsaw," set to music by the Boston-based composer Andrew Vores, was performed together with five poems by poets from different countries as the finale of a recital, first in one of the synagogues in Boston and later in the St. Ignatius Church of Boston College. There were ninety-five people in the Brookline Choir and twenty-five in the orchestra. More than a thousand people attended. When one of the members of the choir came to greet me, he said that for three months of rehearsals he had lived with "The Cry of Warsaw." I thought of Cardinal Krol and of our encounter during the Colloquium in 1973, when I first read "The Cry of Warsaw" for the large audience there and Cardinal Krol had been moved by my poem.

* * *

In the next seven chapters, I continue the story of Pope John Paul II and his tireless work of building bridges between people of different cultures and religions. And I continue my own story and show how the Holy Father's example inspires the work to which I have dedicated my life. These chapters, like some earlier chapters in the book, are written in the form of poetry. Throughout my life, reading and writing poetry has given expression to some of my deepest thoughts and feelings.

In the Plane

In the air circled the plane.

In the air circled thoughts.

Some thoughts float in the air
like a delicate lace,
ingeniously crafted
with shining thread.
These thoughts bless the earth
and kiss the new-born babies
in their little cradles.

In the air circled thoughts.

Some thoughts are brutal,
they shine like the surface
of a sharp knife,
made from the best steel.
These thoughts spread hate,
reach people
who wander
on the roads and paths
of weakness,
and often become victims
of the leaders of evil.
Evil provokes wars

and later on after many years
dances heroically
on the fields of battle
and on the pages of history
of mankind.

In the air circled thoughts.

Thoughts can
in one second
unite people,
they can attain
the distant relics
of a mystery
in human nature.
Thoughts can swim
in one second
on the surface of the oceans
and kiss the drops of dew
with respect
for the transparent truth
of their existence.
Thoughts can create
in one second
the atmosphere
of a warm dream.

Thoughts can dictate
in one second
the words of a prayer
the text of which it
is not possible to find
even in the illuminated
manuscripts.
This prayer allows the pupils
of some chosen people
to see the fringe
of the beauty of God
and sanctify God with love.

In the plane
near the window,
a priest in white attire
was weaving his thoughts.
The priest-poet,
the Holy Father, John Paul II,
was travelling
to his native country.

Why in June 1999
did the guide of 700 million
Catholics,
the guide
who often in his prayers
was thinking of the whole
mankind,
want to come back
even for a few days
to Poland?

The year 2000
was approaching fast,
the new millennium
was throwing a glance
toward all the inhabitants

of the planet earth.
The new millennium
full of riddles,
mysteries, and secrets
once again
was recalling
the past,
this past which left the trace,
the footprints of man
in history,
the trace
of millions of thoughts,
the trace
of dreams,
dreamed sometimes
on the shores of the oceans,
the shores of the lakes,
or streams
in the mountains,
or in the valleys.

Do only people dream?
Maybe, maybe
the trees have their dreams,
and maybe the mountains,
unreachable and magnificent,
pray to remain existent
and sing with the wind
hymns
about the majesty of the
Creator.

Do only people dream?
Maybe the seagulls, the skylarks
and sparrows
have their prayers
and want to have their place
on the earth,

the place that they can call
their nest.
In this nest
the mother gives them life
and after teaches them
how to live.

In the plane
reigned silence.
The Holy Father thought about
his nest.
And maybe the words
of Psalm 84
about home
that "as the sparrow finds a home
and the swallow a nest
to settle her young,
my home is by your altars,
Lord of hosts,
my King and my God."

The Holy Father
was returning
for a few days
to his nest,
to Poland,
to his country.
In this country,
in his family home, in Wadowice
his parents taught their child
how to love God and man.
This child, after many years,
became a pope.

And maybe the words
of the 84th Psalm
came back
with all the force of nostalgia.

This nostalgia
maybe older
than 2000 years:
How to find the altars of God
according to the commandments
offered for safe-keeping
in Sinai.

The past, present,
and future
were meeting
in a poet,
who became a pope.

Pope John Paul II,
the priest in the white attire
thought
that He was listening
to the voices,
sobbing, lamenting –
and to the cry of children.

In the air circled
the tears of the victims
of hate,
prejudices.

In the air circled
millions of unfulfilled dreams,
dreams of people,
who were not allowed
to grow, live, and love.
And a wandering song
of an old black man
from Mississippi
who sang
"Tired of living
and scared of dying,"

the song "Old Man River" also
wandered in the air
of the world.

The songs remain
although the people are gone.
The plane was approaching
Poland.
In the air circled
grains of dust
from the gas chambers
which reached the air
of Europe, Africa, America,
Asia, and Australia.
Like the song of the black man
from Mississippi,
the grains of dust
never will leave the air.
These grains of dust
will remain forever.
The victims for whom
no one erected monuments
after their deaths
left a trace
in the air.
Maybe the wind
says the prayer
for the dead
during cold evenings in winter.
Some tears from the whole world
come back
with the rain,
the tears of the innocents,
persecuted,
Armenians, Gypsies, Jews,
Indians, black people,
Poles, who were hiding
the Jewish children

during the Second World War
a bunch of just people
who were punished
because they were listening
to their conscience,
the tears of Cardinal Saliege in
France
and the tears of Bishop
Lichtenberg
in Germany,
the tears of John Brown
in the United States
who defended blacks
and the tears of those
who were the victims
or witnessed
the massacres in Biafra,
Rwanda, Cambodia, Vietnam,
Sarajevo, and Kosovo,
the tears of the nameless,
who are not remembered
by history.

The victims perished
in the name of injustice,
which was blaspheming
with its existence
against God
and often was leading wars
in the name
of faith.

In the air circled thoughts
and the voices
and the sounds of those
which even the wind
could not muffle.

The plane was approaching
Poland
and suddenly
in his memory
the Holy Father
saw himself
almost 60 years before
in the Wawel Cathedral
on the first day of the war
on the first day of September
1939.
He never forgot this day.
On this memorable Friday
as every month
Karol Wojtyla came for
confession
and Holy Communion.
Father Figlewicz asked the young
student
to serve in the Holy Mass
when from the streets
the sounds of explosions and
bombs
were heard.
The Holy Father never forgot
this morning Mass
from 60 years before
in the year 1939.
Karol Wojtyla did not know
that he would become a pope
but he prayed fervently, ardently
for justice
and that men should be
true men,
men created in the image
of God.

The years passed.

At the threshold
of the new millennium
the Holy Father understood
that really nothing was changed
in him.
He prayed in the plane,
as he had long before
in the Wawel Cathedral,
for men to be true men
created in the image
of God.

The pope-poet
was searching for the dawn,
a new dawn
for the whole of mankind.
In the air circled thoughts
and one ray of sun
touched the pupils
of the passenger
in the white attire.

In the cabin of the plane
the words of the pilot were
heard:
"In a few minutes
we will be landing in Poland."

The poet-pope
prayed fervently, ardently
and the prayer flew
on the wings of the butterflies
high, high . . . .

Jerusalem

Every morning at dawn
Jerusalem repeats
the words of the prophets.
Jerusalem does not forget
the sages
of the olden days.

Every morning
the stones of Jerusalem
recall
the steps of those
who walked
within her borders.

Every morning
from far away
the echo of the prayers
reaches the walls of Jerusalem
and at the gates
some words are retained –
the echo stops there,
but the wind carries onward
the prayers of those
who believe
in One God.

On March 23, 2000
(Adar II 5760
according to the Jewish
calendar),
the wind was strong but gentle.
It became softer
near Mount Herzl.
There on this mount
the greatest dreamer
Theodor Herzl is buried.
He was a modern prophet
who fifty years before
in his dreamer's vision
imagined
the State of Israel.
Theodor Herzl
encouraged the Jews
to come back
to the fields and valleys
of their ancestors
and plant the vineyards
as in the days
of David or Salomon.

The wind stopped
for a while,

paid respect to the great man
and after continued its journey.

The wind circled –

The Mount Memorial
was nearby.

On this mount was built
Yad Vashem
named in memory
of the 6,000,000 Jews
slaughtered in Europe
during the Second World War.

Yad Vashem –

We read in Isaiah 56:5,
"And to them will I give
in my house
and within my walls
a memorial [yad vashem]
that shall
not be cut off."

Were the 6,000,000 Jews cut off
from life, from history –
from mankind – from humanity?
Yes – they were cut off
because
during the war
life became a display
of evil deeds
permitted in the name
of hate.

Were they cut off from history?
Yes – they were

because history
did not remember
the errors and acts of cruelty
of the past.

Were they cut off from mankind?
Yes – they were,
because mankind
was no more mankind –
it was a jungle of beasts
for whom the prey was
an innocent man, a woman or a
child
the martyrs,
who clung
to God from Sinai.

Were they cut off from
humanity?
Yes – they were
because humanity in humans
was asleep –
like the bears in winter –
the conscience of the killers
was drawn into the abyss
of madness.

Yes – they were cut off –
but
when Jews want to deny
reality –
they search in the prophets
for the source of hope
and therefore
they took the words of Isaiah
and built
the Monument and the
Memorial.

The Monument and the
Memorial
in its silence screams.

The scream of silence
is the most frightening
experience.
The souls whisper
but we don't hear them –
we can only feel . . . the souls
as sometimes we feel
the wind touching
our foreheads.

On the day March 23, 2000
(Adar II 5760),
a crowd of people
was waiting.
They were waiting
for the head of the Church,
Pope John Paul II.

And he came
in his long white robe.

He came – a humble priest.
Yes – he was humble.

He entered the Hall of
Remembrance.

In this dark, sombre room
in the heart of suffering
reigned the eternal flame –
delicate, trembling,
the eternal flame
burning
in the memory of the victims.

The Ankor choir,
under the direction
of Dafne ben Johanon,
sang quietly
"We walk to Caesarea."

The voices of the young people
were delicate –
soft – not loud,
respecting the solemn moment –

and then

His Holiness Pope John Paul II
rekindled the eternal flame
and the flame
became stronger –
and the flame gave light
to the wall behind,
the wall made of stones –
large, huge stones –
maybe stones from Galilee –
Suddenly in the room
there were the stones
and the eternal flame –
the stones and the eternal flame
they were strong and powerful.

This flame
was the remembrance
of the victims –
not only of their lives –
this eternal flame
was the remembrance
of the dreams of those
who perished,
the dreams of those
who were killed

only because
they were Jews.

These dreams were
as important as their lives.
When we say 6,000,000
we see 6,000,000
a nameless,
a faceless crowd.

This eternal flame
wanted to give faces to these
people
in light –
this eternal flame
wanted to give them respect
for their dreams
which never came true.

This flame
was recalling
mothers
singing lullabies
to their children.

This flame
was recalling
the thoughts of scientists,
poets, scholars
who wanted to contribute
to understanding
the roads to God's wisdom.

This flame
was recalling
the hands of the tailors,
shoemakers
and the hands of the farmers

who were planting seeds in the
fields
and wanted to see
the harvest.
This flame
was recalling
one and a half million children
who wanted to grow and love.

And there were stones –
the stones of endurance
of centuries.
These indestructible stones
which were the symbols
of those
who in spite of persecution
endured their faith.

Can the endurance of man
be as strong as the endurance
of stones?

The Jews endured hate
in different forms
throughout the centuries.
One form of hate
became the most dangerous –
the sound of voices
repeating:
"You Jews
are the Christ killers."
These words echoed
through space and time.

The Jewish children
were afraid of the cross
the Jewish women
were afraid of the cross,

and the Jewish men
could not defend themselves
when they were called
the Christ killers.

Did the souls
of the people
belonging
to the faceless
and nameless crowd
killed during the Second World
War
come to Yad Vashem?
Maybe they came.
Did other souls
from different centuries come?
Maybe more than 6,000,000
wanted to enter
the dark sombre room
with the eternal flame
and the stones of endurance?

The victims of slaughter
from York in England,
from Blois in France,
from Spain, Portugal,
Ukraine, Russia
were invited to enter the space
in the small room.

The souls do not take
a lot of space
and they are invisible.

They came to listen
to the just, good man.

The silence reigned

for a while.
Then someone read
a letter
describing the memories
of a 14-year-old girl
who after being liberated
from the camp in 1945
decided to walk to Krakow.

At one point –
she understood
that she could not walk anymore.
and then the miracle occurred –
At the moment that she thought
she would die,
a young man came in a brown
robe
– a priest –
she thought he was a priest.
He brought her food
and afterward carried her
on his back
to the railway station.

This was the young seminarian
Karol Wojtyla.
He called her Edita –
there in the camp
she was a number only –
The young man
brought her back
to life.

Edith Zierer
came to Yad Vashem
to thank the man
who saved her life.

In Psalm 8 we read:
"What is the mortal
that thou rememberest him?
and the son of man
that thou thinkest of him?
Yet thou hast made him
but a little less
than angels
and hast crowned him
with honour and glory."

The Pope laid flowers
on the ashes
of the concentration camp
victims.
These ashes came from far away.

The address of the Guide
of the Church
was revealing his emotions.

The words were chosen
each word was meaningful:
"Men, women and children
cry out to us
from the depths
of the horror
that they knew.
How can we fail
to heed their cry?"

Later he continued:

As bishop of Rome
and successor
of the Apostle Peter,
"I assure the Jewish people
that the Catholic Church

motivated by the Gospel law
of truth and love
and by no political
considerations,
is deeply saddened
by the hatred acts
of persecution
and displays of anti-Semitism
directed against the Jews
by Christians at any time
and any place."

The ceremony ended
with the choir
singing
"Ani Ma'amin Ani Ma'amin."

This was the same prayer
that Jews have repeated
for centuries.
Ani Ma'amin
I believe, I believe –
the eternal flame
listened
the eternal stones
listened
and people
in the dark, somber room –

Did the souls repeat
beyond their lives
Ani Ma'amin?
Did the souls disappear
with the voices of the living
singing from generation
to generation
I believe?

After a few days
His Holiness John Paul II
went to the Kotel –
the Western Wall
and with humility
and respect
put his letter
between the crevices
of the stones
of the temple.

The Pontiff stood a while
he bent his head –

The text of the letter was:
"God of our fathers,
you chose Abraham and his
descendants
to bring your name to the
Nations:
we are deeply saddened
by the behaviour of those
who in the course of history
have caused these children
of yours to suffer,
and asking your forgiveness
we wish to commit ourselves
to genuine brotherhood
with the people
of the Covenant.

Jerusalem, 26 March 2000."

Were the flowers of Jerusalem
whispering
that maybe the day of peace
will come
into the world –

or
maybe the flowers
which grow
on Jerusalem soil
were familiar
with the Psalm of David:
"May the Lord bless these
out of Zion: and see
thou the happiness
of Jerusalem
all the days of your life.
And see thou
the children's children:
may there be peace
upon Israel."

When Karol Wojtyla
was a child
his mother said:
"Maybe he will be a priest –
maybe he will be a great man."
John Paul II fulfilled
the wish of his mother –
Her dream came true.

Spring and
the Vanished World

Ottawa
April 22, 1992

Part 1

Dear Betty

"I am going to Poland
in April,"
you told me on the phone.

"I am going to Poland"
resounded in my ears.
Poland, Poland, Poland –
the country of my birth.

I saw the trees –
the trees returned –
the weeping willows,
the maple trees,
the tall poplars,
the chestnut trees
in the park
near our home.

And the flowers came back –
the irises,
the tulips in the gardens.
The lilacs in May
were white and purple.
They were entering my room
through the window.

In the fields grew
red poppies
and the cornflowers,
there,
in the fields,
in the fields of my childhood.

The trees, the flowers,
the fields,
and the sun.
The sunrises and the sunsets.
My first sunrises
and my first sunsets –
and the words, the words,
my first words in Polish,
"tatus," daddy,
"mamusia," mummy
and the word *"usmiech"*
for a smile.

"I am going to Poland,"
you told me on the phone.
"I am going to Poland
in April."

April – a spring,
a Polish spring,
the dandelions
looking up
from the brown soil,
and the buds on the trees,
my trees.

What did I say?
My trees?
Yes, Betty,
they were my trees
and my dandelions
and my first sunrises
and my first sunsets
and my first words in Polish,
tatus and *mamusia*,
and there was *snieg*
the white snow,
the most beautiful of all,
more beautiful
than on Mont Blanc
in the Alps.

I did not know
when I was a child
the summits in Switzerland
covered with snow
but I knew *snieg*,
the white snow in Poland.

And now,
you, my granddaughter,
you have decided to visit
the country
which is not mine anymore.

And the tears flow down
my cheeks,
many, many tears
because
the trees remained.
The poppies and the cornflowers
bloom every year.
My *snieg*,
the white snow,
falls down
from the sky,
but the people
to whom I belonged
are no more there
and therefore
this country
is not mine
anymore.

From the corners
of many streets
in my memory
people appear.

They walk, they smile,
they greet each other,
people, people, people.

On Friday night
I see thousands and thousands
of lights
in the windows.

Through the curtains
I see the flickering flames.
There, the candles are lit.
On Friday night
in Warsaw, Krakow,
Lwow, Surochow,
in Sieniawa, in Jaslo
in Dukla
and in Rymanow.

These lights enter my mind,
these lights enter my heart.

To whom do these lights belong?

These lights belonged
to the Polish Jews.

The tears flow down my cheeks.
I cry, I cry.

The Polish Jews are gone.

I cry for all those
who were killed during the war.

I resembled them.

Why did they not survive?

I survived,
and I remember them
day and night.
Each spring, summer, fall
and winter –
I see them.
They live in my memory.

some I knew by their names,
some are nameless.

And now,
my granddaughter,
you, Betty,
you are going to visit
the vanished world
in spring.

Spring and the vanished world –
how strange these two words
sound together –
spring and the vanished world –
and maybe,
this is not so strange
after all,
because you are spring,
you, the young one
who wants
to remember
the vanished world.

You want to light
a candle,
one candle
for those
who lived in Poland
fifty years ago.

And this candle will be bright
as bright as you, your whole
being –
as bright as your blue,
beautiful eyes,
reflecting the colour
of the sky

and of the eyes
of your paternal grandfather,
Sigmond,
and this candle will shine
like a torch of light
which will never be extinguished
in history
thanks to you
and those who resemble you.

"I am going to Poland,"
you said on the phone.

You will see the trees,
the flowers, the fields,
but you will not see the people,
to whom I belonged.
About these people
and the lights
on Friday nights
I have to tell you.
Promise me, Betty
not to forget.

You and those
who resemble you
are entering the world
which will be built
tomorrow
and when you will not forget
the vanished world,
your world
will never
vanish again.

The lights of the past
will illuminate your thoughts,
and if these lights

will be remembered
when you will light
your own one candle,
you will become
stronger,
my granddaughter.

Part 2

It was many, many years ago
on Sunnyside Avenue
in Westmount, in Quebec.
Your maternal grandmother,
Betty,
who was born in Canada,
asked me about Poland.

We were sitting
in a beautiful room.
Through the window
I saw the St. Lawrence
flowing.
The river was very very far
but this river
reminded me
of other rivers
and time.

The room was blue.
I remember the carpet –
the colour of the St. Lawrence
in spring.

Your grandmother,
in her warm and gentle way,
asked me
about my past,
about the vanished world.

Do you know, Betty,
that your grandmother
would be proud of you.
She cared
for the vanished world
as you do,
you, who carry her name.

Part 3

Do you know, Betty,
what history is?
History is a story of people
and the rivers
flowing softly,
a story of the mountains
and of the forests.
History is a story
of everyday life,
of struggles, of triumphs,
and the downfalls of men.

History is a story
of heroes and of cowards,
of people, who resemble
the angels
of people, who resemble
the devils,
of people who pray
and try to touch
the spark of the divine,
and people
who forget that God is present in
the universe
and in our own being.

How many times
these thoughts
helped me

to accept the cruel time
and immediately after
to make a decision
and fight, fight
for survival.

In June 1941,
Germany attacked the Soviet
Union.
In a few days
we experienced the war
again –
bombing and shooting.

I remember a day
when I stood in the line
for bread .

Suddenly the shooting started
between the Ukrainians
and the Russians.
Many of the Ukrainians
living in Lwow
were friends of Hitler.
One bullet just missed me.
As it passed beside me,
I was scared
but I was not hurt.

The Germans entered Lwow
a few days later.
The suffering began
immediately.

The Jews were taken from the
streets
by Germans.
The humiliation started.

The mockery of the Hasidic Jews
became routine.
People, and especially men,
were disappearing.
Some were shot
and some were taken
to an undisclosed location.

We learned
that "undisclosed location"
meant shooting
on the outskirts of Lwow.

The Jews began
to scrutinize their faces
in the mirror.
Do I look Jewish?
they asked themselves.
How can I walk safely
on the street?

To have dark sad eyes
was an invitation
to persecution and suffering.
More and more people
were disappearing from the
streets.
They never came back.

A few days
after the Germans came
to Lwow,
a good friend of mine
a Pole, Wladyslaw Demianczuk,
came to visit us.
He brought four Roman
Catholic
birth certificates.

He offered these birth
certificates to us
and said,
"Your family does not look
Jewish.
Use these papers
with the false names
and pretend
that you are Poles,
Roman Catholics."

I was very grateful to my friend,
I believed
that it was the best solution.
To be a Jew
during the German occupation
meant persecution.
After my friend
showed us the documents,
my father asked me
to follow him
to the next room.
We left Wladyslaw
who held in his hands
the birth certificates
for my family.

There in the next room
my father said:
"If you
and Adam want
you may take these papers,
but your mother and I
will not use them.
Whatever
will happen
to the Jews in Poland
will happen to us.

I always defended justice,"
my father said,
"I will remain true
to my convictions."

I looked at my father.
I knew
I could not make him
change his mind.

I only said:
"If you don't take these papers
then Adam and I
will remain with you."

We came back to my friend,
we thanked him
for his thoughtfulness,
but we refused to accept
the false papers.

The order to wear the Jewish star
was issued at the end of July.
Even if you did not look Jewish
you were not safe anymore:
The armband indicated
your origin.

We were often hungry
and we decided to move
to a smaller city, Brzezany,
where my mother's family lived.

There are days in our lives
which are engraved
in our beings.
Every hour, every minute
is important.

During the time
of the war
sometimes one moment
played a role
in the "hide and seek" of life.

On the way to Brzezany
we were traveling
in a big truck.
On the road not too far
from Lwow
we were stopped
by the German police.
They were seven Gestapo men.

On the same truck travelled
an elderly Jewish man.
He was wearing
the Jewish armband.
The elderly man had a paper
issued by German authorities
permitting him to travel
to visit his daughter.
We did not have anything.
We were not wearing any arm
bands.

The police ordered us
to step down
and to take our luggage.
In the meantime
the driver of the truck
had to leave.

We were in the middle
of the road
and the first question was
"Are you Jewish?"

I was the first
to answer "No."
One of the policemen
pushed me and my mother
to the side
and asked my father and Adam
to move
to the other side of the road.

I was trembling.
Dividing Jewish men
and Jewish women
was dangerous.
The first step in searching
the Jewish men
was to find out
if they were circumcised.

Suddenly one of the policemen
took my father's leather briefcase
and admired it.
"I will take it for myself,"
he said.
"Let them go."
He ordered his men
to go back
to their van.

We knew that it was dangerous
to remain on the road
in the middle of nowhere
carrying our suitcases.
We did not know
what to do.

The military trucks
heading to the front
were passing fast,

one after another.
Without asking permission
of my parents
I decided to act.

I stopped an empty military
truck.
There were only two soldiers
sitting in the front.
One of them was older.
He stepped down.
I asked him
if he could help us.
He agreed.
He asked me
why we were all alone
on the road.
I decided to tell him
the truth.

"We are Jews," I said,
"The police stopped us."

The soldier was very kind
and slowly said,
"I did not ask you
if you were Jews."

At this moment the other soldier
came.
Suddenly the man
who promised
to take us asked,
"Do you speak
any other foreign language
beside German?"

"Yes," I said, "I speak French."

We started to speak French.
The older soldier
helped us to put
our luggage on the truck.
There were empty benches
and my parents and Adam sat
there.
I got the place
between the two soldiers
in the front.
I was conversing
with the older soldier
in French.
He told me that he came
from Alsace
and he loved the French
language.
Before we approached
the next city, Narajow,
he said that he and his colleague
would have lunch
in a restaurant
designated for Germans.
He invited me to join them.
He asked my parents and Adam
to wait in the truck.

In the restaurant
I observed German soldiers
and German civilians
having a very sumptuous meal,
and while swallowing
my first spoon of soup
to my dismay
I saw the Gestapo men
entering the restaurant.

Since we conversed in French
I stopped for a moment
and then said,
"There are the people
who wanted to arrest us."

I remember my black
plush coat.
I took the coat off,
I pushed the sleeves
of my sweater up.
I remember every move.
I thought
I had to play the role
of a very happy girl.
All this happened
in a few minutes.

The men did not recognize me.

We left the restaurant.
We had driven maybe
30 or 40 kilometres,
when the driver
got a telephone call,
and had to change his itinerary.

Again we were in the middle
of the road.
This time it was a small road
beside a village.
It was a Ukrainian village
and the people of the village
surrounded us
and our luggage,
four suitcases
and a blanket.

One of the peasants offered
to bring us
with his horse and wagon
to Brzezany.

My father agreed.
The man asked my father
to pay in advance.
My father paid
and after he paid him
he overheard the Ukrainian
say to his colleague,
"I will know what to do
when we drive
through the forest."
My father understood
what the men said.
During this time
there were many crimes
committed everywhere.
When we arrived
at the first small town
my father asked the driver
to stop.
After taking our luggage down
my father said,
"My family and I
will spend the night here."
The driver tried
to persuade my father
to continue the journey,
my father refused.

Here we were
in the marketplace
in the city of Narajow.

I spotted
a beautiful black cabriolet
and two magnificent horses.
In the cabriolet
sat one man
in the back
and the driver up front.
I approached the passenger
and asked him
if he would be kind enough
to tell me
where he was going.
He answered that he was going
to Brzezany.

Knowing that we were in danger
I asked him
if he could take my father
and my brother
without any luggage.
He asked me who we were.
I mentioned
that my mother's brother
was the pharmacist in the city.
The man knew him very well.
My uncle, Emil Goldman,
was respected by everyone.
He always helped people
who came
to the pharmacy
and distributed medication
to poor people without asking
for money,
sometimes even providing them
with money for food.
In the meantime
my father
introduced himself.

The man in the cabriolet
was a Ukrainian lawyer
who became mayor of Brzezany.
He told me father
that he was happy he could help
his colleague, a lawyer.
Before leaving he turned to me
and said,
"If in the future you need
any help, please let me know."

How sorry I am
that I don't even remember his
name.
We spent the night
at the home
of the Polish mailman.
The next day I went innocently
to the Ukrainian police
and asked if they could help us
with transportation.

In an hour we got
a very nice driver
with a horse and buggy.
He brought my mother and me
with our luggage
to Brzezany.

I will always remember
September 21, 1941,
a very sunny day.

To Survive or to Die, Why?

Ottawa April 22, 1992
(excerpts from a letter
to my granddaughter Betty)

In Brzezany
we had to register
in the Jewish centre, the
Judenrat.

In the latter part of November
our names appeared on the list
of people to be evacuated
from Brzezany.

One thousand people were on
the
list
men, women, and children.
Many of them were fugitives
from western Poland,
the last who arrived to the city.

On this afternoon
in late autumn
I was walking on the street
when a Jewish policeman
employed by the Judenrat

approached me
and asked me to follow him.
He informed me
that my family was on the list.

The days are grey in November
in Brzezany.
The day seemed grey
like our lives.
I walked beside the policeman.
His name was Heinz
he was in his twenties.
I looked at him,
a man
who to save his skin
followed the most hideous
orders.

The Judenrat, the Jewish Council
established by Germans,
was responsible
for executing the German plans:
1,000 people had to leave.
I walked.
I had an idea.
I asked the policeman

to let me enter the pharmacy
and allow me to buy aspirin.

I said I had a migraine.
The policeman allowed me
to stop.

There in the pharmacy was my
uncle,
the brother of my mother,
the only Jewish pharmacist
who was still working in
Brzezany.
I whispered to him
that my parents and Adam
were in danger.
I asked him
to help them to hide.
I also wrote a few words
to the mayor of the city,
a Ukrainian lawyer.
I had become acquainted with
him
a few weeks before
and he told me
to contact him
if I was in danger.

Then I followed the policeman.
I went to the place
where people were waiting
to be evacuated.

I saw men, women, and children.
Some of them were taken
from the street,
like me.
Some were taken

from their homes.
Those who were taken
from their homes
brought with them
suitcases
and bundles, bundles,
bundles –
a pillow, a blanket.
Suddenly I understood
that when you go into the
unknown
you tend to hold on
to something
from your home –
a pillow, a cover, a blanket
like a child.
A blanket represents home.

So many years after,
I see this group,
this group of people
waiting to be taken.
Where? No one knew.

There were maybe
a hundred people
in the room.
I was with them.
"Do you know
where we are going?"
the people asked.
There were these anxious eyes
and sad faces.
There were children
in the arms of their mothers
and the mothers
wiping their children's tears
and their own.

Do you know, Betty,
what it means to be homeless?
What it means
that a policeman comes
and says:
"Follow me into the unknown"?
No, Betty, you don't know.
No, Betty.
I bless the time
and the country
where you live.
You don't know
what it means
to be homeless,
but I want you
to remember
these people
who became
homeless
in one day.

One hour or two passed by,
then a man came.
a man whom I did not know.
He called my name,
he took me out from the room,
and told me
to leave the building.
I was free now.
The wife of the Ukrainian mayor
intervened on my behalf.
Her husband sent her
to the Judenrat.
She pleaded with the Jewish
authorities
to let me go.

I ran out.
I left the group of people
who became important for me.
I ran out,
but these children, women, and
men
remained there.
I could not help them.

So many years passed,
I never forget
people and bundles,
people and bundles,
the blankets,
and the children
and the voices asking:
Where will we be taken
tomorrow?

I found my parents and Adam
in my friend's house.
These friends were the parents
of Hesio,
a young engineer
whom I knew.
He was my friend.
Were we in love?
I knew that he loved me
and I cared for him.

Hesio was gentle, fine,
delicate, and strong.

Hesio was killed a few years later
in June 1943.
The Germans offered him
freedom –
they needed him;

he knew how to build
the finest bridges
without disturbing
the horizon.
But Hesio chose death,
when his mother
and his two sisters were taken.
He did not let them
go to death
without him.

In the home of Hesio's parents
the decision was made.
Our family had to hide.
I was free,
but my family
was on the list of people
to be evacuated.
A young girl who worked
as the housekeeper
of a German civilian
offered us a place
to hide:
the villa of her employer,
who was temporarily in Berlin.

After a sleepless night,
we went to the villa
at six o'clock in the morning.

When we entered the kitchen
of the villa,
my father said:
"I don't feel safe here,
please let us go down to the
cellar."

My parents and Adam
went to one of the cellars
in the basement.
The girl and I
returned upstairs.

After a few minutes
we heard a knock on the door.
Two Gestapo men came.
They were looking
for Jews hiding
in the villa.
They shouted at the girl.
Suddenly one of the Gestapo
men
addressed me.
He asked me
if I was Jewish.
The girl game me a sign
with her eyes.
It meant: Say no.

I shrugged my shoulders
and said in Polish
that I didn't understand German.
The Gestapo man
asked me
if I knew how to speak
in any foreign language.
I answered that I spoke French.
We conversed for a few minutes
in French.
I told him that I was not Jewish.

There in the cupboard
was my coat
and on the sleeve of my coat
was the Star of David,

my armband.
I tried not to think about it.

The Gestapo men said:
"Since you are not Jewish
I trust you.
Come with me to the cellars.
Show me
where the Jews are hiding."

I went with the Gestapo man
downstairs
I opened all the doors of the
cellars
except one,
where my parents and Adam
were.
We came back upstairs.
A few minutes later
I said:
"I forgot something downstairs."
I left the Gestapo man.
I ran down.
I opened the door
to the cellar
where my family was
and I asked them to leave
immediately.

They went out
from the cellar,
straight to the garden and the
street.

I went back upstairs.
Did my heart beat faster?
I don't know.
I was young,

I knew that each minute
counted.
The German asked the
housekeeper
to leave.
He asked me
to remain in the villa alone.
He trusted me
with the keys to the villa
and promised to come
in an hour.
I stayed, I stayed,
this hour was long
but I knew
that if I left
the Gestapo man
would look for me.

I also knew
that I was lucky.
The Gestapo man
did not ask me for my
documents.
He believed
that I was not Jewish.

When the man from the Gestapo
left,
I opened the cupboard
I took off the armband
from the sleeve
of my coat.

After an hour
the Gestapo man came back.
He took the keys to the villa,
but he demanded
that I come

to the Gestapo office
at 3 o'clock in the afternoon.

I went out
without my armband.
I ran, I ran.
I went first to the pharmacy,
then to my friends.
I asked everyone that I knew
if they had seen my parents
and my brother.
No one knew
where they went.
I heard
that many people
were taken from the streets.
Some of them
were put in prison.
I went to the prison.
There I asked
if the names of my family
appeared on the list of people
taken from the street.

The policeman who was on duty
was Polish.
"What are you doing here?"
he asked,
"Why are you endangering
yourself?
Do you want to lose your life?"

I remember the policeman.
I looked at him
and I said,
"If my family is here
I want to be with them."

I demanded that he check the
list.
The policeman brought the list
of all people
arrested on the street.
The name of my family
was not there.

It was noon.
I walked through the streets of
Brzezany
I loved this city so much.
I had spent so many vacations
there.
My grandmother, my uncles, and
my aunts
lived there in winter,
in summer they resided
on their estate in Kalne.
My mother's family were
landowners.

There in Brezezany was a huge
pond
where I often swam
in summer.
I loved the quiet green waters,
they were soft, gentle
like my life, like my youth
before the war
and now
I made a decision.
If my parents and Adam were
taken
I wanted to end my life.
I longed for these quiet waters.
I knew that I loved life

but only
if my family was alive.

I gave myself a time limit,
to 2 o'clock in the afternoon.

Do you know, Betty,
that I have never described this
day
in writing until now.

Betty, maybe you will not
understand
the meaning of one day
when the danger and love
for my family and love for my
life
were in conflict —
and during this time
of the conflict
I made my choice.
I knew that
my love for the family
was stronger
than my love for life.
I did not want
to survive
alone.

I walked, I walked
through the streets
I did not care anymore
if Heinz, the Jewish policeman,
met me,
I walked and I searched
for my parents and my brother
and on one of the streets
I saw Hesio.

He told me
that when my parents
left the cellar
he met them on the street.
Knowing that being on the street
was dangerous,
he brought them
to his Polish friends.
My parents and Adam
were safe.

I cried, I laughed.
Hesio was holding my hands,
Hesio, my good friend,
my gentle friend,
who later wrote me letters
almost every day
until the day
of his death.
I have these letters
in my home in Philadelphia.
Only the letters are left
and the words of love —
in me.
Does the love of those
who disappeared
accompany our lives?
Yes, Betty,
the love of Hesio
remained in my memory.

We decided,
Hesio and I,
that I had to go
to the Gestapo office.
It was less dangerous
to go there

than to give the Gestapo a
reason
to look for me.

At 3 o'clock in the afternoon
I arrived in the Gestapo office.
The Gestapo man was polite.
He just wanted to talk to me.
We spoke French for half an
hour.
At the end of the conversation
he asked me
to come back
the next day.

My family and I
spent the evening
at Hesio's parents' home.
I remember
how Hesio wanted to treat me
in a special way.
He wanted to give me
something good to eat.
The best that he had
was a piece of bread and honey.

Do you know Betty,
that the best
that exists in the world
is the taste of honey?
I wrote once a poem
about honey
and its taste,
wishing my sons
to have the taste of honey
in life
always.

The dark days came,
they were darker and darker
each day.
We found out
that 1,000 people
who were taken from Brzezany
were shot
near the town of Podhajce
several kilometres away.

There Were a Few Lights –
Lights in the Darkness

Ottawa April 22, 1992
(excerpts from a letter
to my granddaughter Betty)

The dark days were darker
every day.
The nights were sleepless.

I never went back
to the Gestapo.

For several weeks
I stayed in the room
where we lived.

Our best friends,
Helena and Jan Kosiba,
were now in contact with us.
They were sending us
flour, cream of wheat, and kasha.
They knew that we were hungry
very often.
They also knew
that we did not have money
and that we were in danger.

Helena and Jan Kosiba
decided to act.
They were Poles, ardent
Catholics.
They believed in Christ.
They also believed in friendship.

On the morning of Christmas
Eve
December 24, 1941
a stranger knocked on our door.
He came from Jaslo.
550 kilometres
only to take us back
to the city
where we lived
before the war.

I met Hesio
before we left.
We walked together
for a short while.

Behind the house
where we lived
was a little creek

and the bridge.
We stood on this bridge
and we kissed.
My engineer built for me
for a moment
a bridge over hate.

I remember the bridge.
We saw each other there
for the last time.

Late in the afternoon
we started our journey
back west.
Our Polish friends
chose Christmas Eve.
They thought
that the day and the night
of Christmas Eve
would be less dangerous
than any other time
to travel.

Our friends knew
that there were many Jews
who were travelling
from eastern Poland
back to western Poland.
Many of them
were killed
on the spot
on the roads.

We travelled long hours
in the snowstorm.
We had to get out of the car
several times so that we could

push the car forward.
The road was slippery.

The snowflakes were dancing
in the air.
The delicate snowflakes
were showing us
the power of nature.
Instead of twelve hours,
it took us almost twenty-four
to arrive in Jaslo.

Our friends waited.
We were greeted
not as fugitives,
outlawed and miserable Jews.
We were received
with the wine and delicacies
of Christmas Eve dinner.

Helena and Jan Kosiba
and their seven children
celebrated our return
trying to let us forget
the danger.

They prepared a beautiful room
in the hotel which they owned.
They knew that they were
risking
their lives
but in their humaneness
they ignored the general laws
and their consequences.

In this beautiful room
my mother opened her purse
and she discovered

that she had lost
all our documents.

During the snowstorm
while we were pushing the car
she must have lost our papers.
To be a Jew was dangerous
but to have no documents
was even more dangerous.

In Jaslo
there was already
a Jewish district.
The Jews were allowed
to live only
in this prescribed area.

Without our documents
we could not
enter
this Jewish district.
And so we stayed for a week
in the hotel.

One afternoon somebody came
to Kosibas'
and warned them
that although my father was
respected
and did not have any enemies
there were always informers
in the city
who were ready
to bring new victims
to the Germans.

We also knew
that the Poles
who gave shelter
to the Jews
were condemned to death.

I pleaded with my father
to let me get
false documents
as Aryans –
as Roman Catholics.
It was wise
to leave the home of the Kosibas.

My parents found a refuge
in the homes of friends,
first in the home
of the Rybak family,
and later
in the house of Jozef and
Genowefa Mordawski,
teachers.
From the Mordawskis' house
my parents went
to the family of Alfreda
Breitmeier
the principal of a girls' school.

One evening
after a long conversation
with my father
I took the train to Frysztak.

Frysztak was a small city
just thirty-nine kilometres from
Jaslo.
There I met with a man
whose father was a client
of my father.
My father

was remembered in Fryzstak
as a lawyer
who always tried to help people,
especially when they were very
poor.
Ludwik worked
in the mayor's office.
He asked me
to come the next evening
at seven o'clock.

I spent a night
with my father's friends.

The next evening
I had to walk
along the railway tracks
to the mayor's office.

This was a cold winter night.
January 1942 was very cold.
I wore ski boots and slacks.
I was freezing.
I was cold, cold, cold.
I walked alone.
I thought
that these railway tracks
would never end.

It was cold.
The tears running down my
cheeks
froze
like icicles — I thought.

The whole world
seemed to be
like those railway tracks

cold and never ending,
letting the tears flow down
and become
icicles.

So many years passed.
Betty, Betty, Betty,
so often I think
of these rail tracks
and the winter.

I was wandering
and wondering
about the world,
this world
where many innocent people
were dying every day.

The frost and the wind
slapping my face
was less cruel
than the coldness
and indifference
of the majority
of the world.

There however
while walking
on the rail tracks
I saw far away a few lights –
lights in darkness.
Somewhere in the villages
around
and in the city of Frysztak
those lights
meant for me
people
people

who were helping us.
They were lights in darkness:
Kosibas
Rybaks
Mordawskis
and Breitmeiers.

These lights sill existed.
I arrived at the mayor's office
at seven o'clock.
There I got
four sets of identification papers.

From now on
the family Herzig
was no more Herzig.
It was a new false name.
A few days later
the Kosibas hired a German
police car.
They wanted to protect us
as much as possible.
They knew
that every day
Jews were killed
on the roads.

Our friends cared
for our safety.

We took the train
from a small station
30 kilometres from Jaslo.

We began our life
as non-Jews
at the end of January 1942.

A few weeks later
I went back to Jaslo
to bring some warm clothes.
When I arrived
I found out
that a toe on my right foot was
frozen —
It had happened
when I walked
along the railroad tracks
during that cold night.

I stayed with the Kosibas
for four long weeks.
I was treated
as a daughter.
It was too dangerous
for me to stay at their hotel.
I stayed in their small apartment.
I slept in the bed of Helena
Kosiba
whom I called
since this time
Aunt Hela.

Helena Kosiba told me
that they prayed every day
for our survival.
There lying in bed
I understood
that my parents were right
when they taught us to divide
people
only according
to their deeds.

I understood
that what counts

is only the human heart
and nothing else.

So often
I listened
to Helena Kosiba's heart
when we slept together
her heart and mine
were beating,
one close to the other,
in the same rhythm.

Did you ever think, Betty,
about beating hearts:
the fast beating
when we run,
the slow beating
when we are tired —
the hearts, the hearts
taking part
in our loves
and understanding —
the fighting hearts
when our minds
want to rule
our lives —
the quiet hearts
listening
to the hearts of the world
and the breeze
in spring.
Did the breeze in spring
retain
the quiet sound
of millions of hearts
before they
stopped beating
during the war?

Life went on.
We were living now
as Catholics
in the small village Surochow
in southwestern Poland.
Adam started to work
in a lumber mill.
I became a secretary
in the same enterprise.
Our director was German,
sent from Germany.
Ten employees worked
in the office.
They were all Poles
The workers in the mill
were mostly Ukrainians.

My knowledge of German
was limited.
I learned German in school.
At the beginning
when the director
dictated letters
I sometimes wrote
half the word only
and I was lucky
that among my colleagues
was one who knew German
very, very well.
He was a fugitive
from Auschwitz
a very patriotic Pole
who also worked
under an assumed name.

In a few weeks
I learned a lot.
I became acquainted

with the language
and the way of working
with the German precision
of a very demanding director.
Even today,
each time I fold papers
I remember my apprenticeship.
I learned many things
in the most difficult time
of my life.

Adam and I were lucky.
The workers liked Adam
and I was respected
for my friendly attitude
to my colleagues and the
workers.
I was always ready to help
if somebody needed help.

One of my most important tasks
gave me access to information
concerning people
with whom I worked.
I took care of the switchboard
and I tried to listen
to all of the director's
conversations
especially when the calls
came from the Gestapo.

One day I overheard
one of the Gestapo chiefs
discussing
the activities
of our engineer.
The German authorities
were suspicious.

Immediately afterward,
I contacted the engineer
and at night
without saying goodbye
to anybody
he disappeared
together with his wife
and his child.
This man was a Polish officer
before the war
and I suspected
that he was involved
in the underground
organization.

There is another day
which remains
in my memory.
I overheard on the phone
that the Gestapo chief
from Jaroslaw
planned to go
the same afternoon
to the forestry services
in the neighbouring village
and bring the director
to Gestapo headquarters
for interrogation.
I did not know the man
personally.
I only spoke to him
several times
on the phone.
However I decided to act.
I called the forestry
and urged the secretary
to transmit my message.
The man who was supposed

to be interrogated
left immediately.
He went into the forest
and stayed there
until the day
of liberation.
For several weeks
he sent me
blueberries.

On both occasions the director
called me and asked
if anybody was in my office
when the Gestapo called.
Naturally I told him there
was no one there,
and luckily
he never suspected me.

After a few months
our parents arrived.

My father worked for a few
months
in a mountain resort
as supervisor of some work
on the river
but the place where my parents
were
became unsafe
and we decided, Adam and I,
to bring them to Surochow.

All the people
who worked in the office
lived in a special small
compound.

Each of us had a big room and a
kitchen.

When my parents arrived
we already had some friends
and many of these friends
visited us.
They especially appreciated
their conversations with my
father.
My mother became friendly
with the women around
and, despite the awareness
that each day was dangerous,
our life
became like the life of other
Poles
around us.

Since Adam and I were very
young
we attended
parties at Christmas
or on New Year's Eve.
In summer, we often went
swimming
and bicycling.

One of my very good friends
whose brother was a priest
asked me before Easter
why I did not go
to confession.
I remember his words:
"God loves you so much,
why do you not go?"
I simply answered,
"Do you know

my family does not go
to confession."
Later at home I asked,
"How far can you go in lying?"
I did not want to lie.
Today I realize
that it was dangerous.

A year later
a very good friend,
a worker from the mill,
was getting married.
He was Polish
and he asked Adam and me
to be witnesses.
I said to Adam,
"How far can our lies go?"
We politely refused.
We excused ourselves saying
that on this particular Sunday
we had to go
out of town.

A year later
the same couple
asked us
to be the godparents
of their child.
We found another excuse.
Under assumed names
we did not want
to participate
in religious ceremonies.

In my office in Surochow
I often looked through the
window.
Nature entered my being;

the tall poplars across the road
were my messengers
to the Almighty God.
They were watching me.
My own prayers,
my own dreams
were flowing
above the trees.
They entered the universe
and inserted in the air,
they remained
as a part
of the emerging
tomorrow.

Always I was preoccupied
with the dreams of tomorrow –
tomorrow of freedom
and respect.

I remember
one afternoon
in the spring of 1943.
In the German newspaper
I saw the statistics of people
killed
on the battlefields.
I saw numbers, numbers
of the killed soldiers.
The Germans tried to show
that
for every German soldier
there were ten Russian soldiers
killed on the eastern front,
and ten Americans
killed in Africa.
I felt
almost

a physical pain
combined
with my inability
to do anything
to stop the killing.
I did not want the war
to continue,
to kill people
around me,
on the streets,
in prisons,
in camps.
I did not want the soldiers,
any soldiers,
to be killed.
I cannot understand why
but I also remember
that I was thinking
about German soldiers.
In my imagination
I saw a line of people

of different nationalities,
different faces,
different uniforms.
As I visualized them
I promised myself
that if I survived the war
I would try to work
for understanding
among people.
In whatever capacity
large and small
I would try
to promote
respect for life.

I did not forget my promise.

Rome and the Gardens
of the Vatican

The Seven Hills of Rome
watch the city
where the ruins
of the ancient Roman Empire
and the skyscrapers
look at each other
with wonder.

Do the ruins
want to tell their stories?

Do the skyscrapers
want to listen?

The skyscrapers
seem to touch the sky
without understanding
the mystery of ruins
and the history.

Are the skyscrapers lonely
or do they look
at the Cupola
of St. Peter's Basilica
with envy?

The skyscrapers
resemble
one another –
the Cupola is unique
bringing to mind
Michelangelo.

Michelangelo Buonarotti was
unique.

The Cupola
was not finished
during Michelangelo's life
but the Cupola was built
following
his designs –
the Cupola
was his creation.

How very often
the designs,
the thoughts of people
survive
their own lives
and leave a spark of light
for future generations.

God created the world
but God also
sends to the world
those
who continue
his creation
with a noble thought
and designs
guided
by the love of God.

The skyscrapers
grow high, very high.

Do they sing late at night
the glory
of modern man
who does not accept limits,
or were they not taught
how to sing?

If the architect is an artist,
he endows his work
with his own feeling
but if the architect,
while preparing
his first drawing,
considers
the future structures only
as the means to an end —
the harmony
between the horizon
and the structure
is forgotten.

The sense of beauty
and harmony
possesses those

who are humble enough
to offer
to each of their drawings
or ideas
even in the initial stages
a part of themselves,
the reflection
of their conscience.

Therefore
some skyscrapers
know how to sing
with the stars
at night.

The Seven Hills
witness every sound
of yesterday
and today.
They store in their memory
the history
of Rome
and those
who lived and live
in the City of the Seven Hills.

When late at night,
Rome is asleep,
the hills converse
one with the other.

The birds understand
their whisper.
These whispers
the birds retain
as the lyrics
to their melodies.

The most beautiful ballads,
the ballads of life passing by,
are composed
by the birds.

The hills remember
the past.

Emperor Titus
in the year 80
after bringing 12,000 Jewish
captives
from Judea
decided to use them
as slave labor.
They built the Coliseum.

The Coliseum became
the greatest attraction
for the Romans.

The hills remember
the games of cruelty
cheered by 50,000 spectators,
screaming, enchanted
in their fascination
with the spectacles.
The Christian martyrs
and the lions
brought excitement
to the crowd –
the gladiators
killing each other
brought smiles
to Nero.

On the pages of history
all this is recorded –

however some people
want to forget the events
showing evil
in all its power.

There is a Latin saying:
"Homines, quid volunt, credunt"
which means
"Men believe if they want to
believe."

History repeats itself
only
because the acts of inhumanity
are forgotten too soon.

The acts of inhumanity
instead of becoming
a warning
for the future generation
continue their journey
through history.
The trees, the stones,
and the Seven Hills remember.

The Appian Way
built by Emperor
Appius Claudius
as a military road
remembers
one fugitive, St. Peter.

There – not too far from Rome
is a church:
Domine, quo vadis.

This church was built
in memory of St. Peter,

who while fleeing from Rome
had a vision of Christ.

Peter asked him:
"Domine, quo vadis
(Lord, where are you going)?"
and Jesus answered:
"I go to Rome
to be crucified."

St. Peter did not want
to flee anymore,
he went back to Rome.
Nero ordered his crucifixion.

The Basilica of St. Peter
was built in memory
of a man
who asked Jesus
"Lord, where are you going?"

St. Peter brought Christ
to Rome.

Jerusalem is a city
of God and men –
God chose Jerusalem
as the source
for men
who believe in one God.

Rome is a city
of men and God.

Men created a city
for God.

The Basilica of St. Peter

was built
as a source
of spirituality
for Christianity.

Pope Gregory the Great
who lived
in the sixth century
understood
that art is important
when he said:
"Painting can do
for the illiterate
what writing does
for those
who can read."[63]

Before Gregory the Great,
Christians
following
the Second Commandment
which reads:
"You will not have
graven images"
were afraid
to show God
in their works of art.

It was Gregory the Great
who offered Christianity
art.

With the passage of time
many of the successors
of St. Peter,
among them
Pope Julius II,
encouraged

the great artists
to bring meaning
with their thoughts
and their art
to faith.

The Renaissance brought
a breeze of antiquity
and a philosophy
of Neo-Platonism
where the thoughts
of Greek philosophers
and Christianity
were reconciled.

Marcilio Ficino,
a philosopher,
a friend of the de Medici family
in Florence,
influenced many Florentine
artists.

A new art and freedom
made its appearance.

On the ceiling
of the Sistine Chapel,
Michelangelo
painted
the creation of the world.

In the creation of Adam
Michelangelo proved
that with one image
man can start
a dialogue with God.

Michelangelo maybe asked
himself:
"Was the creation of Adam
a triumph of God?"

Was the creation of Adam
the beginning
of man's trials?

Michelangelo was a giant
who tried to touch
with his brush
the heavens
and in his vision
saw the divine
descending
from the celestial kingdom
to his own soul —
when his hands painted
the hand of God
trying to reach
the hand of man —
and his hands painted
the hand of man
trying to reach God.

The city of men and God
was growing.

In the Basilica of St. Peter
La Pieta recalls the sorrow
of a mother.

The artist chiseled
into the stone
the Virgin Mary and Christ —
he endowed the stone
with the love of a mother.

He gave a soul
to the stone.

Michelangelo knew
how to chisel souls.

Millions of people
come every day
and admire a man
who was able
to find a thread
linking beauty
in all its purity
with faith.

There in Rome
in the Church
of St. Peter in Vinculi
(St. Peter in chains)
Michelangelo's *Moses*
sits on a large platform.
The prophet
holds under his arm
the Ten Commandments.

People look at the statue –
the majestic figure
awakens the mystery
of encountering God
in the desert.

This scripture, chiseled
in a huge stone
from Carrara
is powerful
and seeing it

in the Church of St. Peter in
Chains
becomes a symbol.

How often
in the modern world
are there people
who do not have any scruples
even
in endangering
our Planet Earth?

Do they try
to keep
the Ten Commandments
in chains?

Do they dictate
the new commandments
in laboratories
and engrave them
on the tablets of progress?

In the church of St. Peter in
Vinculi
Moses is patient.
He knows
that still in the world
the Ten Commandments fly
over the highest mountains
and touch the conscience
of those
who allow their conscience
to be touched.

Michelangelo,
Botticelli,
Raphael

helped to build
a house of God
in their colours
of faith.

The springs, summers,
autumns, and winters
follow one another –
people are born,
people die –
the issues of mankind
remain the same.
Peace, war.
The fields of wheat
and the battlefields,
the trips to the moon
and the famine
in different places –
and people
in all versions
of their characters.

Each year in the spring
the air
celebrates life.

Spring 2000 came to Rome.
As always,
the buds on the bushes
and the very tiny flowers
were sneaking out
from the branches
or from the brown soil.

In the Gardens of the Vatican
beauty mingled
with spirituality
as in *Primavera*

painted
by Sandro Botticelli
500 years before.

The flowers and the bushes
were revealing dreams
and longings
and with the air
were celebrating life.

In the Square
of the Madonna of Lourdes
with its cement reproduction
of the Grotto,
passersby
were reminded
of the miracles.

In the year 1858,
the Madonna appeared
to Bernadette Soubrious.

St. Bernadette
offers spirituality
and mystery –

St. Bernadette lets people think
about miracles.

These people
who believe in miracles,
even looking
at the Grotto of Lourdes,
they feel the sanctity
of the place –
and they imagine the appearance
which cannot be explained.

The impossibility
of explaining miracles
proves once again
the presence of holiness
depending
on the perception
of the images
which we see
and images
which we do not see –
the images
which we feel
in our inner being.

Our inner being
is strengthened
knowing
of the miracles' existence.

People who believe
in miracles
are happier
than those
who do not believe –
because they can see
very often
for themselves
the miracles of every day
offering them
the flowers
closing their petals
in the evening
and opening the same petals
in the morning.

Often the flowers are planted
in the soil
or sometimes the flowers
are planted
in the minds and hearts of
people.

To visitors
standing in front
of the Grotto of Lourdes
or standing in front
of the replica
of the Grotto,
St. Bernadette
offers comfort
through their own spirituality
awaken in this particular time
and in this particular place.

Men need miracles.
Men have to know
that they have to go through life
without being able
to understand everything.
Instead of understanding,
sincere prayer
lets them receive
the blessing.

Prayer is a blessing of God.
People who know how to pray –
are blessed.

Not too far
from the Grotto of Lourdes
is a small remnant
of the Berlin Wall.

It was a gift
sent to Pope John Paul II
for his efforts
in promoting
freedom
for the family of men.

A few steps farther
an olive tree is growing.
This olive tree
was sent
to the Holy Father
from Israel.

Spring 2000
brought in March
the greetings
from Jerusalem.

The olive tree
is smiling.
The young leaves
recite
the hymn of peace:

"May the flowers grow
in the gardens of humanity
the happy children
who do not know fear . . ."

The Seven Hills
and the skyscrapers
listen . . .

The Cupola of Michelangelo
Watches the Studio of Destinies

The Cupola of Michelangelo
is illuminated every evening.

The night of May 18, 2000,
is calm, serene.

The sublime feeling of mystery
caresses the air
entering the open window
on the fourth floor
of the Apostolic Palace.

At the window
stands the Holy Father,
John Paul II.

He is alone.

In the room on the wall
the image of the Virgin Mary
from Czestochowa
creates an atmosphere
of peace and warmth.

The air enters the room
and touches

the frame of the picture.

There at the window
the man in the white robe
seems to be deep in his thoughts.

Are his thoughts
concerned with his guidance
as a pope?

Do his thoughts
wander from the green meadows
to the sunny valleys
like the thoughts of a poet?

Do his thoughts
reach higher, farther –
and their mysticism
become
the embroidery
for the night
outside the window?

John Paul II
is not only a pope –
he is a poet
and a mystic.

The night outside becomes
a background for his thoughts.
On this dark background
his thoughts are illuminated
not only by the light
coming from the Cupola.

His thoughts are illuminated
by the presence
of his recent visit
to a little village
ninety miles from Lisbon,
Fatima.

In one moment
Fatima
stops being a little village.
Fatima becomes gigantically vast
without limits.

To Fatima
somewhere in the spheres
which man cannot reach or see
was given a gift
of celestial wisdom,
the prophecy
concerning men on earth.

There on May 13, 1917,
three children,
innocent in their purity
were chosen
to become
the messengers
of faith.

Jacinto Marto, six years old,
her brother Francisco, eight
years old,
and their cousin
Lucia de Jerus dos Santos, nine
years old,
witnessed a special light
and in this light appeared
the Virgin Mary.

On the green pastures
so very green in spring
where they were taking care
of their parents' sheep
this beautiful lady
spoke to them.
They knew
that she came from Heaven.
The Virgin Mary asked them
to listen
and after to pray.

The children saw her again –
she appeared to them
a few times
between May 13 and October
13, 1917.

Jacinto and Francisco
did not live long –
Francisco died
on April 4, 1919.
Jacinto died
on July 20, 1920.

Only Lucia survived.

The Virgin Mary predicted
in the first secret
the end of the First World War
and the Second World War.

In the second secret
the Virgin Mary
predicted
the collapse of the Soviet Union.

It was the Virgin Mary
who in her appearance
asked Lucia
to reveal the secret
of the third miracle
in the future.

The third secret
remained with Lucia.

Lucia dedicated her life
to faith —
she entered the convent.

In 1941
before the Jubilee
of the apparition
the bishop of Fatima
asked Sister Lucia
to describe her experience.

She asked the bishop
to transmit the letter
in 1955.
She also said
that the secret could be revealed
in 1960

if the pope would decide
to do so.

Pope Pius XII,
John XXIII,
Paul VI,
and John Paul II
did not reveal
the content of the secret
until the recent visit
on May 13, 2000,
to Fatima.

The secret was revealed
on May 13, 2000.

It was revealed
that "a bishop dressed in white
will fall to the ground
as he would be dead
hit by a firearm."

On May 13, 1981,
Ali Agca, a Turkish terrorist,
tried to assassinate John Paul II.

John Paul II is convinced
that he was protected
by the miracle.

After the Holy Father was
wounded
he said:
"The maternal hand was guiding
the trajectory of the projectile
which stopped
on the threshold of death."

When the Bishop of Fatima
came to see John Paul II
he gave him the bullet
that hit him.
The bullet is inserted
in the golden crown
of the Virgin Mary
in Fatima.

On May 13, 2000,
John Paul II
brought to Fatima
a golden ring
which he received
from the Primate of Poland,
Stefan Wyszynski,
after he became Pope.

He remembers the words
of the Primate
who said:
"The Lord called you
to lead the Church
into the third millennium."

This ring
John Paul II
placed at the foot
of the statue of the Virgin Mary.

Before leaving for Rome
the Pope met Lucia,
93 years old.

The Holy Father, slightly bent,
still stands at the window.

Maybe he thinks
of another miracle
that happened
many, many years ago –
during the war.

On February 29, 1944,
a German truck hit him.
He was lying on the pavement –
unconscious.
A tramway was passing by
and a passenger, Jozefa Florek,
saw the man lying on the street.
She stepped out
she approached him
she did not know
if the man was dead or alive.

At this moment
a German officer
stopped the car
in which he was riding,
came and examined Karol.
He said:
"The man is alive."
Later on
Karol was brought
by a lumber truck
to the hospital.

After he regained consciousness
he was told
that he had a brain concussion
and was unconscious
for nine hours.

One day as Pope,
John Paul II said:

"Providence saved me."

This Providence
gives to the humble man
Karol Wojtyla – the Pope –
courage,
courage to perform deeds
never performed
since the beginning
of Christianity.

This Providence
taught him
how to love people
with all his mind
and with all his heart.

This Providence
guides him in his prayers
and his wanderings
across many seas
and across many deserts –
This Providence taught him
how to swim in the deep waters
of hate
and reach the safe shore –
This Providence dictated to him
the sermons in the deserts
of the minds of people
who forgot
how to be real human beings –
This Providence helped him
to bring consolation
to those who feel abandoned
in their misery
and don't believe anymore
that someone cares.

There are people,
men, women, and children
who look at him
as a source of hope.

It is late at night.

John Paul II
thinks about his drama
Our God's Brother,
which he wrote as a young
priest.
One part of the play is called
"The Studio of Destinies."

In this drama
the studio belongs to a painter
who decided to become
a "servant of God."

There are many people
coming to the studio –
they look at the paintings.
Some of the passersby
try to interpret
in their own way
the works of art.

Some of the passers-by
become inspired
and they retain the paintings
in their beings.

One day –
in the course of the drama –
two friends
have a conversation

in the studio of destinies.
They discuss the essence of art.

In this dialogue
we discover the author's concept
of art.

For Karol Wojtyla
art and conscience
are interwoven.

The spectator,
who watches the drama
takes in
the value of dreams,
in which the conscience
is always present.

Does Pope John Paul II realize
that the room on the fourth floor
of the Apostolic Palace
became a studio of destinies?

Every Sunday
John Paul II
delivers a message
through the open window
to the crowds.

People come and go –
Some of them stop –
they listen.
They are inspired
by the author
of Our God's Brother.

The young priest
who wrote the drama
became a pope.

The young priest
is eighty years old now –
but he retained his dreams –
he pursues his dreams
with a vitality
defying often
his physical frailty.

John Paul II
is strong.

From his own studio of destinies
he teaches the art of living
where conscience
has its place.
He knows
that in the art of living
art and conscience
could be interwoven
with the most beautiful thread
of love.

Eighty years before
when he was born
his mother asked
for the window to be opened –

The mother of Pope John Paul II
implanted in her son
the poetry, the dreams,
the love for the universe
and the love for humanity –

From high above
someone was watching –

The Holy Father
turns his head
toward the illuminated Cupola.
The Cupola watches
the Studio of Destinies.

From far away
across the night
someone is singing.

The voice is beautiful.

"As long as God is with me,
I know where I have to go.

As long as God is with me,
I know where I have to go."

To whom does this voice belong?

John Paul II does not know.

Maybe –
this is his inner voice repeating:

"As long as God is with me,
I know where I have to go."

June 1, 2000

As Long as God Is with Me
I Know Where I Have to Go

When I went to the Vatican for the first time in June 1996, while I was waiting for the first audience with Pope John Paul II, the words of the Polish poet Adam Mickiewicz came back to me. I remembered the sentence from the "Ode to Youth":

"Measure your strength according to your longings and not your longings according to your strength."

These words of the Polish poet became a motto for my life. There in the Vatican I pictured myself during the war in Surochow, when in front of the poplars I made a promise to myself that if I survived the war, I would spread understanding between people of different religions and races.

As I waited in the Vatican I also thought about Ludwig von Beethoven, who read the "Ode to Joy" by Friedrich Schiller when he was twenty-one years old and promised himself that one day he would compose music for it. At the age of fifty-one, when he was completely deaf, he finally composed his *Ninth Symphony*, with its rousing setting of the "Ode to Joy."

The *Ninth Symphony* is Beethoven's powerful exploration of ideas of struggle and victory. A deaf musician, Beethoven somehow managed to fulfil the commitment he made in his youth. He measured strength according to his longings and not his longings according to his strength. He gave us the strength to struggle by composing his symphony.

Years before, when I was in Vienna, I visited the houses where great composers had lived. In one small apartment the guide said, "Here lived Ludwig von Beethoven. During his stay here he composed his *Ninth Symphony*." I approached the window, saw the church, and heard the bells ringing. In that single moment Beethoven became alive for me. I thought about him as if he were present, trying to convey to me not only his powerful music but also his fragility, the fragility of each one of us in our dreams. This symphony has been an inspiration for me for many, many years.

That day in 1996, in the Vatican, I had with me a few of my books written in French and English (the Holy Father had some of my previously published books already). I also brought one long poem I had written in Polish after so many years of writing only in English and French. During my audience with Pope John Paul II, I read him an excerpt from my poem entitled *"Zlocisto-Srebrzyste"* – or "Golden-silverish." He listened very attentively.

I decided to include the beginning of "Golden-silverish" in this autobiographical book because I believe that my poem created the foundation of our friendship, the understanding which can occur when two people (I dare to say) have similar longings.

Golden-silverish
or The Saga of My Life

12 o'clock Sunday
August 20, 1995,
Vesuvius erupted.

Old Vesuvius,
which I saw long ago,
very, very long,
somewhere near Rome
erupted in me.
Old Vesuvius
erupted in my soul,
in my heart
and the lava
started to circulate
in all my veins,
in all the vessels

leading
to the aorta
of my heart
through the thin passages
and big channels
the lava was flowing.
The sand near Vesuvius
is black.
I saw this sand
with my younger son.
My son Jacques
and I
we were walking
on this black sand.
Our feet plunged
in this black sand
on one distant Sunday,
but the lava from Vesuvius
which flows in my veins

is not black.
This lava is transparent
as my tears –
the tears that now
do not flow
down my cheeks.
My cheeks are dry.
Not one drop of my tears
leaves my eyelids.
This lava, lava,
transparent lava,
lava of Vesuvius,
which erupted at night
is overflowing my being.
No – no, no
I will not allow this lava
to overrun with a flood
my strength –
No – no – no.
Gracefully,
I will allow this lava
to give birth in pain
to every word
which I will write now.
I will not allow you, lava,
to overflow
my heart
even with the transparent tears,
like this farmer
in the fields
on a cold day
at the end of winter
who is ploughing
the black soil
and sows, sows grain
and rye
and barley
and corn.

I want to plough
with this heavy plough
controlled
not by the machine.
I want to plough this soil
with my own hand.
I want to plough this soil
black,
black, brown,
reddish,
and sow
something
at the end of the winter.
Yes, this soil is black,
brown, gray,
ashy and reddish –
the soil of life
reddish?
And where is this reddish soil?
The reddish soil
I saw for the first time
from the airplane
of British Airways
when I looked down
on the Spanish land.
Yes, there the soil is reddish
not because
raged the Civil War in Spain
No, because nature
endowed the Spanish earth
with the reddish colour
like in the picture
painted by Francisco de Goya.
This painting shows
the soldiers of Napoleon
carrying out
the death sentence.

The hands of the Spanish
prisoners
are raised to the sky.
The reddish soil –
There not too far from Vesuvius
the soil was black –
On Monte Cassino
during the Second World War
many soldiers were killed
and only red poppies
remained.
There the soil is brown.
There were many Polish soldiers,
who perished.
Many years ago
I heard the song
about the red poppies
on Monte Cassino –
and in Auschwitz
the soil is black,
muddy, soft.
You walk on this soil
as I walked
with my older son Michel
at the beginning of April
not long ago –
five months now.
The soil, the soil, the soil –
and I am ploughing now
with these words
not the soil
but life –
my own life.
Nothing belongs to me
except of my own life.
This is not true –
this is not true.
The lava made a sound

in my being.
This is not true,
this is not true.
These words retained my pen.

Oh, maybe the lava is right.
Maybe my own life
does not belong to me.
Maybe my life
is a fraction, a particle of God –
and of the universe.
How dare you to talk
about your life
as a particle of God?
You are blaspheming –
you are blaspheming,
said the lava.
Oh, yes, the lava is right –
my life is only
one grain of dust
of this earth,
one grain of dust
of this black, brown,
gray, ashy
and reddish soil –
Oh, no,
my life is tinted
with other colours.
My life is golden-
silverish –
Golden-silverish
so beautiful two words in Polish
–

Zlocisto-srebrzyste
The source of poetry
for me
is far away.

It started with Adam Mickiewicz
in Lithuania
and for me
it came
with Julian Tuwim
the poet of my youth,
not Heine and not Goethe,
not Rimbaud
and not Racine,
not Robert Frost
or even Omar Khayyam –
not Homer
and not the prophet Isaiah.

I read the Polish poems
and through my window
I saw
the lilac colour –
and colour of the lilacs –
and I was listening
to the Polish wind.

What is left from these years?
The furious lava
in my veins,
the volcano
in my being
is more
than the dry leaves
of yesterday.
The lava in my being
is dictating to me
these words
on American soil.
The lava in my being,
in my pulse,
is paving for me the road
to my thoughts,

is paving for me a path
to my memories
and from far away
I hear the song.
After this song
my tears flow
down my cheeks.
Why?
Some people in the world
will laugh
if my words reach them
the words of a poem,
of Sunday,
of August.
It does not matter.
May the cynics laugh
but let them be
the witnesses to the tears
of someone
who almost at the end
of the twentieth century
is crying,
is crying sincerely, honestly
and praying ardently
that the world will become
better.
I kneel, God, before you
although Jews do not kneel.
Jews kneel only
once a year
on the Day of Atonement.
I am kneeling before you,
my good, beloved God,
God from Sinai
and from Jerusalem,
God of all people in the world
and I pray for a better world
God, who prays to you –

I
and who am I,
a grain of earth.
I am this dust,
this sand,
the sand golden
as the wheat,
the golden sand
near Costa Brava
not too far from Barcelona
and on the shores
of the Caribbean Islands
I do not want to be
a grain of black sand
near the Vesuvius volcano.

Allow me, my God,
to be
a grain of the golden sand
like the wheat on the fields
in Podolia
near Kalne,
where my grandparents lived.
There in Kalne
my mama grew up.
There in Kalne
my mother was taught
philosophy and French.
She played the piano beautifully
and the roses
in the rose garden
were listening to Chopin.
Allow me, my God,
to be a grain of sand
near Jaslo,
near the city
where I grew up.
There were three rivers,

Jasloka, Wisloka, Ropa.
Yes, God,
I yearn to be
a grain of sand
of the golden earth
like the wheat.

Jean François Millet
painted
a beautiful picture
and he titled the picture:
Angelus.
On this painting
on the field
during the harvest
the man and the woman
interrupt their work
as pious Christians do,
when they listen
to the bell
calling for a prayer
from the nearby church.
This man and woman
join their hands for prayer.
They pray.
As a child
in the dining room
of our apartment
I looked at a reproduction
of the painting
by Jean François Millet.
This painting
was a part of my childhood.
These two Christians
were praying to Christ.
I did not believe in Christ
but Christ existed.
I had respect for this One

whom the Christians call
the Son of God.
I am a Jew.
The Christians are people
as the Jews are,
as Muslims,
as Buddhists,
as Hindus –
people, who could choose
for themselves
if they want to be
a grain of sand
from the black lava
or from the golden sand
as near Barcelona
on Costa Brava
and maybe
as the ears of wheat
near Jaslo.

In February 1998 I visited the Holy Father for the second time. After my arrival in Rome I telephoned Bishop Stanislaw Dziwisz, secretary to Pope John Paul II. (He had just been appointed Bishop by His Holiness. In 2003, His Holiness appointed him Archbishop.) It was early afternoon. My son Jacques was arriving from Ottawa the next afternoon. Bishop Dziwisz greeted me warmly and invited me to come to the Vatican at seven o'clock the next morning for the private Mass celebrated by the Holy Father. When I woke up the next day, Rome was grey. Heavy drops of rain were falling on the large and narrow streets of Rome.

The pope celebrated Mass in the small papal chapel. I found the spirituality of the pontiff very moving. In the book *Gift and Mystery*, written on the occasion of the fiftieth anniversary of his priesthood, Pope John Paul II writes:

As a steward of God's mysteries, the priest is a special witness to the invisible in the world. For he is a steward of invisible and priceless treasures belonging to the spiritual and supernatural order.[68]

I believe that any chaplain who possesses the mystery of spirituality and has the gift of bestowing this spirituality on those whom he meets, fulfills his mission. There in the chapel a small group of people listened to the voice of someone who prays with all his heart.

In the chapel I felt the presence of God, Christ, the Virgin Mary, and the prayer of a good man who does not hesitate to travel extensively to remind people that every human being has the right to freedom and respect.

I thanked God that I could witness the Holy Mass celebrated by the Shepherd of Catholics who tries to teach people around the world that each of us has been given the gift to be ourselves, if we possess a conscience and are guided by it. I wanted to retain in my memory every moment of that Mass. The spirituality of hope was a balm for me, having seen so much injustice in the course of my life. I was filled with many, many thoughts, for those who were persecuted, abandoned, misunderstood – lonely people who still had their dreams. I thought of those for whom every prayer of every good person becomes a spark of hope, a spark of light.

There in the small chapel I prayed ardently, thanking God for the presence of Pope John Paul II near me. This priest with his gift and mystery tried to teach people love. He did not proclaim love for Christians only, he prayed for all his fellow human beings. I prayed that he would continue to spread the seeds of his mission of love with his majestic gift and mystery for many years to come.

When the Holy Father said, "God, forgive us our sins," I was moved. I thought again and again how spirituality transcends religions. I thought that when we repent we can move forward more easily. I thought about how we can find God only through our feelings. I thought about our conscience, the spark of God in each of us.

After celebrating Mass, the Pope exchanged a few words with some of the people who were in the chapel. Bishop Dziwisz asked me to wait in a corner of the room. The Holy Father came to me and we spoke for several minutes. A photographer also arrived. On the way back to my hotel, tears flowed down my cheeks and mingled with the drops of rain falling on the streets of Rome. I thought about how important it is to know that there are good people walking on our planet. A few hours later, I received a very meaningful photograph from the Vatican. The photographer had taken the picture at the very moment when the Holy Father touched my forehead and gave me his blessing.

When Jacques arrived later that afternoon, he saw on the table in my hotel room the photograph of the pope blessing me. He stood for a long while observing this moment in time captured by a skilled photographer.

The next day, Jacques and I were invited to see Bishop Dziwisz. We spent an hour of friendly conversation with him in a small room with a few beautiful paintings and a small table. After our encounter with Bishop Dziwisz we were taken to the private library of the Holy Father where Sister Emilia, who had been born and raised in Poland, offered me a few books in Polish, containing some encyclicals and sermons by the Holy Father.

In the afternoon, Father Mieczyslaw Mokrzycki and Father Marian Babula gave us a private tour of the Gardens of the Vatican. We walked together. The sun was shining, and the delicate spring was in the air. I described my feelings about this garden in my poem "Gardens of the Vatican." There in the garden, rays of light fell on a remnant of the demolished Berlin Wall, on the olive tree sent to the Holy Father from Israel, and on the replica of the Grotto of St. Bernadette from Lourdes.

The next day, a Friday, we were received once again by the Holy Father. Once more, Jacques and I were privileged to speak to someone who, in spite of his heavy schedule and increasing health problems, is able to show concern for others and who knows how to create an atmosphere of friendship. I brought back to Philadelphia a few mementos and the book *Gift and Mystery* in Polish and English, signed by the Holy Father.

Since 1996, Pope John Paul II has written many letters to me that continue to forge our understanding, letters that give me the encouragement to complete this book about my way of seeing the man and the time in which we both live.

When the Holy Father decided to go to Israel in March 2000, I was honoured to be asked to join him there. There in Yad Vashem, where I sat with my son Jacques and we witnessed the testimony of a man who did not hide his emotions, he said:

Men, women and children cry out to us from the depths of the horror that they knew. How can we fail to heed their cry? As a bishop of Rome and successor of the Apostle Peter I assure the Jewish people that the Catholic Church motivated by the Gospel law of truth and love and not by political considerations is deeply saddened by the hatred acts of persecution and displays of anti-Semitism directed against the Jews by Christians at any time and any place.

As I listened to these words, I thought about the Mass I had attended in the papal chapel in February 1998. In the sombre place of Yad Vashem, besides the crowd were also the invisible souls of the past. I believed that they were listening to the words of a man who was suffering with them, with these invisible souls, who came to listen to his words. Afterwards, Father Mokrzycki came to me and brought me to Bishop Dziwisz and there in front of the eternal flame the Holy Father shook my hand and offered me the most beautiful words. These words were for me alone and in them was gift and mystery. Two people met, just like in my poem "The Encounter." Two dreamers – the Holy Father born in Wadowice and me, the woman born in Krakow. There was a blessing of sanctity of the moment. I thanked God.

* * *

On September 11, 2001, the terrorist attack which brought disaster to New York and to the Pentagon, and claimed so many innocent lives in a country built on freedom, started a new era of fighting and intolerance. The struggle for peace will be difficult, but it must strengthen the people of good will who believe in God. We must be united. I am writing these words on September 20, 2001. The memories come back.

So many years ago in my cantata the little boy from the ghetto of Warsaw pleaded with God in heaven to ask people to join their hands. And God cried. I believe that God cries with all the children who became orphans in the United States after September 11, 2001. I believe that if God gave humankind the power to think and the power to love, the choice is ours. This power to think and the power to love has given us the greatest gift of humanity. We do not have the right to surrender to evil. We should measure our strength according to our longings because we know that the struggle will demand from us the commitment of faith. Yes, the commitment of faith that allows us to cherish the gifts of God and not to let them be destroyed. Freedom and justice will prevail. Somewhere in the air vibrates the music of Beethoven's *Seventh Symphony*, the music of power and hope. This music accompanies our struggle. One day we will celebrate justice and freedom for every person on earth. I believe in God and humanity.

Do the dreams and expectations continue their journey?

* * *

On January 22, 2002, I arrived in Rome once more, this time with my sixteen-year-old granddaughter Amanda, Jacques' daughter. It was a very special occasion. The Holy Father had invited representatives of different religions for a day of prayer for peace on January 24. The thought of this gathering had a great significance for me. Only a man of peace could have this idea.

On January 23 we met with Bishop Dziwisz, a man I respect greatly and whose dedication to the pope is another blessing from God. He is wise and warm and these qualities permeate the atmosphere around the Holy Father. Early in the morning Father Konrad and Sister Sabina took us by car to Assisi. During our trip I looked out the window. It was a cold, grey day. The whole time I was thinking about St. Francis of Assisi, about his "Canticle of the Sun" and about Giotto's painting of St. Francis preaching to the birds. I was looking for the birds but did not see any. When we arrived in Assisi, Amanda and I had seats among the places reserved for invited guests.

The meeting took place in a huge, modern tent, built specially for the event. The tent was almost transparent. On the podium in the middle sat the pope, surrounded by members of the hierarchy and clergy of various faiths from all over the world. There were short speeches about uniting all people for the peace of the world. I will never forget that when we were inside the tent, the wind outside was shaking the tent to the point that we could feel the overwhelming power of nature. Was the wind trying to shake all of us, asking us to rethink our deeds and our commitments? Was the wind trying to shake our conscience?

Later, each of us was invited to go to a particular room where people of different faith traditions could pray separately.

I went with Amanda to the room reserved for Jews, where there were a few rabbis from different countries. We were the only women there. We conversed in English and French and afterwards we prayed.

It was very moving. From the neighbouring room we could hear the Buddhists chanting.

After the prayer we went for lunch. I sat near a Mennonite clergyman from Indonesia. After ten minutes of conversation we understood how much we have in common. Each of the guests received a gift: a medallion and beautifully created olive leaf. At four o'clock in the afternoon we returned to Rome. As we were walking back to the car, the rain began to fall. Maybe, I thought, in this rain were the prayers of all those who were persecuted because of prejudice. Maybe this rain tried to awaken our feelings in the name of God, and not only for one day.

The next evening Amanda and I spent more time with the Holy Father.

We were with Bishop Dziwisz and Father Mokrzycki, and we were treated like friends. God! How grateful I was for this evening. We spoke in Polish but the Holy Father also spoke in English to Amanda. When Amanda and I got back from the Vatican to the hotel, I knew that she had been very moved, just as her father, Jacques, had been when we met the pope for the first time in 1996.

When Amanda had fallen asleep, I opened the door to the balcony and went out. I stood there, looking at the illuminated Cupola of Michelangelo. The light graced the Roman sky. Somehow, the music of Chopin and Beethoven was in the air. Their music accompanied the words of Adam Mickiewicz. In the Vatican a strong man, Pope John Paul II, measures his strength according to his longings, no matter how difficult this can be. Pope John Paul II started to build bridges. This is only the beginning. I believe there will be more bridges to build.

In my poem "The Cupola of Michelangelo Watches the Studio of Destinies," I wrote, "As long as God is with me, I know where I have to go."

In October 2002, when I finished the original version of *Building Bridges*, I concluded it with these words:

The river of my thoughts
whispers:
As long as God is with me
I know where I have to go,
As long as God is with me
I know where I have to go.

2002-2004 ... and the Radiant Path in the Sky

B*uilding Bridges* first saw the light of day in 2002. Now, as I reread this book, memories and images come to me. The days are passing by, the tumultuous events of the twentieth century weave their way through these pages.

The violent history of the past century makes it clear that we simply do not learn the lessons of the past. Throughout this fragile world, animosities continue to ignite, inflaming hatred and death. Politicians around the world strive to appease the pain of those who suffer and try to ignite, often against all logic, the hope and expectations of people on our planet. The risk of terrorism has increased, but at the same time we have improved our methods of overcoming it. The fact remains that we live with terrorism, we have to face the truth and go forward, building our future no matter in what condition.

Many years ago, I wrote a song called "World on Fire." Today I ask myself if our world is even more inflamed now than it was when I first wrote that song. Hate abounds, and wars, together with ignorance and religious and idealogical conflicts, continue to destroy the lives of children and other innocent victims. Our greatest strength is to know that there are people around the world who continue to work tirelessly for peace.

I sit at the piano, touching the keys, trying to find a simple melody and lyrics that might give me hope. A song begins to take shape about paving a road where there is no road. The words enter my being as if they were sent from somewhere far away:

How to pave the road where there is no road
How to find a home where I can go,
How to pray to God without any words,
Without asking why I have to grow.

The grass grows, the trees grow
The spring blooms in the air
The storms pass, the rainbow comes
And I don't know why.

Forget yourself, my friend
And listen to your heart
And then the voice will come
And tell you how to start.

And you will find your home
And you will pave your road
Which will be built for you
By angels sent from God.

How to pave the road where there is no road
How to find a home where I can go,
How to pray to God without any words,
Without asking why I have to grow.

Yes, each one of us has to grow, no matter what age we are. We have to go forward, and not stagnate.

In the last two years, I have visited Pope John Paul II three more times. In November 2002, I went to Rome with my son, Michel, and his two children, Betty and Sigmond, where I had been invited to celebrate my birthday with the Holy Father. There we were, in the company of Bishop Dziwisz and young Father Mokrzycki, as the Holy Father sang *"Sto lat"* – Happy Birthday – to me in Polish. This *"Sto lat"* was a blessing of hope that entered my whole being. It filled my lifelong commitment to work for peace and joy among all people, everywhere in our fragile world.

In June 2003, I visited the Holy Father once more, with my son Jacques. Together, we presented Pope John Paul II with a copy of the first edition of *Building Bridges*. He held the book in his hands, looked at me and smiled. It was a simple smile, but one that continues to hold a lot of meaning for me. For six years I had struggled to find the right words to describe his gift to the world: his commitment to building bridges, brick by brick, bridges that encircle our vulnerable planet and the fragile humanity it contains.

Then, in January 2004, I was back in Rome again, this time to attend a unique interfaith event organized by the Vatican: the Concert of Reconciliation. The Holy Father had invited me and members of my family. I brought along my niece Elise, my brother Adam's daughter, and Michel's son, my grandson Loren.

The Concert of Reconciliation brought three faith groups together in the Aula Paulo VI, the giant auditorium at the Vatican where the Pope holds his weekly public audiences. Christians, Jews, and Muslims had been invited, as the invitation explained in Italian, English, Hebrew, and Arabic, to hear music "chosen to reflect two fundamental tenets of faith common to adherents of Christianity, Judaism, and Islam: a reverence for one Patriarch, Abraham, and our belief in the concept of resurrection from death."

Choirs from Ankara, Krakow, London, and Pittsburgh joined the Pittsburgh Symphony Orchestra under the baton of Sir Gilbert Levine to perform music by the contemporary American composer, John Harbison, and Symphony number 2, "The Resurrection Symphony," by Gustav Mahler.

The final notes of this powerful music still echoed in the auditorium as Pope John Paul II spoke. His words resounded like a hymn of understanding and respect for three religions believing in one God.

There in the auditorium a memory came back to me. Years before, when I was in Jerusalem, I had entered what has often been called the Mosque of Omar, but which is more commonly known as the Dome of the Rock. I took off my shoes. I looked at the beautiful carpets, and standing in this sacred place, I thought that every sanctity has its own meaning, and that if we respect this sanctity and respect other religions, we will find peace of mind, peace within ourselves and peace in our world.

Years, years ago, I was in Bethlehem at Christmas time and there in the Church of the Nativity, similar feelings came to me. With these feelings came melodies of Polish carols, sung at Christmas time in Poland.

I also remember the Western Wall in Jerusalem. I remember the stones, the old, old stones, a remnant of the Temple of Solomon. There between these stones I saw the letters, letters to God from people who are longing for the Almighty. There, between the crevices, was also one letter written by the Holy Father, who during his visit to Jerusalem in the year 2000 came and placed his letter between the stones.

Three religions meet in Jerusalem.

The sounds of the Concert of Reconciliation still vibrated in the air of Rome on this night of January 24, 2004. In my heart I blessed the destiny that allowed me to see these holy places and feel their sanctity in my lifetime.

The next evening, I met with the Holy Father once again. In the corner of the room the lights of a Christmas tree flickered with simple joy. I sat at a table, facing a great and kind human being, a man whose words and actions, throughout his career, have demonstrated his love for all of humanity, and the importance of building bridges across a divided world.

* * *

Yesterday, from Philadelphia, I spoke to my son Jacques about the last chapter of this book. In my memory appeared that small café in Rome, during our first visit together in 1996. It was there that Jacques first encouraged me to write about building bridges. Eight years had passed by. This time Jacques said, "Make sure you write about the generation of tomorrow." He is right, and I am grateful for his advice.

Jacques also reminded me of my own youth. In my office in Surochow in the spring of 1943, I promised myself that if I survived the war, I would promote understanding in the world. The poplars across the road were watching me. They were my witnesses. I kept my promise. Perhaps these poplars were my messenger to the almighty God.

I realize that throughout my life, in my books, in my songs, and in my teaching I am fulfilling the promise I made to those poplars. Not long ago, a friend visited Surochow and saw the same tall poplars trying to reach the sky.

The same sky I see now I saw years ago.

In Psalm 121 we read:

> I lift my eyes unto the mountains
> Where shall come my help
> My help is from the Lord
> The Maker of heaven and earth.

* * *

Two days ago at twilight, I looked through the window and I saw one part of the sky covered with pink clouds. I knew that I had to go out on to the balcony. I saw the pink clouds, each more beautiful than the other. There in the sky, I discovered the most beautiful sanctuary. I knew that this sanctuary would not last long. I followed the pink clouds moving slowly through the radiant path, and there between them appeared a light blue cloud. For me it looked like a lake, a round blue lake, surrounded by pink clouds. After a while I saw the pink clouds building a bridge through the lake – there in the sky I saw the radiant path.

As long as God is with me, I know where I have to go.

Yes, I lift my eyes to the sky with a sense of wonder and trust that from there can come the greatest help of all – the gift of understanding ourselves and others. If we have a bridge with heaven, then any bridge we try to build with others will be strong.

But this is only the beginning. You, the generations of tomorrow, you can make this world brighter, safer, more accepting, more loving. You can make this world happier. You hold the key to open up new horizons for yourselves and for the children who will be here long after you. It depends on you. You can do it! You can continue building bridges in the light from above!

Sunday, August 15, 2004

Letters from Pope John Paul II to Lena Allen-Shore

Vatican, June 20, 1996
Dear Madam,
Thank you for the letter which you wrote expressing how impressed you were with your and your son's meeting with me. I am happy that your stay in Rome and the view of the world from the Cupola of St. Peter brought you and your son nearer to God and allowed you to "cross the threshold of hope." I wish you the courage to "be yourself," to have good will in looking at your fellow man and the whole world, to help goodness overcome evil, to assuage antagonistic feelings among people with loving kindness. May peace and joy reign in your heart.

I entrust you and your son to the care of the Holy Mother and I am sending you sincere blessings for your dear family.
Jan Pawel II

Vatican, June 27, 1997
Dear Mme. Professor,
Thank you for your letter, which expressed your spiritual presence during my pilgrimage to the beautiful soil of Poland. These were extraordinary days. I was able to visit the graves of my parents, remembered in your letter of All Souls Day, and to look at "Morskie Oko" described in your poem. May God bless you.

Sincere greetings
May Christ bless you and your sons.
Johannes Paulus II

Vatican, October 23, 1998
Dear Mme. Professor,
I am grateful for the wishes you expressed in the poem "The Apostle of Hope" which you sent to me on the occasion of the twentieth anniversary of my pontificate.
The expression of your sincere feelings is shown in the effort you have put into "building bridges" through your written and spoken words to your students.
May the blessing of God make your efforts fruitful.
Sincere greetings to Mme. Professor and those near to her.
Jan Pawel II

Christmas card (first part)
Vatican, December 7, 1998
Dear Mme. Professor,
Thank you sincerely for your letter with your poem "The Apostle of Hope" in Polish, English, and French versions. I am grateful to Mme. Professor for the kind words of her letter and prayers, which wandered from the grave of Cardinal Krol to the graves of my parents on All Souls Day.
For the coming Holiday and New Year, I wish peace, joy, and God's blessing for Mme. Professor and her dear ones, Jacques and Michas (Michel in French).
Sincere regards,
Jan Pawel II

Vatican, Easter 2000
Dear Mme. Professor,
Thank you for your faxed letter which was written following my pilgrimage to the Holy Land where you, Mme. Professor, were also present.
Thank you for your prayers, which accompanied me during those days.
I am sending you Holiday wishes. May the Pascal joy of the Jubilee Year shine upon your every day effort and strengthen faith and faithfulness to the grace of God.
My sincere greetings to Mme. Professor and those near to her.
Jan Pawel II

Vatican, Sept. 9, 2000
Dear Mme. Professor,

Two letters reached me from July 8 and August 14 with the English version of your book. Thank you for so much work and effort. Together with loving kindness which was the inspiration of creativity.

Thank you for your prayers for a good vacation. The stay in the mountains was very successful and the beauty of nature was favourable to the atmosphere of relaxation and rest.

I wish you a good rest after the hard work with the youth this summer.

I return the expression of respect and sincere greetings for you Mme. Professor, your sons and your brother. May God bless you all.

Jan Pawel II

Vatican, November 4, 2001
Dear Mme. Professor

Thank you for your letter containing thoughts and wishes on the occasion of the twenty-third anniversary of my pontificate. Thank you for your prayers and the expression of your feelings which have accompanied me over the years.

November brought the second letter with your memories of Cardinal Krol of saintly memory, about whom you expressed your gratitude, The Day of All Spirits and the Day of All Saints especially draws us to prayers for the dead.

Your birthday, November 17, is approaching.

I wish you the vital graces of God and good health for long years to come.

May God bless you, your sons, and your brother.

Jan Pawel II

Vatican, Christmas 2001
Dear Mme. Professor,

Thank you for your letter with the "Whisper of the Vistula," the Psalm of David, and the words of Christ. I reciprocate your heartfelt wishes.

May the song of the angels proclaiming love and joy fill your heart with peace and confidence in God's care which guides the world and will not permit evil to win.

I share with you the Christmas Eve wafer and wish you God's protection in the New Year of 2002.

I am sending you sincere regards and blessings.

Jan Pawel II

Vatican, Easter 2002

Thank you for your letter written in your thoughts and on your paper.

You have come back again to your deep feelings awoken in Assisi and Rome. Thank you for your concern for my health and for your prayers.

I wish for you, Mme. Professor, that your words take on life in the hearts of your students with goodness and truth and may God's blessing accompany you every day.

Please pass on my heartfelt greetings to Amanda, your brother, and your sons, Mme. Professor, and I wish all of you a blessed and happy Holiday.

John Paul II

Notes and Acknowledgments

1   Morskie Oko is the name of a lake in the Tatra Mountains.

2   Karol Wojtyla, *The Place Within: The Poetry of John Paul II,* translated by Jerzy Peterkiewicz (London: Hutchinson, 1982), p. ix.

3   Ibid., p. 103.

4   Pope John Paul II, *Crossing the Threshold of Hope,* Jenny McPhee and Martha McPhee, trans. (New York: Knopf, 1994), p. 18.

5   Karol Wojtyla, *Easter Vigil and Other Poems,* translated by Jerzy Peterkiewicz (New York, Random House, 1979), p. 75.

6   *The Place Within,* pp. 4–5.

7   Pope John Paul II, *Dominum et Vivificantum,* Section 5.

8   *Crossing the Threshold of Hope,* pp. 95-96.

9   *The Place Within,* pp. 7–8.

10 Luigi Accattoli, *When a Pope Asks Forgiveness: The Mea Culpa's of John Paul II* (Boston: Pauline Books and Media, 1998), pp. 160–161.

11 Adam Bujak and Michael Rozek, *Wojtyla* (Wroclaw: Wydanictwo Dolnoslaskie, 1997), pp. 19–20.

12 *The Place Within,* pp. 6-7.

13 *The Place Within,* p. 141.

14 *The Place Within,* pp. 141–149.

15 *Francis and Clare: The Complete Works: The Classics of Western Spirituality* (New York: Paulist Press, 1982), p. 38.

16 *Basic Writings of Nietzsche,* Modern Library, Modern Library Classics, Walter Arnold Kaufmann, ed., 1992.

17 Adapted from Lena Allen-Shore, *Ten Steps in the Land of Life: A Step by Step Guide to Meaning and Happiness in Life* (Philadelphia: Lena Allen-Shore Center, 1990), p. 34.

18   Karol Wojtyla, *Collected Poems* (New York: Random House, 1982), p. 174.

19   Tad Szulc, *Pope John Paul II: The Biography* (New York: Scribner, 1995), pp. 80–81.

20   Adam Mickiewicz, *Master Thaddeus or The Last Foray in Lithuania* (New York: J.M. Dent: 1931), pp. 321–326.

21   Thomas Merton, *Seeds of Contemplation* (New York: Dell, 1953), p. 11.

22   Thomas Merton, *New Seeds of Contemplation* (New York: New Directions, 1962), p. 161.

23   *Marcus Aurelius and His Times: The Transition from Paganism to Christianity* (New York: Black, 1945), pp. 90–93.

24   Lena Allen-Shore, *Langue universelle: fraternité et culture* (Montreal, 1970).

25   Cyprian Kamil Norwid, *Poezia I dobroc* (Warsaw: Panstowy Instytut Wydanawniczy, 1981), p. 343.

26   *Crossing the Threshold of Hope*, pp. 35–36

27   *Poezia I dobroc*, pp. 355–356.

28   Quoted in Julian Kryzanowski, *A History of Polish Literature* (Warsaw: PWN, Polish Scientific Publishers, 1978), p. 300.

29   *Collected Plays and Writings on Theatre* (Berkeley, CA: University of California Press, 1987), pp. 227ff.

30   Ibid.

31   Lena Allen-Shore, *Thinking of Rembrandt and … Life – On the Canvas of Your Soul* (Philadelphia: Lena Allen-Shore Center, 1992).

32   *When a Pope Asks Forgiveness*, p. 168.

33   Ibid., p. 186.

34   Ibid., pp. 158–159.

35   Ibid., p. 118.

36   Lena Allen-Shore, *Ne me demandez pas qui je suis* (Montreal: Librairie La Québécoise, 1965).

37   Lena Allen-Shore, *The Singing God – Le Dieu qui Chant* (Montreal: Éditions Aries, 1970).

38   Ibid., pp. 97–106.

39   Quoted in Will Durant, *The Story of Philosophy* (New York: Pocket Books, 1937), p. 417.

40   Quoted in Walter Kaufman, *Religion from Tolstoy to Camus* (New York: Harper, 1961), p. 195.

41   Quoted in Karl Jaspers, *The Great Philosophers* (New York: Harcourt Brace, 1957), p. 311.

42   Nora Levin, *The Holocaust: The Destruction of European Jewry 1933–1945* (New York: Schocken Books, 1973), p. 504.

43   Ibid.

44   *John Paul II: A Panorama of His Teachings* (New York: New City Press, 1989), p. 130.

45   Ibid.

46   Karl Barth, *The Church and the World* (New York: MacMillan, 1944).

47   Quoted in André Froissard, *Giovanni Paulo II* (Milan, 1983), pp. 13–14.

48   Cardinal Glemp, "Human Work: John Paul II – A Panorama of His Teachings" (Concepcion, April 5, 1987).

49   *The Place Within*, pp. 63–64.

50   Ibid., p. 6.

51   George Blazynski: *Pope John Paul II* (New York: Dell, 1979).

52   *When a Pope Asks Forgiveness,* xii–xvii.

53   Ibid.

54   Ibid.

55   Ibid.

56   Dante Alighieri, *The Divine Comedy*, Lawrence Grand White, trans. (New York: Pantheon, 1948), p. 1.

57   Ibid, p. 2.

58   Blazynski, *Pope John Paul II.*

59   *Collected Works of John of the Cross*, Kieran Kavanagh, ed. (Washington: ICS, 1973), p. 37.

60   Ibid, p. 640.

61   Ibid, p. 641–2.

62   Ibid, p. 577.

63   Michel M.J. Shore, *Jerusalem Breezes* (New York: Shengold Publishers, 1981).

64   Quoted in Lucinda Vardey, *God in All Worlds* (New York: Knopf, 1996), p. 396.

65   Lena Allen-Shore, *Forty Years After Darkness* (Philadelphia: Lena Allen-Shore Center, 1991), pp. 83–85.

66   Ibid.

67   Lena Allen-Shore, *May the Flowers Grow* (New York: Shengold, 1969), pp. 8–11.

68   Pope John Paul II, *Gift and Mystery* (New York: Doubleday, 1999), p. 87.

Lena Allen-Shore is the author of the following books:

L'orage dans mon coeur
(poetry) 1963

Le pain de la paix
(poetry) 1964

Ne me demandez pas qui je suis
(fiction) 1965

May the Flowers Grow
(poetry) 1969

The Singing God – Le dieu qui chante
(poetry) 1970

Langue universelle: fraternité et culture
1970

Ten Steps in the Land of Life: How to Find Meaning in Life
1980

Roots and Wings (In collaboration with my father Jakub Herzig)
1982

40 Years After Darkness
1985

Dix pas dans le pays de la vie
1985

Thinking of Rembrandt and ... Life – On the Canvas of Your Soul
1992

Rendezvous with Love
1993

Building Bridges: Pope John Paul II and the Horizon of Life
2003 and 2004